LAW, CRIME AND LAW ENFORCEMENT

THE PERSISTENCE OF HUMAN TRAFFICKING

LAW, CRIME AND LAW ENFORCEMENT

Additional books in this series can be found on Nova's website
under the Series tab.

Additional E-books in this series can be found on Nova's website
under the E-book tab.

CRIMINAL JUSTICE, LAW ENFORCEMENT AND CORRECTIONS

Additional books in this series can be found on Nova's website
under the Series tab.

Additional E-books in this series can be found on Nova's website
under the E-book tab.

THE PERSISTENCE OF HUMAN TRAFFICKING

PERRY SIMMONS FOSTER

AND

KAYLA BRADY

EDITORS

publishers
New York

Library of Congress Cataloging-in-Publication Data

ISBN: 978-1-62257-773-6

Published by Nova Science Publishers, Inc. ✠ *New York*

CONTENTS

PREFACE

Trafficking in persons, or human trafficking, refers to the subjection of men, women, and children to exploitative conditions that can be tantamount to slavery. Reports suggest that human trafficking is a global phenomenon, victimizing millions of people each year and contributing to a multi-billion dollar criminal industry. It is a centuries-old problem that, despite international and U.S. efforts to eliminate it, continues to occur in virtually every country in the world. Human trafficking is also an international and cross-cutting policy problem that bears on a range of major national security, human rights, criminal justice, social, economic, migration, gender, public health, and labor issues. This book examines the international dimensions and foreign policy issues for Congress of human trafficking.

Chapter 1 – Trafficking in persons, or human trafficking, refers to the subjection of men, women, and children to exploitative conditions that can be tantamount to slavery. Reports suggest that human trafficking is a global phenomenon, victimizing millions of people each year and contributing to a multi-billion dollar criminal industry.

It is a centuries-old problem that, despite international and U.S. efforts to eliminate it, continues to occur in virtually every country in the world. Human trafficking is also an international and cross-cutting policy problem that bears on a range of major national security, human rights, criminal justice, social, economic, migration, gender, public health, and labor issues.

The U.S. government and successive Congresses have long played a leading role in international efforts to combat human trafficking. Key U.S. foreign policy responses include the following:

- Foreign Country Reporting to describe annual progress made by foreign governments to combat human trafficking, child soldiers, and forced labor.
- Foreign Product Blacklisting to identify goods made with convict, forced, or indentured labor, including forced or indentured child labor.
- Foreign Aid to support foreign countries' efforts to combat human trafficking.
- Foreign Aid Restrictions to punish countries that are willfully noncompliant with anti-trafficking standards.
- Conditions on Trade Preference Program Beneficiaries to offer certain countries export privileges to the United States, only if they also adhere to international standards against forced labor and child trafficking.

- Preventing U.S. Government Participation in Trafficking Overseas to punish and deter trafficking-related violations among U.S. government personnel and contractors.

Although there is widespread support among policy makers for the continuation of U.S. anti-trafficking goals, ongoing reports of such trafficking worldwide raise questions regarding whether sufficient progress has been made to deter and ultimately eliminate the problem, the end goal of current U.S. anti-trafficking policies. This report explores current foreign policy issues confronting U.S. efforts to combat human trafficking, the interrelationship among existing polices, and the historical and current role of Congress in such efforts.

The 112th Congress has introduced and taken action on several bills related to human trafficking, including bills to reauthorize the Trafficking Victims Protection Act (TVPA), the cornerstone legislative vehicle for current U.S. policy to combat human trafficking, beyond FY2011 (S. 1301, H.R. 2830, and H.R. 3589).

Given recent challenges in balancing budget priorities, the 112th Congress may choose to consider certain aspects of this issue further, including the effectiveness of international anti-trafficking projects, interagency coordination mechanisms, and the monitoring and enforcement of anti-trafficking regulations, particularly as they relate to the activities of U.S. government contractors and subcontractors operating overseas. See the Appendix for further discussion of legislative activity in the 112th Congress.

Chapter 2 – Trafficking in persons (TIP) for the purposes of exploitation is believed to be one of the most prolific areas of international criminal activity and is of significant concern to the United States and the international community. According to U.S. government estimates, roughly 800,000 people are trafficked across borders each year. If trafficking within countries is included in the total world figures, some 2 million to 4 million people may be trafficked annually. As many as 17,500 people are believed to be trafficked into the United States each year, and some have estimated that 100,000 U.S. citizen children are victims of trafficking within the United States. Notably, TIP is a modern form of slavery and does not have to include the movement of a person.

Through the Trafficking Victims Protection Act of 2000 (TVPA, Div. A of P.L. 106-386), and its reauthorizations (TVPRAs), Congress has aimed to eliminate human trafficking by creating grant programs for both victims and law enforcement, appropriating funds, creating new criminal laws, and conducting oversight on the effectiveness and implications of U.S. anti-TIP policy. Most recently, the TVPA was reauthorized through FY2011 in the William Wilberforce Trafficking Victims Protection Reauthorization Act of 2008 (TVPRA of 2008, P.L. 110-457).

Two of the bills introduced in the 112th Congress to reauthorize the TVPA have received action. S. 1301 was reported by the Senate Judiciary Committee, and H.R. 2830 was ordered reported by the House Foreign Affairs Committee. The bills would make changes to the act and extend authorizations for some current programs. S. 1301 would extend TVPA authorizations through FY2015, and H.R. 2830 through FY2013. As Congress considers reauthorization of the TVPA, the current budget situation has heightened interest in oversight and funding of current efforts to fight TIP. Obligations for global and domestic anti-TIP programs, not including operations and law enforcement investigations, totaled approximately $109.5 million in FY2010. The TVPRA of 2008 authorized $191.3 million in global and domestic anti-TIP programs for FY2011.

Overall, issues related to U.S. anti-TIP efforts include the effectiveness of current programs, whether there is duplication among these programs, and whether there is sufficient oversight of monies spent on anti-trafficking activities. Ongoing international policy issues include how to measure the effectiveness of the U.S. and international responses to TIP, the U.S. Department of State's annual country rankings and the use of unilateral sanctions, and how to prevent known sex offenders from engaging in international child sex tourism. Domestic issues include whether there is equal treatment of all victims—both foreign nationals and U.S. citizens, as well as victims of labor and sex trafficking; and whether current law and services are adequate to deal with the emerging issue of domestic child sex trafficking (i.e., the prostitution of children in the United States). Other overarching issues include whether all forms of prostitution (i.e., children and adults) fit the definition of TIP, and whether sufficient efforts are applied to addressing all forms of TIP, including not only sexual exploitation, but also forced labor and child soldiers.

In June 2011, the State Department issued its annual, congressionally mandated TIP Report. In addition to outlining major trends and ongoing challenges in combating TIP, the report provides a country-by-country analysis and ranking, based on what progress countries have made in their efforts to prosecute traffickers, protect victims, and prevent TIP. The report categorizes countries according to the government's efforts to combat trafficking, with the worst-performing countries at risk of losing selected non-humanitarian, nontrade-related U.S. foreign assistance. For FY2012, TIP sanctions were fully imposed on three of the worst-performing countries: Eritrea, Madagascar, and North Korea.

Chapter 3 - Trafficking in persons (TIP) for the purpose of exploitation is a lucrative criminal activity that is of major concern to the United States and the international community. According to the most recent U.S. State Department estimates, roughly 800,000 people are trafficked across borders each year. If trafficking within countries is included in the total world figures, official U.S. estimates are that some 2 million to 4 million people are trafficked annually. While most trafficking victims still appear to originate from South and Southeast Asia or the former Soviet Union, human trafficking is also a growing problem in Latin America.

Countries in Latin America serve as source, transit, and destination countries for trafficking victims. Latin America is a primary source region for people trafficked to the United States. In FY2010, for example, primary countries of origin for the 449 foreign trafficking victims certified as eligible to receive U.S. assistance included Mexico, Honduras, Haiti, El Salvador, and the Dominican Republic (along with India and Thailand).

Since enactment of the Victims of Trafficking and Violence Protection Act of 2000 (TVPA, P.L. 106-386), Congress has taken steps to address human trafficking by authorizing new programs and reauthorizing existing ones, appropriating funds, creating new criminal laws, and conducting oversight on the effectiveness and implications of U.S. anti-TIP policy. Most recently, the TVPA was reauthorized through FY2011 in the William Wilberforce Trafficking Victims Protection Reauthorization Act of 2008 (P.L. 110-457). Obligations for U.S.-funded anti-TIP programs in Latin America totaled roughly $17.1 million in FY2010.

On June 27, 2011, the State Department issued its 11th annual, congressionally mandated report on human trafficking. The report categorizes countries into four "tiers" according to the government's efforts to combat trafficking. Those countries that do not cooperate in the fight against trafficking (Tier 3) have been made subject to U.S. foreign assistance sanctions. While Cuba and Venezuela are the only Latin American countries ranked on Tier 3 in this year's TIP report, seven other countries in the region—Barbados, Costa Rica, Dominican Republic, Ecuador, Panama, St. Vincent and the Grenadines, and the Bahamas—are on the Tier 2 Watch List. Unless those countries make significant progress, they could receive a Tier 3 ranking in the 2012 report.

Activity on combating TIP has continued into the 112th Congress, particularly related to efforts to reauthorize the TVPA and oversee TIP programs and operations, including U.S.-funded programs in Latin America. Congress may also consider increasing funding for anti-TIP programs in the region, possibly through the Mérida Initiative for Mexico, the Central America Regional Security Initiative (CARSI) or through other assistance programs. Congress is likely to monitor new trends in human trafficking in the region, such as the increasing involvement of Mexican drug trafficking organizations in TIP and the problem of child trafficking in Haiti, which has worsened since that country experienced a devastating earthquake on January 12, 2010.

Chapter 4 – The trafficking of individuals within U.S borders is commonly referred to as domestic human trafficking, and it occurs in every state of the nation. One form of domestic human trafficking is sex trafficking. Research indicates that most victims of sex trafficking into and within the United States are women and children, and the victims include U.S. citizens and noncitizens alike. Recently, Congress has focused attention on domestic sex trafficking, including the prostitution of children—which is the focus of this report.

Federal law does not define sex trafficking per se. However, the term "severe forms of trafficking in persons," as defined in the Victims of Trafficking and Violence Protection Act of 2000 (TVPA, P.L. 106-386) encompasses sex trafficking. "Severe forms of trafficking in persons" refers, in part, to "[s]ex trafficking in which a commercial sex act is induced by force, fraud, or coercion, or in which the person induced to perform such act has not attained 18 years of age...." Experts generally agree that the trafficking term applies to minors whether the child's actions were forced or appear to be voluntary.

The exact number of child victims of sex trafficking in the United States is unknown because comprehensive research and scientific data are lacking. Sex trafficking of children appears to be fueled by a variety of environmental and situational variables ranging from poverty or the use of prostitution by runaway and "thrown-away" children to provide for their subsistence needs to the recruitment of children by organized crime units for prostitution.

The TVPA has been the primary vehicle authorizing services to victims of trafficking. Several agencies have programs or administer grants to other entities to provide specific services to trafficking victims. Despite language that authorizes services for citizen, lawful permanent resident, and noncitizen victims, appropriations for trafficking victims' services have primarily been used to serve noncitizen victims. U.S. citizen victims are also eligible for certain crime victim benefits and public benefit entitlement programs, though these services are not tailored to trafficking victims. Of note, specialized services and support for minor victims of sex trafficking are limited. Nationwide, organizations specializing in support for these victims collectively have fewer than 50 beds. Other facilities, such as runaway and homeless youth shelters and foster care homes, may not be able to adequately meet the needs of victims or keep them from pimps/ traffickers and other abusers.

In addition, it has been suggested that minor victims of sex trafficking—while too young to consent to sexual activity with adults—may at times be labeled as prostitutes or juvenile delinquents and treated as criminals rather than being identified and treated as trafficking victims. These children who are arrested may be placed in juvenile detention facilities instead of environments where they can receive needed social and protective services.

Finally, experts widely agree that any efforts to reduce the prevalence of child sex trafficking—as well as other forms of trafficking—should address not only the supply, but also the *demand*. Congress may consider demand reduction strategies such as increasing public awareness and prevention as well as bolstering investigations and prosecutions of those who buy illegal commercial sex ("johns"). In addition, policy makers may deliberate enhancing services for victims of trafficking. The 112th Congress may address these and other issues if policy makers choose to take up the reauthorization of the TVPA , which expires at the end of FY2011.

In: The Persistence of Human Trafficking
Editors: Perry Simmons Foster and Kayla Brady

ISBN: 978-1-62257-773-6
© 2013 Nova Science Publishers, Inc.

Chapter 1

TRAFFICKING IN PERSONS: INTERNATIONAL DIMENSIONS AND FOREIGN POLICY ISSUES FOR CONGRESS[*]

Liana Sun Wyler

SUMMARY

Trafficking in persons, or human trafficking, refers to the subjection of men, women, and children to exploitative conditions that can be tantamount to slavery. Reports suggest that human trafficking is a global phenomenon, victimizing millions of people each year and contributing to a multi-billion dollar criminal industry.

It is a centuries-old problem that, despite international and U.S. efforts to eliminate it, continues to occur in virtually every country in the world. Human trafficking is also an international and cross-cutting policy problem that bears on a range of major national security, human rights, criminal justice, social, economic, migration, gender, public health, and labor issues.

The U.S. government and successive Congresses have long played a leading role in international efforts to combat human trafficking. Key U.S. foreign policy responses include the following:

- Foreign Country Reporting to describe annual progress made by foreign governments to combat human trafficking, child soldiers, and forced labor.
- Foreign Product Blacklisting to identify goods made with convict, forced, or indentured labor, including forced or indentured child labor.
- Foreign Aid to support foreign countries' efforts to combat human trafficking.
- Foreign Aid Restrictions to punish countries that are willfully noncompliant with anti-trafficking standards.
- Conditions on Trade Preference Program Beneficiaries to offer certain countries export privileges to the United States, only if they also adhere to international standards against forced labor and child trafficking.

---

[*] This is an edited, reformatted and augmented version of a Congressional Research Service publication, CRS Report for Congress R42497, prepared for Members and Committees of Congress, from www.crs.gov, dated July 6, 2012.

- Preventing U.S. Government Participation in Trafficking Overseas to punish and deter trafficking-related violations among U.S. government personnel and contractors.

Although there is widespread support among policy makers for the continuation of U.S. anti-trafficking goals, ongoing reports of such trafficking worldwide raise questions regarding whether sufficient progress has been made to deter and ultimately eliminate the problem, the end goal of current U.S. anti-trafficking policies. This report explores current foreign policy issues confronting U.S. efforts to combat human trafficking, the interrelationship among existing polices, and the historical and current role of Congress in such efforts.

The 112th Congress has introduced and taken action on several bills related to human trafficking, including bills to reauthorize the Trafficking Victims Protection Act (TVPA), the cornerstone legislative vehicle for current U.S. policy to combat human trafficking, beyond FY2011 (S. 1301, H.R. 2830, and H.R. 3589).

Given recent challenges in balancing budget priorities, the 112th Congress may choose to consider certain aspects of this issue further, including the effectiveness of international anti-trafficking projects, interagency coordination mechanisms, and the monitoring and enforcement of anti-trafficking regulations, particularly as they relate to the activities of U.S. government contractors and subcontractors operating overseas. See the Appendix for further discussion of legislative activity in the 112th Congress.

INTRODUCTION

Trafficking in persons, or human trafficking, refers to the subjection of men, women, and children to exploitative conditions that some equate with slavery. It is a centuries-old problem that, despite international and U.S. efforts to eliminate it, continues to occur in virtually every country in the world. Common forms of human trafficking include trafficking for commercial sexual exploitation and trafficking through forced labor and debt bondage. Other forms of human trafficking also include trafficking for domestic servitude and the use of children in armed conflict (e.g., child soldiers).

The modern manifestation of this trafficking problem is driven by the willingness of labor and service providers to violate anti-trafficking laws and regulations in the face of continued international demand for cheap labor and services and gaps in the enforcement of such rules. Ongoing demand is particularly concentrated among industries and economic sectors that are low-skill and labor-intensive. To address the complex dynamics at issue in human trafficking, policy responses are cross-cutting and international, bringing together diverse stakeholders in the fields of foreign policy, human rights, international security, criminal justice, migration, refugees, public health, child welfare, gender issues, urban planning, international trade, labor recruitment, and government contracting and procurement.

In the United States, Congress has enacted legislation to address aspects of the problem, including the Trafficking Victims Protection Act of 2000 (TVPA, Division A of P.L. 106-386, as amended); TVPA reauthorizations (TVPRAs of 2003, 2005, and 2008); the Child Soldiers Prevention Act of 2008 (CSPA of 2008, Title IV of P.L. 110-457); and the Tariff Act of 1930 (Title III, Chapter 497, as amended). Other trafficking-related provisions have also been enacted through the Trade Act of 1974 (Title V of P.L. 93-618, as amended), the Trade and Development Act of 2000 (TDA, P.L. 106-200, as amended), and several additional trade preference programs authorized by Congress.

Although the United States has long supported international efforts to eliminate various forms of human trafficking, a new wave of contemporary action against international human trafficking galvanized in the late 1990s as news stories drew attention to the discovery of trafficked women and children from the former Soviet Union forced to participate in the commercial sex industries in Western Europe and North America. Across the international community, the transnational nature of the phenomenon highlighted the need for improved international coordination and commitment to halting trafficking flows. To this end, the United Nations (U.N.) adopted in 2000 the Protocol to Prevent, Suppress and Punish Trafficking in Persons, Especially Women and Children (hereinafter U.N. Trafficking Protocol), a supplement to the U.N. Convention Against Transnational Organized Crime. The U.N. Trafficking Protocol is not the first or only multilateral mechanism to address human trafficking; it was, however, the first to define trafficking in persons and require States Parties to criminalize such activity.[1]

Since the U.N. Trafficking Protocol entered into force in 2003, the international community has seen an uptick in the number of countries enacting laws that prohibit and criminally punish human trafficking. While observers note that continued vigilance is required to encourage the remaining 46 U.N. members to become States Parties to the U.N. Trafficking Protocol, emphasis from the U.S. foreign policy perspective has also been placed on improving the implementation and enforcement of anti-trafficking laws. According to the U.S. State Department's 2011 *Trafficking in Persons Report* (hereinafter *TIP Report*), 62 countries have yet to convict a trafficker under laws in accordance with the U.N. Trafficking Protocol.[2]

Continued public attention and academic research suggest that human trafficking remains a problem—a key rationale for the repeated reauthorization and enactment of further legislative enhancements to the TVPA, most recently through the TVPRA of 2008 (P.L. 110-457). Data on the global scope and severity of human trafficking continue to be lacking, due in large part to uneven enforcement of anti-trafficking laws internationally and related challenges in identifying victims. According to the International Labor Organization (ILO), some 20.9 million individuals worldwide today are likely subjected to forced labor, including labor and sex trafficking as well as state-imposed forms of forced labor.[3] The sources of victims have diversified over time, as have the industries in which such trafficking victims are found. Known flows involve victims originating not only from Eastern and Central Europe, but also from South and Southeast Asia, North and West Africa, and Latin America and the Caribbean. Observers, however, debate whether existing anti-trafficking efforts worldwide have resulted in appreciable and corresponding progress toward the global elimination of human trafficking.

The 112th Congress has remained active on international human trafficking issues, particularly with appropriations identified for anti-trafficking assistance purposes, pending legislation in both chambers to reauthorize the TVPA, and an active record of committee hearings. Given current challenges in balancing budget priorities, Congress may choose to further explore possible gaps and redundancies in international anti-trafficking projects, whether there is a need for enhanced interagency coordination mechanisms for funding and programming prioritization, and what prospects may exist to invigorate the monitoring and enforcement of anti-trafficking laws and policies, particularly as they relate to U.S.

government contractors and subcontractors. See the *Appendix* for further discussion of pending legislation in the 112th Congress on international human trafficking.

U.S. FOREIGN POLICY FRAMEWORK

Current U.S. foreign policy approaches for addressing human trafficking are a modern off-shoot of anti-slavery policies that centered initially on reinforcing international prohibitions on forced labor during the first half of the 20th century. With time, U.S. and international perspectives on the global scope of human trafficking have expanded to cover a broader range of victims and prohibited activities, including sex trafficking and the exploitation of children in labor, armed conflict, and the commercial sex industry. The ultimate goal of current U.S. anti-trafficking policy is to eliminate the problem and support international efforts to abolish human trafficking worldwide.

The U.S. government has long played a leading role in international efforts to combat human trafficking, with Congress in particular driving contemporary U.S. foreign policy responses. Several major sources of foreign policy legislation and executive branch guidance frame current U.S. responses to the problem. They include the following:

- *Executive Memorandum on Steps to Combat Violence Against Women and Trafficking in Women and Girls.* In March 1998, President William J. Clinton identified trafficking in women and girls as an international problem with domestic implications in the United States. In the memorandum, President Clinton establishes the goals of increasing human trafficking awareness, providing protection to victims, and enhancing the "capacity of law enforcement worldwide to prevent women and girls from being trafficked" to ensure that traffickers are punished.
- *Trafficking Victims Protection Act of 2000.* The cornerstone legislative vehicle for current U.S. policy on combating international human trafficking is the Trafficking Victims Protection Act of 2000 (TVPA), as amended and reauthorized (TVPRAs).[4] Among other provisions, the TVPA formalized the overall U.S. approach to anti-trafficking through an emphasis on prevention of severe forms of human trafficking, prosecution of traffickers, and protection of victims (the three Ps) both domestically and internationally. It establishes minimum standards for the elimination of trafficking and specific criteria to assess whether such standards have been met. The TVPA also established several key elements in the U.S. foreign policy response to human trafficking, including the State Department Office to Combat and Monitor Trafficking in Persons; interagency entities to coordinate anti-trafficking policies across U.S. agencies, such as the Senior Policy Operating Group (SPOG) and President's Interagency Task Force (PITF); several reporting requirements to Congress; authorities to provide anti-trafficking foreign aid; and mechanisms to withhold U.S. aid to countries that fail to achieve progress in combating human trafficking.
- *National Security Presidential Directive 22.* Highlighting the impact of human trafficking on U.S. national security, President George W. Bush in December 2002 issued National Security Presidential Directive 22 on Combating Trafficking in

Persons (NSPD-22).[5] NSPD-22 is "based on an abolitionist approach to trafficking in persons," establishing as a U.S. government-wide goal the eradication of international trafficking in persons, including a zero tolerance policy among U.S. government employees and contractors.[6] NSPD-22 also notably identifies prostitution and several related activities as "contributing to the phenomenon of trafficking in persons"—and thus to be opposed as a matter of U.S. government policy.

- *Tariff Act of 1930.* Section 307 of the Tariff Act of 1930, as amended, prohibits the import of all foreign "goods, wares, articles, and merchandise mined, produced, or manufactured wholly or in part" by convict or forced or indentured labor.[7] The U.S. Department of Homeland Security (DHS) implements the provisions of Section 307 by maintaining a public list of such prohibited goods and barring entry of such products into the United States.[8]

- *Executive Order 13126.* On June 12, 1999, President William J. Clinton issued Executive Order 13126, the Prohibition of Acquisition of Products Produced by Forced or Indentured Child Labor (EO 13126). This executive order prohibits U.S. government contractors from using or procuring "goods, wares, articles, and merchandise mined, produced, or manufactured wholly or in part by forced or indentured child labor." The U.S. Department of Labor, with consultation from DHS and the State Department, implements the provisions of EO 13126 by maintaining a public list of offending products, as well as a list of the countries from which such products originate.[9]

- *Trade Preference Program Eligibility.* Select countries receive temporary, non-reciprocal, duty-free U.S. market access for certain exports on condition that they adhere to "internationally recognized worker rights," including prohibitions on forced labor, as well as eliminate the "worst forms of child labor," including child trafficking.[10] Such congressionally authorized preference programs include the Generalized System of Preferences (GSP);[11] Caribbean Basin Economic Recovery Act (CBERA), as amended and extended through the U.S. Caribbean Basin Trade Partnership Act (CBTPA);[12] Andean Trade Preference Act (ATPA), as amended and extended through the Andean Trade Promotion and Drug Eradication Act (ATPDEA);[13] and African Growth and Opportunity Act (AGOA).[14]

- *Child Soldiers Prevention Act of 2008.* Addressing the specific issue of children in armed conflict, the Child Soldiers Prevention Act of 2008 (CSPA of 2008) mandates the U.S. Department of State to annually publish a list of countries in violation of international standards to condemn the conscription, recruitment, and use of children in armed conflict and punish such countries by prohibiting the provision of certain types of U.S. military assistance.

Key U.S. entities involved in combating international trafficking in persons include the Department of State, Department of Labor, Agency for International Development (USAID), Department of Defense (DOD), and the Department of Homeland Security (DHS). These departments and agencies are among the participants in interagency coordination mechanisms to combat international human trafficking through the SPOG and the PITF and may also issue agency-specific guidelines against human trafficking that implement enacted laws, federal regulations, and presidential determinations, directives, and executive orders.

The U.S. government also participates in multilateral and regional anti-trafficking efforts conducted by the international community, including through organizations such as the United Nations, the International Labor Organization (ILO), the International Organization for Migration (IOM), and the Organization for Security and Cooperation in Europe (OSCE), among many others. See *Table 1* for a list of multilateral treaties related to human trafficking in which the U.S. government participates.

Table 1. Key International Treaties Addressing Trafficking in Persons Which the United States Has Ratified or Acceded To

Date of U.S. Accession, Signing, or Ratification	Name of Convention or Protocol	Entry into Force
December 6, 1967 (accession)	1956 U.N. Supplementary Convention on the Abolition of Slavery, the Slave Trade, and Institutions and Practices Similar to Slavery	April 30, 1957
December 13, 2000 (signed)	2000 U.N. Protocol to Prevent, Suppress and Punish Trafficking in Persons, Especially Women and Children, Supplementing the U.N.	December 25, 2003
November 3, 2005 (ratified) July 5, 2000 (signed) December 23, 2002 (ratified)	Convention Against Transnational Organized Crime 2000 U.N. Optional Protocol to the Convention on the Rights of the Child on the Sale of Children, Child Prostitution and Child Pornography	January 18, 2002
July 5, 2000 (signed) December 23, 2002 (ratified)	2000 U.N. Optional Protocol to the Convention on the Rights of the Child on the Involvement of Children in Armed Conflict	February 12, 2002
September 25, 1991 (ratified)	1957 ILO Convention No. 105 on the Abolition of Force Labor	January 17, 1959
February 12, 1999 (ratified)	1999 ILO Convention No. 182 on the Worst Forms of Child Labor	November 19, 2000

Sources: CRS presentation of data contained in the U.N. Treaty Collection, Status of Treaties, http://treaties and ILO Database of International Labor Standards, http://www.ilo.org/ ilolex/english/ newrat frameE.htm.

Key Trafficking Terms in U.S. Foreign Policy Context

As various terms are defined and used in international treaties as well as domestic statutes, choice in the application of these terms may trigger different policy consequences. The following section identifies and compares several terms frequently used in the context of foreign policy discussions related to human trafficking.

Human Trafficking

"Human Trafficking" is a generic term to describe what the U.N. Trafficking Protocol defines as "trafficking in persons" and the TVPA in U.S. statute defines as "severe forms of trafficking in persons."

The U.N. and U.S. terms share similarities, but are applied in different policy contexts. They are both precedent-setting, as two of the earliest official definitions broadly conceived to describe human trafficking as a combination of prohibited acts (e.g., recruitment, harboring, or transportation of victims) and prohibited methods or means of procuring commercial sex and other labor or services (e.g., force, fraud, or coercion). Both afford enhanced protections for children against victimization in the commercial sex industry, as well as protections against their subjection to work under conditions of involuntary servitude, peonage, debt bondage, or slavery. Neither the U.S. nor the U.N. definition requires trafficking victims to be physically moved across international borders.

In general, the U.S. term defined in the TVPA is considered more restrictive than the U.N. definition, resulting in a less expansive basis for the concept of human trafficking and a more narrowly defined scope for U.S. foreign policy activities to combat human trafficking. The intended foreign policy purposes of the definitions also differ.

The U.N. term was created to facilitate international cooperation for legal and technical assistance. The U.S. term is used to measure and rank foreign countries' progress in combating trafficking. It can trigger unilateral U.S. government restrictions on foreign aid to countries with a record of poor performance to combat severe forms of human trafficking.

Additionally, it can also affect federal contracting and procurement policies. Domestically, the U.S. term also has implications for the criminal justice system and immigration status categories.

Forced Labor

The U.N. Trafficking Protocol does not define forced labor. Instead, the primary international definition of forced labor can be found in ILO Convention No. 29, the Forced Labour Convention of 1930, which defines "forced or compulsory labour" as "all work or service which is exacted from any person under the menace of any penalty and for which the said person has not offered himself voluntarily." The TVPRA of 2008 (P.L. 110-457) amends the *U.S. Criminal Code* and indirectly defines "forced labor" by describing the circumstances under which an individual could be punished for knowingly providing or obtaining the labor or services of a person.[15]

The ILO term for forced labor is broader than both the U.N. and U.S. definitions of human trafficking.

The ILO term is relevant in the U.S. anti-trafficking policy context, as it is the governing definition for the U.S. import ban on foreign goods produced with convict, forced, or indentured labor (§307 of the Tariff Act of 1930).

The ILO definition also applies to U.S. decisions to apply or revoke trade preference beneficiary status to select foreign countries (e.g., GSP, CBERA/CBTPA, ATPA/ATPDEA, and AGOA).

The U.S. Department of Labor also applies the international definition in its preparation of two additional mandates: (1) a list of foreign goods produced with exploitative child labor that may not be used in federal contractor supply chains (EO 13126), and (2) a list of foreign goods produced by forced labor or child labor (TVPRA of 2005; P.L. 109-164).

Worst Forms of Child Labor

ILO Convention No. 182, the Worst Forms of Child Labor Convention of 1999, defines "the worst forms of child labour" to include child slavery and prostitution, as well as use of children in illicit activities, such as drug trafficking, and other work, which by its nature, is likely to harm the health, safety, or morals of children. This term is used in the U.S. foreign policy context in decisions to apply or revoke trade preference beneficiary status to foreign countries. It is also the governing definition used by the Labor Department for its annual report on *Findings of the Worst Forms of Child Labor* (hereinafter *Worst Forms of Child Labor Report*). However, not all of the ILO-specified worst forms of child labor necessarily constitute human trafficking, as defined by either the U.N. or the TVPA. This term is to be distinguished from other terms used in U.S. foreign policy contexts, including "forced and indentured child labor" (as is used by EO 13126) and "child labor" (as is used to develop a list of foreign goods produced by forced or child labor, pursuant to the TVPRA of 2005).

FOREIGN POLICY ISSUES

Overall, U.S. foreign policy to address and eliminate international human trafficking includes several dimensions that are not mutually exclusive. They are summarized below, and key issues associated with each line of activity are discussed in the subsequent sections.

- *Foreign Country Reporting.* Congress requires the U.S. Departments of State and Labor to report annually on foreign country efforts against human trafficking, child soldiers, and the worst forms of child labor, as well as country efforts to support human rights, including prohibitions on forced and compulsory labor and child trafficking.
- *Foreign Product Blacklisting.* Congress mandates the U.S. Departments of Labor and Homeland Security to maintain, respectively, a list of foreign goods produced with child or forced labor and a list of foreign products made with convict, forced, or indentured labor to be barred entry at U.S. ports. Additionally, the President, through EO 13126, requires the Department of Labor to maintain a list of foreign goods made with forced or indentured child labor prohibited from use in federal procurement supply chains.
- *Foreign Assistance and Related Projects to Support Anti-Trafficking Efforts Abroad.* Congress authorizes and appropriates to the U.S. Department of State, U.S. Agency for International Development (USAID), and the U.S. Department of Labor funds to support foreign countries' efforts to combat human trafficking. Between FY2005 and FY2010, these departments and agencies obligated a total of $493 million for international anti-trafficking activities, including assistance to foreign governments, NGOs, and civil society organizations, as well as researchers.
- *Restrictions on Foreign Assistance to Poor-Performing Countries.* Congress requires that non-humanitarian, nontrade-related foreign aid be denied to countries that are willfully noncompliant with anti-trafficking standards. Separately, Congress also

requires that certain types of U.S. military assistance be denied to countries that harbor or recruit child soldiers.

- *Conditions on Foreign Country Trade Preference Beneficiary Status for Anti-Trafficking Purposes.* Through several legislative vehicles, Congress authorizes certain countries to export to the United States specified products duty-free. Eligibility for this privilege, however, is conditioned on whether such countries are committed to certain foreign policy goals, including internationally recognized worker rights, such as prohibiting forced labor, and the elimination of the worst forms of child labor, such as child trafficking.

- *Prevention of Trafficking in U.S. Operations Overseas.* Congress and the White House have issued several policies and regulations emphasizing prohibitions on trafficking-related activities among U.S. military personnel, contractors, peacekeepers, and post-conflict and humanitarian aid workers. For U.S. contractors operating overseas, for example, anti-trafficking laws and regulations bar not only "severe forms of human trafficking," as defined by the TVPA, but also procurement of commercial sex (e.g., prostitution) while contracted with the U.S. government and use of forced labor in the performance of the contract.

These lines of activity reflect a long-standing and broad-based set of U.S. policy commitments to eliminate international human trafficking. The problem of human trafficking, however, continues to persist—challenging policy makers to modify and improve existing U.S. foreign policy responses to the problem. Persistent reports of human trafficking worldwide may also challenge policy makers to evaluate whether anti-trafficking programs can achieve current U.S. foreign policy goals within a realistic time frame.

Foreign Country Reporting

One line of U.S. foreign policy activity to combat human trafficking is through foreign country reporting. Congress has mandated that the Departments of State and Labor regularly report on foreign countries' policy responses to human trafficking and forced labor, identify countries that recruit and harbor child soldiers, and evaluate efforts made by foreign countries to eliminate the worst forms of child labor, including child trafficking.

The most targeted of these reports is the State Department's *TIP Report*, which reviews the status of foreign countries in achieving the TVPA's minimum standards to eliminate severe forms of trafficking in persons.[16] In the *TIP Report*, countries ultimately receive one of four possible ranking designations: Tier 1 (best), Tier 2, Tier 2 Watch List, and Tier 3 (worst). Only Tier 1 countries are fully compliant with the TVPA's minimum standards, while the rest are noncompliant and vary in terms of the level of effort to improve. Other congressionally mandated foreign country reporting includes two reports, the *Findings of the Worst Forms of Child Labor* (hereinafter *Worst Forms of Child Labor Report*) and the *Country Reports on Human Rights Practices* (hereinafter *Human Rights Report*), as well as an additional list, published in conjunction with the *TIP Report*, of countries involved in recruiting and using child soldiers (see *Table 2* below). For two of these reporting requirements—the *TIP Report* and the list of countries involved in recruiting and using child soldiers—the worst-performing countries may, in turn, be subject to restrictions on certain types of U.S. foreign assistance (see section below on "Foreign Aid Restrictions").

Table 2. Summary of Foreign Country Reporting Requirements

Reporting Requirement	Legislative Source	Description
TIP Report	Section 110(b) of the TVPA, as amended; 22 U.S.C. 7107(b).	Due each June and issued annually since 2001, the centerpiece of the TIP Report is a country-by-country analysis and ranking, based on progress countries have made in their efforts to prosecute, protect, and prevent human trafficking.
List of Countries Involved in Recruiting and Using Child Soldiers	Section 404(b) of the CSPA; 22 U.S.C. 2370c-1(b)	Beginning in 2010, the State Department annually publishes a list of countries that recruit or use child soldiers in their armed forces, or that harbor non-government armed forces that recruit or use child soldiers. Following these guidelines, the State Department identified six such countries in both 2010 and 2011: Burma, Chad, Democratic Republic of the Congo (DRC), Somalia, Sudan, and Yemen. In 2012, Chad was removed from the list, but two more were added—Libya and South Sudan—for a total of seven listed countries.
Worst Forms of Child Labor Report	Section 412(d) of the TDA, as amended; 19 U.S.C. 2464	Since 2002, the Labor Department has issued an annual report on the progress made by certain specified countries to eliminate the worst forms of child labor. The most recent report, released in September 2011, covers 144 countries and territories designated as current or previous beneficiaries of trade preference programs.
Human Rights Report	Section 504 of the Trade Act of 1974 (19 U.S.C. 2464) and Section 104 of the TVPA (22 U.S.C. 2151n)	Congress also requires the State Department to include in its annual Human Rights Report sections for each country on the status of the "prohibition of forced or compulsory labor" as well as on trafficking in persons. In the 2011 edition, the State Department reported on 196 countries. The 2011 edition cross-referenced the TIP Report for details on human trafficking and also stated that most countries faced challenges associated with implementing and enforcing prohibitions against forced or compulsory labor.

Sources: CRS presentation of data from the Legislative Information System (LIS); DOS, J/TIP, 2012 TIP Report; DOL, 2011 Worst Forms of Child Labor Report; and DOS, 2011 Human Rights Report.

These annually updated analyses provide regular reporting and country-level detail that are not otherwise published. As public documents, the information contained in them has created diplomatic opportunities for engagement with foreign counterparts, as well as for increased public awareness of human trafficking as an international problem. Some officials and outside observers value these reports as an effective means through which to praise countries that have implemented best practices, criticize those that have balked at reform, and offer support to those that could benefit from foreign donor assistance.

In contrast, the State Department's Office of Inspector General (OIG) describes several of these reports as resource-intensive, unnecessarily "encyclopedic in detail and length," largely redundant, and at times the cause of more diplomatic harm than good.[17] Although the actual number of pages devoted to each individual country narrative tends to be relatively few, OIG criticized the length of the State Department's *TIP Report*, which in 2012 totaled

396 pages, and the Department of Labor's *Worst Forms of Child Labor Report*, which in 2011 totaled 855 pages. The State Department's OIG described the *TIP Report* as among the most cost-intensive in terms of personnel resources both at U.S. diplomatic posts abroad and at headquarters in Washington, DC.

To illustrate such criticisms, the OIG highlighted the experience of U.S. Embassy Bridgetown, located in Barbados. In addition to Barbados, Embassy Bridgetown is responsible for diplomatic relations with six additional governments in the Eastern Caribbean, including Antigua and Barbuda, Dominica, Grenada, St. Kitts and Nevis, St. Lucia, and St. Vincent and the Grenadines. All are covered by either the *TIP Report* or the *Worst Forms of Child Labor Report*, or both. Embassy Bridgetown reportedly estimated that approximately 200 person-hours were required to resolve questions and differences in its submission to Washington for the 2009 *TIP Report* and an additional 200 person-hours for "dealing with negative political, media, and public reactions."[18] Some, however, may consider such time and personnel resources committed to human trafficking issues appropriate, given the perceived magnitude and seriousness of the problem.

Other concerns have centered on the lack of consistent reporting quality across countries, as well as questions regarding discrepancies in data collection and the reliability of report findings. For example, the Labor Department's *Worst Forms of Child Labor Report* identifies a substantially larger number of countries associated with child soldiers, compared to the State Department's list. A rationale for this discrepancy may be that, in most cases, reports of child soldiers are often associated with unsanctioned rebel groups beyond the control of state policies. However, in the case of Afghanistan, the Department of Labor reports that children have joined its national military and police forces.

Foreign Product Blacklisting

A second line of foreign policy activity to combat human trafficking is through foreign product blacklisting. Through two acts (the Tariff Act of 1930 and the TVPRA of 2005) and an executive order (EO 13126), the Departments of Labor, State, and Homeland Security are required to maintain lists of foreign products that have been produced by forced labor, child labor, indentured labor, forced or indentured child labor, and convict labor.

- Pursuant to the *Tariff Act of 1930*[19] and implementing regulations, DHS may prohibit certain types of goods from import into the United States when it is determined that (1) the goods are produced, mined, or manufactured with the use of convict, forced, or indentured labor; and (2) such goods had been or are likely to be imported into the United States. According to DHS's Customs and Border Protection (CBP), currently banned products include specified furniture, clothes hampers, and palm leaf bags from a state penitentiary in Tamaulipas, Mexico, as well as specified diesel engines, machine presses, sheepskin and leather products, and malleable iron pipe fittings from a combination of factories and prisons in Yunnan, Xuzhou, Qinghai, and Tianjin, China.[20]
- Pursuant to *EO 13126*, issued by President Clinton on June 12, 1999, the Department of Labor, in consultation with the State Department and DHS, is required to jointly publish and maintain a list of countries and products that are likely to have been

mined, produced, or manufactured by forced or indentured child labor. The appearance on the list triggers an additional requirement for U.S. federal contractors to certify that they have made good faith efforts to ensure that their products and services to the U.S. government do not involve forced or indentured child labor. The most recent version of the list identifies 46 products from 21 countries.[21]

- The *TVPRA of 2005* mandates the Department of Labor to "develop and make available to the public a list of goods from countries that the Bureau of International Labor Affairs has reason to believe are produced by forced labor or child labor in violation of international standards."[22] Pursuant to this mandate, the Department of Labor initially published a list in 2009 and subsequently updated the list in 2010 and 2011. There are currently 130 goods from 71 countries identified by the Department of Labor as likely produced by child labor or forced labor.[23]

Although not all of the blacklisted products pursuant to these provisions are necessarily indicative of human trafficking, they are often included today as a dimension of U.S. policy to combat international human trafficking and described in recent State Department *TIP Reports* as a component of the overall U.S. anti-trafficking policy regime.[24] The consequences of being identified as a blacklisted product vary, depending on which list a product is placed.

These lists can be viewed as innovative policy responses to prevent labor-related human trafficking, often considered an under-emphasized and under-prioritized dimension of the trafficking in persons problem. They may, however, be criticized by some as duplicative, while also not sufficiently tailored or utilized as a tool to combat human trafficking, given variations in the standards, definitions, and criteria used for each blacklist. The direct correlation between blacklisted products and human trafficking is therefore imprecise, as none of the three lists specify whether blacklisted products are indicative of human trafficking as defined by either the U.N. or the TVPA (see *Table 3* below).

Foreign Aid and International Anti-Trafficking Projects

A third line of foreign policy activity to combat human trafficking is through provisions of aid to foreign countries. For more than a decade, Congress has authorized and appropriated foreign assistance and international grants to combat human trafficking. From FY2005 through FY2010, the U.S. government obligated a total of $493 million for international anti-trafficking projects outside the United States. Given the transnational nature of human trafficking, these anti-trafficking programs are viewed by proponents as crucial tools to build the capacity and capability of other countries to prevent trafficking, protect victims, and prosecute traffickers (commonly referred to as the three Ps).

Improved foreign efforts to eliminate trafficking could, in turn, translate into fewer legal, political, and physical safe havens for international traffickers to exploit.

Such international projects, however, are also challenged by limitations in measuring effectiveness and developing meaningful measures of progress. Given the general absence of data to formulate a baseline estimate for the scope of the human trafficking problem, it is often difficult to specify how anti-trafficking aid programs have improved the situation.

Table 3. Foreign Product Blacklisting Terms Used in Comparison

Legislative Source	Implementing Agency	Convict Labor	Child Labor[a]	Forced Labor[b]	Forced Child Labor[c]	Indentured Labor	Indentured Child Labor[c]	Human Trafficking	Consequence of Blacklisting
Tariff Act of 1930	DHS	X		X	X	X	X	N/A	Import Ban
EO 13126	DOL, in consultation with DOS and DHS				X		X	N/A	Procurement Ban
TVPRA of 2005	DOL		X	X	X			N/A	N/A

Sources: Section 307 of the Tariff Act of 1930 (Title III, Chapter 497, as amended; 19 U.S.C. 1307), EO 13126 (June 12, 1999), Section 105 of the TVPRA of 2005 (P.L. 109-164; 22 U.S.C. 7112), and U.S. Department of Labor, Bureau of International Labor Affairs (ILAB), Frequently Asked Questions, Trafficking Victims Protection Reauthorization Act (TVPRA), "What Definitions of Child Labor and Forced Labor are Used in Developing the List?" http://www.dol. gov/ilab/faqs2.htm#tvpra3. N/A=not applicable; DHS= Department of Homeland Security, DOS=Department of State, DOL=Department of Labor.

[a] Child labor is undefined in the TVPRA of 2005, but the Department of Labor defines "child labor" as "all work performed by a person below the age of 15" and includes all work performed by a person below the age of 18 under circumstances that fit the ILO's definition of the "worst forms of child labor" (ILO Convention No. 182). ILO Convention No. 182 defines the "worst forms of child labor" as "(a) all forms of slavery or practices similar to slavery, such as the sale and trafficking of children, debt bondage and serfdom and forced or compulsory labour, including forced or compulsory recruitment of children for use in armed conflict; (b) the use, procuring or offering of a child for prostitution, for the production of pornography or for pornographic performances; (c) the use, procuring or offering of a child for illicit activities, in particular for the production and trafficking of drugs as defined in the relevant international treaties; (d) work which, by its nature or the circumstances in which it is carried out, is likely to harm the health, safety or morals of children."

[b] Section 307 of the Tariff Act of 1930 defines "forced labor" consistent with ILO Convention No. 29. ILO Convention No. 29 defines forced labor as "all work or service which is exacted from any person under the menace of any penalty for its nonperformance and for which the worker does not offer himself voluntarily."

[c] EO 13126 defines "forced or indentured child labor" as all work or service (1) exacted from any person under the age of 18 involving forced labor as defined by ILO Convention No. 29; or (2) performed by any person under the age of 18 pursuant to a contract the enforcement of which can be accomplished by process or penalties.

For example, the U.N. Office on Drugs and Crime (UNODC) stated in a 2009 report that "without a sense of the magnitude of the problem, it is impossible to prioritize human trafficking as an issue relative to other local or transnational threats, and it is difficult to assess whether any particular intervention is having effect."[25] In lieu of specifics, anti-trafficking assistance programs are often described as providing diffuse capacity-building benefits for governance, civil society, and general public awareness. Such factors, however, are difficult to measure and, even if they were to be measured, may claim only tenuous links to any specific anti-trafficking program. In the past, the U.S. Government Accountability Office (GAO) has reported on problems with coordinating, evaluating, and monitoring the effectiveness of U.S. foreign aid projects to combat human trafficking.[26]

Table 4. Assistance to Combat Trafficking in Persons in the State Department's Foreign Operations Budget
(in current U.S. $ thousands)

	FY2009 Actual	FY2010 Actual	FY2011 Actual	FY2012 Estimate	FY2013 Request
Africa	900	435	750	1,500	1,550
East Asia and Pacific	4,505	2,818	4,180	5,150	4,302
Europe and Eurasia	5,894	2,136	4,556	5,943	4,450
Near East	300				2,000
South and Central Asia	3,834	4,930	5,404	5,338	4,260
Western Hemisphere	1,565	1,150	1,396		700
DOS/J-TIP	19,380	21,262	16,233	18,720	18,720
DOS/INL					425
USAID/DCHA			1,600	1,500	1,800
USAID/EGAT	1,567	900			
TOTAL	38,445	34,631	34,119	38,151	38,207

Sources: DOS, responses to CRS request, December 21, 2011 and April 4, 2012; DOS, CBJ, Volume 2: Foreign Operations, Fiscal Year 2012-2013 (revised).

Notes: USAID=U.S. Agency for International Development; DCHA=USAID Bureau for Democracy, Conflict, and Humanitarian Assistance, DOS=U.S. Department of State, EGAT=USAID Bureau for Economic Growth, Agriculture and Trade; J-TIP=DOS Office to Monitor and Combat Trafficking in Persons; INL=DOS International Narcotics and Law Enforcement Affairs Bureau, Estimates are rounded up to the nearest thousand. Foreign assistance spigots included in this chart encompass Assistance for Europe, Eurasia, and Central Asia (AEECA), Development Assistance (DA), Economic Support Fund (ESF), and International Narcotics Control and Law Enforcement (INCLE) funds. U.S. Department of Labor and DOS Educational and Cultural Exchange (ECE) assistance funds are listed separately. The State Department has in the past reported that some non-quantified amount of Migration and Refugee Assistance (MRA) is obligated in support of projects related to anti-trafficking. but the anti-trafficking component of such projects could not be disaggregated.

Accounting for the annual amount of U.S. funding for international projects to combat human trafficking can also present difficulties. Executive branch agencies receive anti-trafficking funding through several appropriations accounts that are not necessarily linked to TVPA authorities. State Department aid for anti-trafficking is broken down on a country and regional basis, rather than allocated according to the TVPA's specified authorities. For each fiscal year from FY2008 through FY2011, the TVPRA of 2008 authorized a total of $63.8 million in foreign assistance to the State Department and to the President for combating trafficking in persons.[27] Yet, differing sources provide a varied portrait of how much the U.S. government spent on anti- trafficking aid projects in that period. The State Department, for example, reported that it budgeted a total of $34.63 million in anti-trafficking foreign aid for FY2010 (see Table 4). Separately, the State Department also reported that, in FY2010, the U.S. government obligated $85.27 million for approximately 175 international anti-trafficking projects benefitting more than 80 countries (see Figure 1).28 The latter figure for obligated funds in FY2010 includes funding for projects that are allocated to agencies and for purposes beyond those referenced in the TVPA, such as Department of Labor funds for combating the worst forms of child labor.

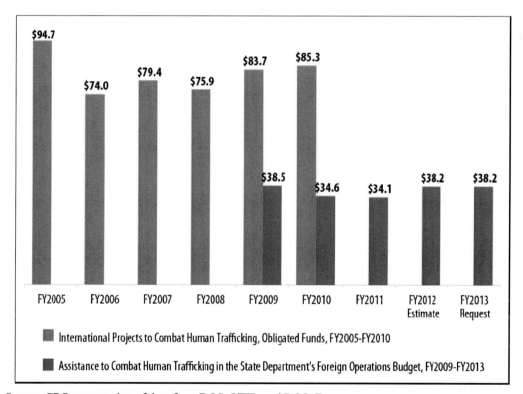

Source: CRS presentation of data from DOS, J/TIP, and DOS, F.
Note: Numbers are rounded to the nearest decimal.

Figure 1. International Anti-Trafficking Obligations and Foreign Operations Budget (in current U.S. $ millions).

Further, it is not clear from annual budget request documents why certain countries are selected for aid projects and what role the *TIP Report's* country rankings play in such selections.

According to the State Department's FY2013 congressional budget justification (CBJ) for anti-trafficking foreign assistance, priority countries to receive such assistance include those that have not achieved the TVPA's minimum standards for eliminating severe forms of trafficking in persons (i.e., countries designated as Tier 3, Tier 2 Watch List, and Tier 2 in the

State Department's annual *TIP Report*) provided that such countries have a demonstrable need for external assistance and that they show the political will to address deficiencies in their anti-trafficking policies. The CBJ, however, does not provide information on how aid recipient countries are selected among other countries ranked by the *TIP Report*. For a comparison of the State Department's budget request for FY2013 anti-trafficking aid and the most recent *TIP Report* ranking for those countries selected to receive such aid, see the *text box* below.

FY2013 Foreign Aid Request Compared to Country Rankings in the 2012 TIP Report

For FY2013, the State Department is requesting a total of $38.2 million in anti-trafficking foreign aid funding to at least 28 countries. Of these, two were designated as Tier 1 in the 2012 TIP Report, 18 were Tier 2, seven Tier 2 Watch List, and one Tier 3. This represents about 15% of all countries ranked in the TIP Report.

- Tier 1 (2 of a total of 33 Tier 1 countries in the 2012 *TIP Report*): Georgia and Macedonia.
- Tier 2 (18 of 93 total Tier 2 countries): Albania, Armenia, Bangladesh, Bosnia and Herzegovina, Cambodia, Egypt, Guatemala, Indonesia, Kazakhstan, Kosovo, Moldova, Montenegro, Mozambique, Nepal, Philippines, Tajikistan, Ukraine, and Vietnam.
- Tier 2 Watch List (7 of 42 total Tier 2 Watch List countries): Azerbaijan, Belarus, Lebanon, Malaysia, Russia, Thailand, and Uzbekistan.
- Tier 3 (1 of 17 total Tier 3 countries): Democratic Republic of Congo.

Foreign Aid Restrictions

Restrictions on foreign assistance are also used to combat human trafficking. Congress has enacted two provisions through which to deny certain types of foreign aid to countries that are not advancing U.S. and international community anti-trafficking goals. One of these provisions, pursuant to the TVPA, seeks to restrict non-humanitarian, nontrade-related foreign aid from certain governments that do not show progress in eliminating human trafficking.[29] Under this provision, countries that receive a Tier 3 ranking in the *TIP Report* are ineligible to receive non-humanitarian, nontrade-related aid in the following fiscal year. The second provision, which first went into effect in 2010 pursuant to the CSPA of 2008, seeks to restrict certain U.S. military assistance from countries known to recruit or use child soldiers in their armed forces, or that host non-government armed forces that recruit or use child soldiers.[30] For both provisions, the President may reserve the option of waiving aid sanctions in cases where the continuation of aid would promote U.S. national interests that supersede anti-trafficking policy goals.

The goal of these aid restriction mechanisms is to induce foreign governments to enhance their commitments to combat human trafficking. Withholding or denying U.S. aid, it is argued, can be an effective point of leverage for countries that would like to continue receiving such aid. Some, however, perceive aid sanctions as a potentially blunt policy tool that can interfere with or undermine other U.S. interests in such countries.

Table 5. Aid Restrictions and Waivers Pursuant to the TVPA, FY2004-FY2012

	Non-humanitarian, Non-Trade Aid Restricted	In the Absence of Aid to Restrict, Exchange Programs Restricted	Full National Interest Waivers	Partial National Interest Waivers	Waivers Due to Subsequent Compliance
FY2004	none	Burma, Cuba, North Korea	none	Liberia, Sudan	Belize, Bosnia and Herzegovina, Dominican Republic, Georgia, Greece, Haiti, Kazakhstan, Suriname, Turkey, Uzbekistan
FY2005	none	Burma, Cuba, North Korea	none	Equatorial Guinea, Sudan, Venezuela	Bangladesh, Ecuador, Guyana, Sierra Leone
FY2006	none	Burma, Cuba, North Korea	Ecuador, Kuwait, Saudi Arabia	Cambodia, Venezuela	Bolivia, Jamaica, Qatar, Sudan, Togo, UAE
FY2007	Burma	Cuba, North Korea	Saudi Arabia, Sudan, Uzbekistan	Iran, Syria, Venezuela, Zimbabwe	Belize, Laos
FY2008	Burma	Cuba	Algeria, Bahrain, Malaysia, Oman, Qatar, Saudi Arabia, Sudan, Uzbekistan	Iran, North Korea, Syria, Venezuela	Equatorial Guinea, Kuwait
FY2009	Burma, Syria	Cuba	Algeria, Fiji, Kuwait, Papua New Guinea, Qatar, Saudi Arabia, Sudan	Iran, North Korea	Moldova, Oman
FY2010	North Korea	Cuba	Chad, Kuwait, Malaysia, Mauritania, Niger, Papua New Guinea, Saudi Arabia, Sudan	Burma, Eritrea, Fiji, Iran, Syria, Zimbabwe	Swaziland
FY2011	none	North Korea, Eritrea	DRC, Dominican Republic, Kuwait, Mauritania, Papua New Guinea, Saudi Arabia, Sudan	Burma, Cuba, Iran, Zimbabwe	none
FY2012	none	North Korea, Eritrea, Madagascar	Algeria, CAR, Guinea-Bissau, Kuwait, Lebanon, Libya, Mauritania, Micronesia, Papua New Guinea, Saudi Arabia, Sudan, Turkmenistan, Yemen	Burma, Cuba, DRC, Equatorial Guinea, Iran, Venezuela, Zimbabwe	none

Source: Presidential Determination (PD) with Respect to Foreign Governments' Efforts Regarding Trafficking in Persons, PD nos. 2003-35, 2004-46, 2005-37, 2006-25, 2008-4, 2009-5, 2009-29, 2010-15, and 2011-18.

With the discretion to partially or fully waive sanctioned countries from experiencing the full effect of the aid restrictions, Presidents have sought to balance the impact of the aid restrictions with consideration of other U.S. foreign policy interests that may be at play (see *Table 5* and *Table 6*). An issue for debate is the extent to which the waiver option should be exercised and whether extensive use of the waiver option can have a negative effect on international commitments against human trafficking.

Observers have questioned whether the aid restrictions are effective in prompting countries to improve their efforts to combat human trafficking. It may be too soon to assess the impact of the child soldiers-related aid restriction.

With regard to the aid sanctions program pursuant to the TVPA, however, few countries have improved from Tier 3, the worst-performing category, to Tier 1, the highest-performing category, since the aid restriction program first went into effect almost a decade ago. Many more countries have either maintained the same tier ranking over the years, or are middling in their performance ratings without clear trends toward significant improvement. To this end, some commentators have questioned whether the existing aid restrictions are sufficient. See *text box* below on "TIP Report Ranking Trends: Measurable Signs of Improvement?"

Congress sought to increase the consequences associated with consistent poor performance in the *TIP Report* through the TVPRA of 2008, which included a new provision to automatically downgrade to Tier 3 those countries that have stayed on the "Tier 2 Watch List" for two consecutive years (unless the President issues a waiver to block the downgrade).[32] FY2012 is the first year in which this provision resulted in automatic downgrades to Tier 3 and posed a subsequent risk of aid denial. Of the 22 countries that were at risk of a downgrade to Tier 3 in the 2011 *TIP Report*, all received waivers to avoid full sanctions on aid in FY2012.[33]

Even if aid restrictions were fully applied to all poor-performing countries, however, such an action would not necessarily indicate that U.S. aid to those countries has stopped because the existing aid denial provision exempts several categories of foreign aid.

Table 6. Aid Restrictions and Waivers Pursuant to the CSPA of 2008, FY2011-FY2012

Aid Restricted		Partial National Interest Waivers	Full National Interest Waivers	Waivers Due to Subsequent Compliance
FY2011	Burma and Somalia	none	Chad, DRC, Sudan, and Yemen	none
FY2012	Burma, Somalia, and Sudan	DRC	Yemen	Chad

Source: Presidential Determination (PD) with Respect to Section 404(c) of the Child Soldiers Prevention Act of 2008, PD 2011-4, PD 2012-01.

TIP Report Ranking Trends: Measurable Signs of Improvement?

Since 2001, the State Department's *TIP Report* has been ranking countries on the basis of their efforts to combat human trafficking. In the 2012 report, a total of 185 countries were ranked.

Only Tier 1 countries are compliant with achieving the TVPA's minimum standards for eliminating trafficking. The rest, totaling approximately 83.5% of all countries ranked in the 2012 *TIP Report*, are listed as non-compliant—variously receiving designations as Tier 2, Tier 2 Watch List, or Tier 3, depending on their level of effort in achieving the minimum standards. Following are trends in country rankings over the course of the TIP Report's existence:

- Consistent top performers, having always received a Tier 1 designation in annual TIP Reports, include Australia, Austria, Belgium, Colombia, Denmark, Germany, Italy, Luxembourg, the Netherlands, New Zealand, Norway, Spain, the United Kingdom, and the United States of America (first ranked in 2010).[31]
- Most improved countries, having previously been ranked as a Tier 3 countries and eventually attaining Tier 1 status in 2012, include South Korea (from Tier 3 in 2001 to Tier 1 since 2002), Georgia (from Tier 3 in 2003 to Tier 1 since 2007, and Israel (from Tier 3 in 2001 to Tier 1 in 2012).
- Middling countries, having always received a Tier 2 designation, include Antigua and Barbuda, Aruba (first ranked in 2011), Botswana, Bulgaria, Burkina Faso, Chile, El Salvador, Kosovo, Marshall Islands (first ranked in 2011), Mongolia, Palau, St. Lucia (first ranked in 2011), Timor-Leste, Tonga (first ranked in 2011), Uganda, and Uruguay.
- Consistent worst performers, having always received a Tier 3 designation, include Cuba, Eritrea, North Korea, and Sudan.
- Countries that have backslid, having previously attained Tier 2 status but are now listed in the current 2012 TIP Report as a Tier 3 countries, include Algeria, DRC, Equatorial Guinea, Guinea-Bissau, Iran, Kuwait, Lebanon, Libya, Madagascar, Saudi Arabia, Syria, Yemen, and Zimbabwe.

Conditions on Country Beneficiary Status for Trade Preference Programs

A further line of foreign policy activity to combat human trafficking is the designation of foreign countries as U.S. trade preference program beneficiaries, provided they adhere to international anti-trafficking commitments. For decades, the U.S. government has implemented a variety of unilateral trade preference programs designed to promote exports among selected developing countries.[34] Through such trade preference programs, designated beneficiary countries are provided duty-free entry for specified products into the United States. The first such program, in existence since 1976, is the Generalized System of Preferences (GSP).[35]

Beneficiary countries may be designated (or removed) based on eligibility criteria specified in the relevant authorizing legislation. Such eligibility criteria include commitments to "internationally recognized worker rights," such as prohibiting the "use of any form of forced or compulsory labor," as well as commitments to eliminate the "worst forms of child labor," such as child trafficking.[36]

In theory, conditioning preferential trade status on foreign policy goals, including prohibiting forced labor and the worst forms of child labor, may serve to encourage country compliance with international efforts to combat human trafficking. According to GAO, government officials as well as representatives from non-governmental organizations and the private sector consider the process of conditioning beneficiary status for trade preference programs valuable in raising awareness about problems in foreign countries related to workers' rights.[37] Some, however, question whether U.S. trade policies may nevertheless at times work at cross-purposes with U.S. anti-trafficking policies, offering trade benefits to countries that have not effectively enforced national policies to combat forced labor and the worst forms of child labor, including child trafficking. The U.S. Trade Representative is not a member of interagency coordination mechanisms on human trafficking, such as the SPOG and the PITF.

In the past, GAO has criticized the trade preference programs' country beneficiary review processes as disconnected with U.S. anti-trafficking policy.[38] Further, the criteria used to determine whether countries have committed to prohibiting forced labor and eliminating the worst forms of child labor appear to be set at a different threshold or standard than the ranking process established by either the State Department's annual *TIP Report* to measure country performance in combating severe forms of trafficking in persons or the Department of Labor's annual report listing countries and goods associated with child or forced labor. According to a GAO report, U.S. Trade Representative officials stated that "there is not a specific link" between eligibility criteria for trade preference programs and the State Department's *TIP Report*.[39] The GAO report further states that "while following statutory requirements, agencies' approaches to monitoring compliance with program criteria nevertheless result in disconnected review processes that are separate from ongoing U.S. efforts to [among other purposes] ... combat trafficking in persons."[40]

Among those countries eligible for trade preference programs in 2012, eight were designated by the State Department's 2012 *TIP Report* as Tier 3, the worst-performing category of countries, described as not having achieved the minimum standards for eliminating severe forms of human trafficking and not making significant efforts to do so.[41] Similar discrepancies appear between the trade preference program beneficiary countries and those listed by the Department of Labor as producing goods with either child labor, forced labor, or both. A total of 21 beneficiary countries are reported by the Department of Labor as producing goods with both forced and child labor.[42] Such contrasts may raise questions regarding both the credibility and impact of the State Department's *TIP Report* ranking process and the Department of Labor's annual list of goods produced by child or forced labor, as well as the effectiveness of the administrative reviews for beneficiary status for trade preference programs.

Preventing U.S. Government Participation in Trafficking Overseas

A final dimension of foreign policy activity to combat human trafficking addressed in this report is efforts to prevent U.S.-facilitated trafficking from occurring abroad. U.S. government personnel, diplomats, peacekeepers, and contractors operate overseas and represent U.S. interests abroad at U.S. embassies, consulates, military bases, and other posts located in foreign countries where domestic anti-trafficking laws and the enforcement of such laws may vary significantly.

In recent decades, news reports have unearthed a range of international sex and labor trafficking schemes that have allegedly involved U.S. representatives overseas as the traffickers and exploiters and the end-user consumers of services provided by trafficking victims. Current focus has centered on allegations at U.S. installations in Iraq and Afghanistan, as well as at U.S. embassy missions, where third-country nationals (TCNs) are hired by subcontractors to perform low-skill, labor-intensive jobs.43 Such schemes involving U.S. personnel apparently occur despite NSPD-22, discussed above, which established a "zero tolerance" policy toward all U.S. government employees and contractor personnel overseas who engage in human trafficking violations.

TVPA: Contractor Prohibitions and Reporting Requirements

The TVPA requires the President to authorize federal agencies and departments to terminate, without penalty, grants, contracts, and cooperative agreements if the grantee, subgrantee, contractor, or subcontractor (1) engages in severe forms of trafficking in persons while the grant, contract, or cooperative agreement is in effect; (2) procures a commercial sex act while the grant, contract, or cooperative agreement is in effect; or (3) uses forced labor in the performance of the grant, contract, or cooperative agreement.[44]

Also pursuant to the TVPA, actions to enforce the U.S. government's zero-tolerance policy against human trafficking in contracts are reported in an annual report to Congress prepared by the Attorney General.[45]

Subsequently, the TVPRA of 2008 mandated additional reporting requirements for the OIGs for the Departments of State and Defense and USAID.[46] This provision directed the OIGs to investigate, over the course of three years from FY2010 through FY2012, a series of contracts and subcontracts at any tier under which contractors and subcontractors are at heightened risk of engaging in acts related to human trafficking. Specified high-risk activities include confiscation of employee passports, restriction on an employee's mobility, abrupt or evasive repatriation of an employee, and deception of an employee regarding the work destination.

Although the OIG reports submitted to Congress pursuant to the TVPRA of 2008 collectively documented few instances of likely contractor involvement in severe forms of human trafficking, solicitation of commercial sex acts, sex trafficking, or involuntary servitude,[47] several of them identified contractor management practices that increased the risk of human trafficking and related violations. The State Department's OIG, for example, found instances of contractor coercion at recruitment and destination points and exploitative conditions at work, including frequent instances in which workers paid recruiters brokerage fees and employers regularly confiscated employee passports, withheld wages, used confusing calculations to determine earnings, provided unsafe or unsanitary living conditions for workers, and participated in deceptive recruitment practices that exploited workers' lack of language, education, and information.[48] The DOD's OIG evaluated selected contracts in the U.S. Pacific Command and U.S. Central Command areas of responsibility and revealed problems with ensuring that contracts had the appropriate anti-trafficking clauses.[49]

Although the U.S. government reports that it continues to investigate alleged cases of trafficking involving U.S. officials and contractors, many experts have questioned why such cases rarely result in criminal prosecution or other enforcement measures. Regarding federal contractors, allegations are generally corrected internally by the contractor before more severe contracting penalties are imposed by the U.S. government, such as contract termination, or contractor disqualifications, suspensions, and debarments. Though there are anti-trafficking laws, regulations, and zero-tolerance policies in place, some question whether they are effectively enforced.[50] In war zones and overseas contingency operations, enforcement capacity is particularly challenged by factors such as the unreliability of host nation capacity to enforce its domestic rule of law, the need for low-cost and quickly recruited government contractors in large volumes, the prioritization of investigating human trafficking violations relative to other possible national security priorities in such operations, and the general absence of security, such that investigators and contracting officer representatives (CORs) are unable to travel to sites for inspection and audit. The 112th Congress has introduced several bills that seek to improve the enforcement of anti-trafficking regulations among federal contractors.[51] For further discussion of trafficking-related legislation in the 112th Congress, see the *Appendix*.

CONCLUSION

Human trafficking is an inherently transnational and multi-dimensional issue that touches on a broad combination of foreign policy, human rights, criminal justice, and national security priorities. Despite U.S. and international efforts, perpetrators continue to persist in victimizing men, women, and children worldwide through commercial sexual exploitation, forced labor, debt bondage, domestic servitude, and the use of children in armed conflict. Although there remains widespread support among policy makers and outside observers for the continuation of U.S. and international anti-trafficking goals, reports of ongoing exploitation of trafficking victims worldwide appear to fundamentally question the effectiveness and prioritization of current responses to the trafficking problem. In the face of persistent reports of human trafficking worldwide, policy makers remain challenged to evaluate whether U.S. goals to eradicate human trafficking worldwide are achievable and whether current international anti-trafficking programs are measured against realistic expectations.

This report has explored issues related to several U.S. foreign policy responses to human trafficking, including (1) foreign country reporting, (2) foreign product blacklisting, (3) foreign aid, (4) foreign aid restrictions, (5) conditions on trade preference program beneficiaries, and (6) preventing U.S. government participation in trafficking overseas. These U.S. approaches to international human trafficking highlight a series of initiatives, often implemented unilaterally, that exceed the international commitments set forth in treaties such as the U.N. Trafficking Protocol. Issues discussed in this report have centered on challenges associated with how well these policy mandates connect with and reinforce each other, and whether resources devoted to combating human trafficking are allocated effectively and efficiently. Several generations of legislative activity address aspects of human trafficking as currently conceptualized by the U.N. Trafficking Protocol and TVPA, but they are neither necessarily or easily integrated in current anti-trafficking policy nor implemented smoothly across federal agencies. Given recent reports suggesting that U.S. government personnel and contractors have been implicated in trafficking schemes overseas, some may also question the credibility of the United States as an international leader against trafficking in persons.

As the 112th Congress considers action on international human trafficking issues related to pending legislation in both chambers to reauthorize the TVPA, the FY2013 budget and appropriations cycle, and upcoming executive branch report submissions to Congress, illustrative questions of congressional interest may include the following:

- *Congressionally Mandated Reports: Redundancies and Resource Costs.* In October 2010, the State Department's OIG released a report that singled out the *TIP Report* as among the most cost-intensive in terms of personnel resources both at U.S. diplomatic posts abroad and at headquarters in Washington, DC. It also pointed to redundancies among other congressionally mandated reports that reference human trafficking-related concerns, including the Labor Department's annual *Worst Forms of Child Labor Report*. Is there value in requiring the executive branch to submit multiple reports to Congress with similar information? To what extent have these reports provided Congress with relevant information needed to make policy decisions?

- *U.S. Military Aid to Countries with Child Soldiers.* Beginning with the 2010 *TIP Report*, the State Department has been mandated by Congress to identify countries that recruit or harbor child soldiers. Yet, some of the listed countries continue to receive various types of U.S. military assistance, pursuant to presidential national interest waivers. Other countries that receive U.S. military assistance, such as Afghanistan, have also been variously reported by the Department of Labor and non-governmental groups as having recruited and harbored minors in their armed forces. What factors are taken into consideration when balancing the priorities of providing U.S. military assistance to key partner countries and combating the practice of child soldiers? Are current U.S. restrictions on military aid effective in preventing and deterring countries from recruiting child soldiers? What policy options might exist to further induce foreign countries to halt such practices?

- *Effectiveness of U.S. Aid Restrictions to "Tier 3" Countries.* For FY2012, President Obama authorized the full force of anti-human trafficking aid restrictions to be applied to 3 of 23 Tier 3 countries listed in the 2011 *TIP Report*: Eritrea, Madagascar, and North Korea. None of these countries, however, were anticipated to receive U.S. assistance that could have been sanctioned in FY2012. Have congressionally authorized anti-trafficking aid restrictions been effectively used by the executive branch? What additional policy options might exist to reach poor-performing countries that do not receive much U.S. foreign aid?

- *Interagency Consistency in the Implementation of Anti-Trafficking Policy.* Through the TVPA, Congress mandated the creation of two senior-level interagency coordinating bodies, including the SPOG and the PITF, to de-conflict and ensure consistency among international anti-trafficking initiatives. Yet, some interagency inconsistencies persist. For example, U.S. trade preference programs in 2012 continue to list as among its beneficiaries 12 Tier 3 countries listed in the 2011 *TIP Report* and 8 Tier 3 countries from the 2012 *TIP Report*. Additionally, 21 trade preference program beneficiary countries are listed by the Department of Labor as producing goods with a combination of both forced and child labor. Although there are no specific requirements to ensure consistency among U.S. trade policies and anti-trafficking policies, how do such discrepancies affect the effectiveness of efforts to combat human trafficking?

- *Enforcement of Anti-Trafficking Policies Among U.S. Contractors Overseas.* Recent OIG reports submitted to Congress by the Departments of State and Defense and USAID identified several contractor management practices that increased the risk that human trafficking and related violations might occur, including instances of contractor coercion at recruitment and destination points and potentially exploitative conditions at work, such as unregulated recruitment fees, regular confiscation of employee passports, withheld wages, confusing calculations of earnings, unsafe or unsanitary living conditions, and deceptive recruitment practices that exploit workers' lack of language, education, and information.[52] What policy options should Congress consider in reducing the possibility of U.S. government funds and representatives from facilitating severe forms of trafficking in persons?

- *Multilateral Policy Options: Potential for Redundancy or Efficiency Gains?* As discussed in this report, the U.S. government implements a series of unilateral policy responses to combat international human trafficking. The United States is also an active participant in multilateral anti-trafficking initiatives. To what extent do such multilateral initiatives enhance or render redundant existing U.S. efforts? Do other countries and international organizations consider U.S. foreign policy responses to combat human trafficking an effective model? Given the common goal of eliminating trafficking in persons, what can or should the U.S. government do, if anything, to enhance its support of multilateral anti-trafficking initiatives?

See the *Appendix* for further discussion of pending legislation in the 112th Congress on international human trafficking.

APPENDIX. SELECTED LEGISLATION IN THE 112TH CONGRESS

The 112th Congress has considered issues related to international trafficking in persons in the form of hearings and authorization and appropriations bills, as well as other oversight actions.

This appendix identifies pending bills in the 112th Congress that would have an impact on U.S. foreign policy responses against human trafficking. Overall, key provisions have centered on themes related to funding levels for anti-trafficking initiatives, country and region-specific human rights issues, adjustments to existing trafficking-related reporting requirements and aid sanctions programs, prevention of labor trafficking in U.S. supply chains, and allegations associated with U.S. contractors operating overseas.

Trafficking Victims Protection Reauthorization Act of 2011

The 112th Congress has introduced three bills to reauthorize the TVPA beyond FY2011: two House bills, the Trafficking Victims Protection Reauthorization Act of 2011 (H.R. 2830 and H.R. 3589), and one Senate bill, the Trafficking Victims Enhanced Protection Act of 2011 (S. 1301).

For a comparison of funding provisions, see *text box* below on "House and Senate Authorization of Appropriations in Comparison."

H.R. 2830, H.R. 3589, and Related Provisions

Representative Smith introduced H.R. 2830 on August 30, 2011, as well as H.R. 3589 on December 7, 2011. Both bills would reauthorize appropriations for the TPVA for an additional two fiscal years: FY2012 and FY2013. The House Committee on Foreign Affairs marked up H.R. 2830 on October 5, 2011, and amended the bill as introduced in the nature of a substitute. Included in the marked-up version of H.R. 2830 were four amendments agreed upon en bloc, including amendments offered by Representatives Murphy, Fortenberry, Royce, and Bass. One notable omission in the marked-up version of H.R. 2830 included the removal of a provision to authorize the establishment of a DOD Director of Anti-Trafficking Policies.

H.R. 3589 includes the text of H.R. 2830 as amended in the October 5, 2011, following committee markup (at Sections 106, 108, 109, and 110). It also includes an additional provision at Section 303 related to the eligibility of faith-based organizations to receive assistance pursuant to the TVPA. H.R. 3589 was referred on December 14, 2011, to the House Subcommittee on Crime, Terrorism, and Homeland Security.

Notable provisions in H.R. 2830, as marked up, and H.R. 3589, as introduced, addressing foreign policy issues to combat international trafficking in persons include the following (as applicable, similarities among other bills introduced in the 112th Congress, including S. 1301, are also described below):

- *Section 102. Office to Monitor and Combat Modern Slavery and Other Forms of Human Trafficking.* This provision would rename the State Department's Office to Monitor and Combat Trafficking in Persons the "Office to Monitor and Combat Modern Slavery and Other Forms of Trafficking in Persons."

- *Section 103. Prevention of Trafficking.* This provision would incorporate human trafficking-related elements of H.R. 2524, Microenterprise Empowerment and Job Creation Act of 2011.[53] It would also prioritize assistance to particularly vulnerable categories of persons, including stateless, marginalized, and internally displaced, as well as assistance to address post-conflict and humanitarian emergencies.

- *Section 104. Reports to Congress.* This provision would require, among other provisions, two additional sections in the annual *TIP Report* issued by the State Department pursuant to Section 110 of the TVPA. One new section would be entitled "Best Practices in Slavery Eradication" and a second section would be entitled "Refugee-Trafficking Connection." Section 106 of S. 1301 as reported out of the Senate Judiciary Committee also includes a similar provision "Best Practices in Trafficking in Persons Eradication," which would mandate the State Department to include in its annual *TIP Report* a new section on "exemplary governments and practices in the eradication of trafficking in persons."[54]

- *Section 106. Additional Activities to Monitor and Combat Forced Labor and Child Labor.* This provision incorporates the amendment offered by Representative Murphy to the marked-up version of H.R. 2830. The provision would incorporate similar provisions in H.R. 2759, introduced by Representative Maloney, entitled the Business Transparency on Trafficking and Slavery Act. It would encourage publicly traded or private entities with business operations in the United States and having annual global receipts in excess of $100 million to voluntarily disclose on their websites measures to identify and address "conditions of forced labor, slavery, human trafficking and the worst forms of child labor" within their supply chains.

- *Section 108. Sense of Congress on Human Trafficking.* This provision incorporates the amendment offered by Representative Royce to the marked-up version of H.R. 2830, which would provide a Sense of Congress that Cambodia should be designated a Tier 3 country in the State Department's annual *TIP Report.*

- *Section 109. Prohibition on Peacekeeping Operations Assistance to Countries that Recruit and Use Child Soldiers and Revision to National Interest Waiver Under the Child Soldiers Prevention Act of 2008.* This provision incorporates the amendment offered by Representative Fortenberry to the marked-up version of H.R. 2830 to bar assistance through the Peacekeeping Operations (PKO) foreign aid account from countries designated by the State Department as recruiting and using child soldiers. This provision would incorporate similar provisions in H.R. 2519, introduced by Representative Fortenberry on July 13, 2011, and the companion bill S. 1259, introduced by Senator Durbin on June 22, 2011. Section 109 of S. 1301 as reported out of the Senate Judiciary Committee also includes a similar provision to bar PKO funds from states designated as recruiting and using child soldiers. In contrast to the House bill, S. 1301 exempts from restriction PKO programs that "support military professionalization, security sector reform, heightened respect for human rights, peacekeeping preparation, or the demobilization and reintegration of child soldiers." Several additional bills and enacted appropriations in the 112th Congress include similar provisions barring certain types of military assistance to countries that recruit or use child soldiers.[55]

- *Section 201 of H.R. 2830 and Section 202 H.R. 3589. Interagency Task Force to Monitor and Combat Trafficking.* Among other purposes, this provision would require the annual report prepared for Congress by the Attorney General on U.S. anti-trafficking programs, pursuant to Section 105(d)(7) of the TVPA,[56] to include additional information on federal agencies' enforcement of the U.S. government zero-tolerance policy, pursuant to NSPD-22, against trafficking in persons, including termination, discipline, and prosecution of government contractors and subcontractors. Section 112 of S. 1301 as reported out of the Senate Judiciary Committee includes related amendments to Section 105(d)(7) of the TVPA to require additional information on Defense Department reporting of trafficking cases, including those by defense contractors.

S. 1301 and Related Provisions

S. 1301, the Trafficking Victims Enhanced Protection Act of 2011, was introduced on June 29, 2011, by Senator Leahy. On November 17, 2011, the bill was reported favorably in the nature of a substitute out of the Senate Judiciary Committee (S.Rept. 112-96). Notable provisions include the following:

- *Section 101. Regional Strategies for Combating Trafficking in Persons.* This provision would require each regional bureau to compile a list of anti-trafficking goals and objectives for each country in its area of responsibility.

- *Section 102. Regional Anti-Trafficking Officers.* This provision would authorize the Secretary of State to appoint at U.S. embassies overseas officers with specific responsibility to coordinate anti-trafficking diplomacy, initiatives, and programs.

- *Section 103. Partnerships Against Significant Trafficking in Persons.* This provision would amend the TVPA and insert a new section, Section 105A, intended to promote collaboration and cooperation among U.S. government, foreign government, civil society actors, and private sector entities to combat human trafficking. This section would also introduce a new mechanism, Child Protection Compacts, through which foreign countries may receive assistance to combat child trafficking. Initially introduced under S. 185, Child Protection Compact Act of 2011, by Senator Boxer on January 25, 2011, prospective country recipients would be required to meet certain eligibility criteria and assistance would be provided in the form of grants, cooperative agreements, or contracts with recipient country governments or relevant NGOs or private entities with expertise in combating child trafficking.[57]

- *Section 105. Minimum Standards for the Elimination of Trafficking.* This provision would amend Section 108(b) of the TVPA to include additional criteria for determining whether a country has achieved the minimum anti-trafficking standards, such as effective bilateral, regional, and multilateral coordination and cooperation on trafficking route information and effective policies and laws regulating foreign labor recruiters.

- *Section 106. Best Practices in Trafficking in Persons Eradication.* This provision would amend Section 110(b) of the TVPA to, among other purposes, require that the State Department, in its annual *TIP Report*, include a new section on "Exemplary Governments and Practices in the Eradication of Trafficking in Persons." As discussed above, this provision incorporates aspects of S. 1362, Trafficking in Persons Report Improvement Act of 2011, introduced by Senator Webb on July 13, 2011.[58] Additionally, a similar provision is incorporated into Section 104 of H.R. 3589.

- *Section 108. Prevention of Child Trafficking Through Child Marriage.* This provision would require the Secretary of State to prepare a strategy to prevent child marriage and incorporate information on the status of child marriage in the State Department's annual *Human Rights Report*.

- *Section 109. Child Soldiers.* As discussed above under Section 109 of H.R. 3589, this provision would bar certain PKO funds from states designated as recruiting and using child soldiers.

- *Section 110. Presidential Award for Technological Innovations to Combat Trafficking in Persons.* This provision would amend Section 112B(a) of the TVPA to include as possible recipients of the Presidential Award for Extraordinary Efforts to Combat Trafficking in Persons private sector entities and units of national, regional, and local governments. Such recipients may qualify for the award not only for having contributed extraordinary effort in combating trafficking, but also for contributing to technological innovation.

- *Section 111. Contracting Requirements.* This provision would elaborate on existing authorities for the federal government to terminate grants, contracts, and cooperative agreements if human trafficking-related acts take place during or in the performance of the grant, contract, or agreement. This provision would also mandate that a contract compliance plan be in place for grants, contracts, and cooperative agreements valued at more than $1 million and that take place mainly overseas in support of contingency operations.

- *Section 112. Department of Defense Reporting of Trafficking in Persons Claims and Violations.* As discussed above under Section 201 of H.R. 2830 and Section 202 of H.R. 3589, this provision would require in the annual report prepared for Congress by the Attorney General on U.S. anti-trafficking programs, pursuant to Section 105(d)(7) of the TVPA,[59] additional information on Defense Department reporting of trafficking cases, including those by defense contractors.

- *Section 222. Reporting Requirements for the Secretary of Labor.* This provision would amend Section 105(b) of the TVPRA of 2005[60] to require that the list of goods from countries that are reasonably believed to have been produced by forced or child labor in violation of international standards be updated no later than December 2, 2012, and every two years thereafter. Although the Department of Labor has updated the list three times since the TVPRA of 2005 first mandated the list, there is no provision in current law that specifies whether and how frequently the list should be updated.

- *Section 223. Information Sharing to Combat Child Labor and Slave Labor.* This provision would require the Secretary of State to share on a regular basis with the Department of Labor information related to child labor and forced labor used to produce goods in violation of international standards.

- *Section 225. GAO Report on the Use of Foreign Labor Contractors.* This provisions would require the U.S. Government Accountability Office (GAO) to submit a report, within two years of enactment of the act, on the use of foreign labor contractors both domestically and overseas.

House and Senate Authorization of Appropriations in Comparison

Title III of H.R. 2830, as marked up; H.R. 3589, as introduced; and S. 1301, as reported, address authorization of appropriations for anti-trafficking initiatives and programs.

For the most part, Title III of H.R. 2830 and H.R. 3589 authorize appropriations for FY2012 and FY2013 for international programs at the same levels as in the previous TVPRA ending FY2011.[61] One notable change is to the authorization of appropriations for the Presidential Award for Extraordinary Efforts to Combat Trafficking in Persons pursuant to Section 112B of the TVPA.[62] In current law, for each of the fiscal years 2008 through 2011, "such sums as may be necessary to carry out this section" are authorized to be appropriated. Section 301 of H.R. 2830 and H.R. 3589 would amend this to specify that $500,000 may be appropriated for each of the fiscal years 2012 and 2013.

In contrast, Title III of S. 1301 authorizes appropriations for four fiscal years: FY2012 through FY2015. S. 1301 zeros or reduces authorized funding several programs and initiatives previously authorized for appropriations. S. 1301 also omits reference to some other programs and initiatives authorized for appropriations in the TVPRA of 2008. For example:

- *Programs zeroed out* include a USAID pilot program for victim rehabilitation facilities.[63] This program was previously authorized under P.L. 110-457 at $2.5 million for FY2011. H.R. 2830 and H.R. 3589 authorize $1.5 million for each fiscal year 2012 and 2013 for such purposes. Also zeroed out are authorized expenses for Interagency Task Force receptions, previously authorized for appropriations at $3,000 for FY2011.[64] H.R. 2830 and H.R. 3589 maintain authorized appropriations at the previously authorized level.

- *Programs for which authorized funding levels are reduced* by S. 1301 include funding in support of the Interagency Task Force,[65] from $5.5 million in FY2011 to $2 million in each fiscal year 2012 through 2015; funding for foreign victim assistance,[66] from $15 million in FY2011 to $7.5 million in each fiscal year 2012 through 2015; and funding for foreign assistance to meet the minimum standards to eliminate trafficking in persons,[67] from $15 million in FY2011 to $7.5 million in each fiscal year 2012 through 2015.

- *Programs omitted from reference* in S. 1301, which in current law are authorized only through FY2011, include funding for additional personnel to staff the Interagency Task Force (for which $1.5 million is authorized in current law);[68] funding for foreign law enforcement training assistance (for which $250,000 is authorized in current law);[69] research on human trafficking (for which $2 million is authorized in current law);[70] and the Presidential Award for Extraordinary Efforts to Combat Trafficking in Persons (for which "such sums as may be necessary" is authorized in current law).[71]

Other Anti-Trafficking Bills

Other bills in the 112th Congress that address foreign policy issues to combat international trafficking in persons include the following:

- *H.R. 1410, the Vietnam Human Rights Act of 2011.* H.R. 1410 was introduced on April 7, 2011, by Representative Smith. On March 7, 2012, the bill was marked up and ordered to be reported. The bill would prohibit an increase in non-humanitarian foreign aid to Vietnam over FY2011 levels unless, among other provisions, the President determines and certifies to Congress that "[n]either any official of the Government of Vietnam nor any agency or entity wholly or partly owned by the Government of Vietnam was complicit in a severe form of trafficking in persons, or the Government of Vietnam took all appropriate steps to end any such complicity and hold such official, agency, or entity fully accountable for its conduct."

- *H.R. 2583, the Foreign Relations Authorization Act, Fiscal Year 2012.* H.R. 2583 was introduced on July 19, 2011, by Representative Ros-Lehtinen. The bill was reported favorably by the House Committee on Foreign Affairs on September 23, 2011 (H.Rept. 112-223). H.R. 2583 includes human trafficking related provisions of H.R. 1410, the Vietnam Human Rights Act of 2011, and also would mandate the U.S. Department of State to establish a code of conduct to prevent trafficking in persons, which among other provisions, would "outline necessary steps to ensure that

Department of State contractors and subcontractors do not engage in trafficking in persons."

- *S. 1426, the Foreign Relations Authorization Act, Fiscal Years 2012 and 2013.* S. 1426 was introduced on July 27, 2011, by Senator Kerry. The bill would authorize foreign police assistance with respect to combating trafficking in persons to address sexual and gender-based violence, reduce corruption, prevent conflict, and respond to disasters.

- *H.R. 3253, the International Megan's Law of 2011.* H.R. 3253 was introduced by Representative Smith on October 24, 2011. It was referred on November 2, 2011, to the House Subcommittee on Immigration Policy and Enforcement. The bill would amend the criteria for determining whether countries have achieved the minimum standards for eliminating severe forms of human trafficking to specify that government-to-government cooperation on trafficking investigations and prosecutions include cooperation in the reporting of its own citizens who are suspected of engaging in severe forms of human trafficking in another country. Among other provisions, H.R. 3253 would establish an International Sex Offender Travel Center and encourage the use of anti-trafficking assistance authorized by Section 134 of the Foreign Assistance Act of 1961 to support foreign governments in the establishment of systems to identify sex offenders and share and receive information related to such individuals' travel plans abroad. The bill would also mandate additional reporting requirements related to the plans and status of international mechanisms to track and monitor traveling child sex offenders.

- *S. 2318 and H.R. 4077, the Department of State Rewards Program Update and Technical Corrections Act of 2012.* S. 2318 and H.R. 4077 were introduced by Senator Kerry and Representative Royce, respectively. Among other provisions, the bills would authorize the publication and distribution of rewards for information leading to the arrest or capture of selected transnational criminals. The bills specified that it is the sense of Congress that the expanded rewards program would cover trafficking in persons, among other crimes.

- *S. 2234 and H.R. 4259, the End Trafficking in Government Contracting Act of 2012.* S. 2234 and H.R. 4259 were both introduced on March 26, 2012, by Senator Blumenthal and Representative Lankford, respectively. The provisions of S. 2234 and H.R. 4259 were also incorporated into two other bills in the 112th Congress.[72] Among other provisions, the bills would enhance the existing authority provided in Section 106(g) of the TVPA to terminate or take other remedial action against contractors and subcontractors who are found destroying, concealing, removing, or confiscating an employee's immigrations documents without consent; failing to repatriate an employee upon the end of employment in certain circumstances; offering employment by means of materially false or fraudulent pretenses; charging recruited employees exorbitant placement fees; and providing inhuman living conditions. The bills would also amend 18 U.S.C. 1351 to expand the penalties for fraud in foreign labor contracting to include work outside the United States.[73]

End Notes

[1] Other key international treaties addressing human trafficking, which the United States has ratified or acceded to, include the 1956 Supplementary Convention on the Abolition of Slavery, the Slave Trade, and Institutions and Practices Similar to Slavery; the 2000 U.N. Optional Protocol to the Convention on the Rights of the Child on the Sale of Children, Child Prostitution, and Child Pornography; the 2000 U.N. Optional Protocol to the Convention on the Rights of the Child on the Involvement of Children in Armed Conflict; the 1957 International Labor Organization (ILO) Convention No. 105 on the Abolition of Forced Labour; and the 1999 ILO Convention No. 182 on the Worst Forms of Child Labour.

[2] U.S. Department of State (DOS), Office to Monitor and Combat Trafficking in Persons (J/TIP), Trafficking in Persons Report 2011, June 27, 2011. Hereinafter cited as TIP Report (2011).

[3] ILO, ILO Global Estimate of Forced Labour: Results and Methodology, June 2012. ILO estimates the range of victims to be between 19.5 million and 22.3 million, with a 68% level of confidence.

[4] The TVPA has been amended and reauthorized through the Trafficking Victims Protection Reauthorization Act of 2003 (TVPRA of 2003), P.L. 109-162; the Trafficking Victims Protection Reauthorization Act of 2005 (TVPRA of 2005), P.L. 109-164; and the William Wilberforce Trafficking Victims Protection Reauthorization Act of 2008 (TVPRA of 2008), P.L. 110-457. Additional provisions, amending the TVPA are also located at Section 682 of Division A (Department of State Authorization Act, Fiscal Year 2003), Title VI, Subtitle G of the Foreign Relations Authorization Act, Fiscal Year 2003 (P.L. 107-228); and Section 804 of Title VIII, Subtitle A of the Violence Against Women and Department of Justice Reauthorization Act of 2005 (P.L. 109-162). The TVPA is codified at 22 U.S.C. 7101-7112. Unless otherwise noted, all subsequent references to the TVPA are assumed to refer to the TVPA, as amended.

[5] President George W. Bush, National Security Presidential Directive 22 (NSPD-22), Combating Trafficking in Persons, December 16, 2002, partially declassified for publication as "Appendix C" in U.S. Department of Defense (DOD), Office of the Inspector General (OIG), Inspections and Evaluations: Evaluation of DOD Efforts to Combat Trafficking in Persons, Report No. IE-2007-002, November 21, 2006.

[6] Ibid.

[7] Section 307 of Title III, Chapter 497 (46 Stat. 689); 19 U.S.C. 1307. Unless otherwise noted, all subsequent reference to the Tariff Act of 1930 are assumed to refer to the Act, as amended.

[8] U.S. Department of Homeland Security (DHS), Customs and Border Protection (CBP), Convict, Forced, or Indentured Labor Product Importations, December 10, 2009, http:// www.cbp.gov/xp/cgov/trade/ trade_outreach/ convict_importations.xml.

[9] U.S. Department of Labor, International Labor Affairs Bureau (ILAB), Executive Order 13126, http://www.dol.gov/ ILAB/regs/eo13126/main.htm.

[10] The definition for "internationally recognized worker rights" was first incorporated into U.S. statutes through Section 507, Title V (Trade Act of 1974), of the Trade Reform Act (P.L. 93-618), as added by Section 1952(a), Title I (GSP Renewal Act of 1996) of the Small Business Job Protection Act of 1996 (P.L. 104-188). The definition for "worst forms of child labor" was first incorporated into U.S. statutes through Section 412(b), Title IV of the Trade and Development Act of 2000 (TDA, P.L. 106-200). Both terms are codified at 19 U.S.C. 2467.

[11] Title V (Trade Act of 1974) of the Trade Reform Act (P.L. 93-618), as amended; 19 U.S.C. 2462-2467.

[12] CBERA was first enacted through the Title II of P.L. 98-67 ("An act to promote economic revitalization and facilitate expansion of economic opportunities in the Caribbean Basin region, to provide for backup withholding of tax from interest and dividends, and for other purposes"), and subsequently amended. CBTPA was first enacted through Title II of the TDA (P.L. 106-200), and subsequently amended. Both provisions are codified at 19 U.S.C. 2701-2707.

[13] ATPA was first enacted through Title II (Trade Preference for the Andean Region) of the Andean Trade Preference Act (P.L. 102-182) and subsequently amended. ATPDEA was first enacted through Division C, Title XXXI of the Trade Act of 2002 (P.L. 107-210), and subsequently amended. Both provisions are codified at 19 U.S.C. 3201-3206.

[14] Title I (Extension of Certain Trade Benefits to Sub-Saharan Africa) of the TDA (P.L. 106-200); 19 U.S.C. 3701-3706 and 19 U.S.C. 2466a-b.

[15] 18 U.S.C. 1589.

[16] Section 108(a) of the TVPA, as amended; 22 U.S.C. 7106(a).

[17] DOS and Broadcasting Board of Governors (BBG), Office of Inspector General (OIG), Inspection of Department-Required and Congressionally Mandated Reports: Assessment of Resource Implications, Report of Inspection, Report Number ISP-I-11-11, October 2010.

[18] Ibid.

[19] Section 307 of the Tariff Act of 1930 (Title III, Chapter 497, as amended; 19 U.S.C. 1307).

[20] DHS, CBP, Convict, Forced, or Indentured Labor Product Importations, December 10, 2009, http://www.cbp.gov/ xp/cgov/trade/trade_outreach/convict_importations.xml.

[21] U.S. Department of Labor, ILAB, EO 13126, Current List of Products and Countries on EO 13126, current as of May 31, 2011, http://www.dol.gov/ILAB/regs/eo13126/.

[22] Section 105(b)(2)(C) of the TVPRA of 2005 (P.L. 109-164; 22 U.S.C. 7112(b)(2)(C)). Section 110 of the TVPRA of 2008 (P.L. 110-457) reiterates this reporting requirement (no corresponding U.S. Code citation).

[23] U.S. Department of Labor, ILAB, List of Goods Produced by Child Labor or Forced Labor, 2011.

[24] The original purpose of enacting these provisions was not necessarily designed to serve specifically as a policy response to trafficking in persons, but rather to condemn foreign labor practices in contravention to international labor standards.

[25] U.N. Global Initiative to Fight Human Trafficking (UNGIFT) and U.N. Office on Drugs and Crime (UNODC), Global Report on Trafficking in Persons, February 2009.

[26] U.S. Government Accountability Office (GAO), Human Trafficking: Better Data, Strategy, and Reporting Needed to Enhance U.S. Anti-Trafficking Efforts Abroad, GAO-06-825, July 18, 2006. In 2007, GAO followed up with a second report with similar conclusions, but indicated that progress in addressing GAO's recommendation, though mixed, was generally positive. According to GAO, the executive branch continues to remain in the process of responding to several of its recommendations to improve anti-trafficking program monitoring, effectiveness, and coordination. GAO, Human Trafficking: A Strategy Framework Could Help Enhance the Interagency Collaboration Needed to Effectively Combat Trafficking Crimes, GAO-07-915, July 26, 2007.

[27] P.L. 110-457; not included in this total are additional funds authorized to the President for research ($2 million, pursuant to Section 113(e)(3) of the TVPA) and to the State Department for the interagency task force, additional personnel, and official reception and representation expenses (approximately $7 million, pursuant to Section 113(a) of the TVPA).

[28] DOS, J/TIP, U.S. Government Anti-Trafficking in Persons Program Funding, June 27, 2011. This document warns, however, that the total figure for international anti-trafficking projects "may be overstated" because funds through the Department of Labor to address the worst forms of child labor, including but not limited to child trafficking, cannot be disaggregated. Obligated totals for international anti-trafficking projects include funding budgeted separate from the foreign operations appropriations process, including some Educational and Cultural Exchange (ECE) programs funded by the State Department as well as some international, bilateral, and multilateral technical assistance to combat exploitative child labor internationally provided by the Department of Labor's Bureau for International Labor Affairs (ILAB).

[29] Section 110(a) of the TVPA, as amended, 22 U.S.C. 7107(a).

[30] Title IV of the TVPRA of 2008 (P.L. 110-457); 22 U.S.C. 2151 note, and 2370c through 2370c-2. Prohibited aid, pursuant to the CSPA of 2008 include international military education and training (IMET); foreign military financing (FMF); excess defense articles; other DOD-funded aid, including aid provided pursuant to Section 1206 of the National Defense Authorization Act of FY2006 (P.L. 109-163), as amended and extended; and the issuance of direct commercial sales of military equipment.

[31] The TVPA does not require the TIP Report to include and rank the United States in its country-by-country evaluations. The State Department, however, has voluntarily chosen to do so. Separately, the TVPA requires the Attorney General to submit a report each year to Congress on specified actions by the U.S. government to combat human trafficking, pursuant to Section 105(d)(7) of the TVPA, as amended (22 U.S.C. 7103(d)(7)).

[32] Section 107 of the TVPRA of 2008 (P.L. 110-457); 22 U.S.C. 7105a. This provision allows the President to waive the Tier 3 downgrade for up to two years.

[33] The 10 countries automatically downgraded in the 2011 TIP Report to Tier 3 included Algeria, Central African Republic (CAR), Equatorial Guinea, Guinea-Bissau, Lebanon, Libya, Micronesia, Turkmenistan, Venezuela, and Yemen. Twelve other countries remained listed as Tier 2 Watch List after the Secretary of State issued a waiver to prevent these countries from receiving the automatic downgrade to Tier 3, including Azerbaijan, Bangladesh, Cameroon, China, Guinea, Iraq, Mali, Qatar, Republic of Congo, Russia, St. Vincent and the Grenadines, and Uzbekistan. According to the 2011 TIP Report, such waivers were issued in cases in which the government in question has a written plan that "would constitute making significant efforts to comply with the TVPA's minimum standards for the elimination of trafficking," if implemented, and that there is credible

evidence that the government in question is "devoting sufficient resources to implement the plan." In the 2012 TIP Report, one country dropped to Tier 3 after receiving a Tier 2 Watch List designation for the previous two years: Syria. Thirteen other countries were at risk of auto-downgrade in the 2012 TIP Report (Afghanistan, Azerbaijan, Barbados, Chad, China, Republic of Congo, Iraq, Malaysia, Mauritania, Niger, Russia, Thailand, and Uzbekistan), but the Secretary of State waived their auto-downgrades.

[34] For an overview of trade preference programs, see CRS Report R41429, Trade Preferences: Economic Issues and Policy Options, coordinated by Vivian C. Jones.

[35] Title V (Trade Act of 1974) of the Trade Reform Act (P.L. 93-618), as amended; 19 U.S.C. 2462-2467.

[36] Countries may be removed from beneficiary status on the basis of periodic administrative reviews for each trade preference program, either initiated by the executive branch or as a result of external petitions from outside, nongovernmental organizations. In the past, countries have been petitioned by such groups for removal and ultimately removed from beneficiary status due to worker rights issues, although it is unclear how many of such removals were specifically due to poor government commitments to combat forced labor or the worst forms of child labor.

[37] GAO, U.S. Trade Preference Programs Provide Important Benefits, but a More Integrated Approach Would Better Ensure Programs Meet Shared Goals, GAO-08-443, March 2008. Hereinafter cited as GAO-08-443.

[38] Based on a review of trade preference programs from 2001 through 2007. GAO, An Overview of Use of U.S. Trade Preference Programs by Beneficiaries and U.S. Administrative Reviews, GAO-07-1209, September 27, 2007.

[39] GAO-08-443.

[40] Ibid.

[41] These 8 countries include Algeria, CAR, DRC, Eritrea, Madagascar, Papua New Guinea, Yemen, and Zimbabwe. See U.S. International Trade Commission, Harmonized Tariff Schedule of the United States (2012) – Supplement 1, USITC Publication 4339, effective July 1, 2012.

[42] These countries include Afghanistan (bricks), Angola (diamonds), Benin (cotton), Bolivia (brazil nuts/chestnuts and sugarcane), Brazil (cattle and charcoal), Burkina Faso (cotton and gold), DRC (cassiterite and coltan), Cote d'Ivoire (cocoa and coffee), Ethiopia (hand-woven textiles), Ghana (tilapia/fish), India (bricks, carpets, cottonseed/hybrid, embroidered textiles/zari, garments, rice, and stones), Kazakhstan (cotton and tobacco), Malawi (tobacco), Mali (rice), Nepal (bricks, carpets, embroidered textiles/zari, and stones), Nigeria (cocoa, granite, and gravel/crushed stones), Pakistan (bricks, carpets, and coal), Russia (pornography), Sierra Leone (diamonds), Thailand (garments and shrimp), and Uzbekistan (cotton). Paraguay reportedly produces goods with both child and forced labor, but not in combination to make a single item.

[43] Third-country nationals (TCNs) include non-local, non-U.S. citizen workers temporarily hired to work by federal contractors for the U.S. government overseas. There is concern that they are particularly susceptible to trafficking schemes, according to recent news and U.S. inspector general reports. As neither U.S. citizens nor citizens of the host nation where they are working, such TCNs are vulnerable due to distance and isolation from their home communities, the possibility of language barriers, and dependence on their employers to procure and maintain current visas and work permits. The U.S. government is often heavily reliant on such contractors for support in providing services at its overseas posts related to facilities maintenance, gardening, construction, cleaning, food, and local guard forces. Often, such TCNs are hired to perform labor for significantly lower cost than would be required to hire local staff. See for example DOS and BBG, OIG, Middle East Regional Office (MERO), Performance Evaluation of Department of State Contracts to Assess the Risk of Trafficking in Persons Violations in Four States in the Cooperation Council for the Arab States of the Gulf, Report No. MERO-I-11-06, January 2011.

[44] Section 106(g) of the TVPA, as amended; 22 U.S.C. 7104(g).

[45] Section 105(d)(7) of the TVPA, as amended; 22 U.S.C. 7103(d)(7). Although not congressionally mandated to report on anti-trafficking progress made by the U.S. government in the TIP Report, the 2011 edition reports that allegations of U.S. defense contractor violations were investigated and ultimately resulted in the dismissal of one employee by a DOD contractor. TIP Report (2011), "Country Narrative for the United States."

[46] Section 232 of the TVPRA of 2008 (P.L. 110-457).

[47] DOS and BBG, OIG, Performance Evaluation of Department of State Contracts to Assess the Risk of Trafficking in Persons Violations in the Levant, Report No. MERO-I-11-07, March 2011; Report to the House Committee on Foreign Relations, January 15, 2010; and Report of Inspection, Embassy Riyadh and Constituent Posts, Saudi Arabia, Report No. ISP-I-10-19A, March 2010.

[48] DOS and BBG, OIG, Performance Evaluation of Department of State Contracts to Assess the Risk of Trafficking in Persons Violations in Four States in the Cooperation Council for the Arab States of the Gulf, Report No. MERO-I-11- 06, January 2011; Report to the House Committee on Foreign Relations, January 15, 2010; and

Performance Audit, The Bureau of Diplomatic Security Baghdad Embassy Security Force, Report No. MERO-A-10-05, March 2010.

[49] DOD, OIG, Evaluation of DOD Contracts Regarding Combating Trafficking in Persons, Report No. IE-2010-001, January 2010; and Evaluation of DOD Contracts Regarding Combating Trafficking in Persons: U.S. Central Command, Report No. IE-SPO-2011-002, January 18, 2011.

[50] See for example U.S. House of Representatives, Committee on Oversight and Government Reform, Subcommittee on Technology, Information Policy, Intergovernmental Relations, and Procurement Reform, Hearing, Are Government Contractors Exploiting Workers Overseas? Examining Enforcement of the Trafficking Victims Protection Act, November 2, 2011.

[51] See for example S. 2234 and H.R. 4259, the End Trafficking in Government Contracting Act of 2012 and S. 2139, the Comprehensive Contingency Contracting Reform Act of 2012.

[52] U.S. Department of State and the BBG, OIG, Performance Evaluation of Department of State Contracts to Assess the Risk of Trafficking in Persons Violations in Four States in the Cooperation Council for the Arab States of the Gulf, Report No. MERO-I-11-06, January 2011; Report to the House Committee on Foreign Relations, January 15, 2010; and Performance Audit, The Bureau of Diplomatic Security Baghdad Embassy Security Force, Report No. MERO-A-10- 05, March 2010.

[53] H.R. 2524, Microenterprise Empowerment and Job Creation Act of 2011, introduced by Representative Smith on July 13, 2011. It was referred to the House Foreign Affairs Committee on July 13, 2011. The bill would authorize foreign assistance, pursuant to Section 252(a) of the Foreign Assistance Act of 1961, as amended, to include "sustainable poverty-focused programs" whose beneficiaries would include "victims or potential victims of severe forms of trafficking in persons or women who are victims of or susceptible to other forms of exploitation and violence."

[54] Note that S. 1301 incorporates the provision in S. 1362, Trafficking in Persons Report Improvement Act of 2011, introduced by Senator Webb on July 13, 2011, that would mandate the State Department to include in its annual TIP Report a new section on "exemplary governments and practices in the eradication of trafficking in persons."

[55] These include the Department of Defense and Full-Year Continuing Appropriations Act, 2011 (P.L. 112-85); the Consolidated Appropriations Act, 2012 (P.L. 112-74); the Foreign Relations Authorization Act, Fiscal Year 2012 (H.R. 2583); the Arms Sales Responsibility Act of 2012 (H.R. 5749); the Department of State, Foreign Operations, and Related Programs Appropriations Act, 2013 (S. 3241 and H.R. 5857); and the Department of State, Foreign Operations, and Related Programs Appropriations Act, 2012 (S. 1601).

[56] 22 U.S.C. 7103(d)(7).

[57] S. 185, the Child Protection Compact Act of 2011, was referred to the Senate Committee on Foreign Relations on January 25, 2011. This bill specified that a country may receive up to $15 million in assistance through a Compact.

[58] S. 1362, the Trafficking in Persons Report Improvement Act of 2011,was referred on July 13, 2011, to the Senate Committee on Foreign Relations. In addition to mandating a new section in the TIP Report on "exemplary governments and practices in the eradication of trafficking in persons," S. 1362 would amend Section 110 of the TVPA, relating to the country designations as Tier 1, Tier 2, Tier 2 Watch List, or Tier 3, to implement a new ranking scheme. One category of countries would be identified as fully compliant with the minimum standards to eliminate severe forms of trafficking in persons and the countries in this category would be sorted and ranked according to their relative adherence to the minimum standards. A second category of countries would be identified as non-complaint with the minimum standards and similarly sorted and ranked relative to other countries in this second category.

[59] 22 U.S.C. 7103(d)(7).

[60] 22 U.S.C. 7112(b).

[61] The previous TVPRA was the TVPRA of 2008, P.L. 110-457.

[62] 22 U.S.C. 7109B.

[63] 22 U.S.C. 7105 note.

[64] 22 U.S.C. 7110(a).

[65] 22 U.S.C. 7105 note.

[66] 22 U.S.C. 7110(e)(1).

[67] 22 U.S.C. 7110(e)(2).

[68] 22 U.S.C. 7105 note.

[69] 22 U.S.C. 7110(d)(B).

[70] 22 U.S.C. 7110(e)(3).

[71] 22 U.S.C. 7109(d).

[72] These include S. 2139, the Comprehensive Contingency Contracting Reform Act of 2012, introduced on June 12, 2012, by Senator McCaskill and H.R. 4310, the National Defense Authorization Act for Fiscal Year 2013, introduced on March 29, 2012, by Representative McKeon, and later passed by the House on May 18, 2012.

[73] This latter provision also appears in an earlier version of Senator McCaskill's bill, the Comprehensive Contingency Contracting Reform Act of 2012 (S. 2139), introduced on February 29, 2012.

In: The Persistence of Human Trafficking
Editors: Perry Simmons Foster and Kayla Brady

ISBN: 978-1-62257-773-6
© 2013 Nova Science Publishers, Inc.

Chapter 2

TRAFFICKING IN PERSONS: U.S. POLICY AND ISSUES FOR CONGRESS[*]

Alison Siskin and Liana Sun Wyler

SUMMARY

Trafficking in persons (TIP) for the purposes of exploitation is believed to be one of the most prolific areas of international criminal activity and is of significant concern to the United States and the international community. According to U.S. government estimates, roughly 800,000 people are trafficked across borders each year. If trafficking within countries is included in the total world figures, some 2 million to 4 million people may be trafficked annually. As many as 17,500 people are believed to be trafficked into the United States each year, and some have estimated that 100,000 U.S. citizen children are victims of trafficking within the United States. Notably, TIP is a modern form of slavery and does not have to include the movement of a person.

Through the Trafficking Victims Protection Act of 2000 (TVPA, Div. A of P.L. 106-386), and its reauthorizations (TVPRAs), Congress has aimed to eliminate human trafficking by creating grant programs for both victims and law enforcement, appropriating funds, creating new criminal laws, and conducting oversight on the effectiveness and implications of U.S. anti-TIP policy. Most recently, the TVPA was reauthorized through FY2011 in the William Wilberforce Trafficking Victims Protection Reauthorization Act of 2008 (TVPRA of 2008, P.L. 110-457).

Two of the bills introduced in the 112th Congress to reauthorize the TVPA have received action. S. 1301 was reported by the Senate Judiciary Committee, and H.R. 2830 was ordered reported by the House Foreign Affairs Committee. The bills would make changes to the act and extend authorizations for some current programs. S. 1301 would extend TVPA authorizations through FY2015, and H.R. 2830 through FY2013. As Congress considers reauthorization of the TVPA, the current budget situation has heightened interest in oversight and funding of current efforts to fight TIP. Obligations for global and domestic anti-TIP programs, not including operations and law enforcement

---

[*] This is an edited, reformatted and augmented version of a Congressional Research Service publication, CRS Report for Congress RL34317, prepared for Members and Committees of Congress, from www.crs.gov, dated January 12, 2012.

investigations, totaled approximately $109.5 million in FY2010. The TVPRA of 2008 authorized $191.3 million in global and domestic anti-TIP programs for FY2011.

Overall, issues related to U.S. anti-TIP efforts include the effectiveness of current programs, whether there is duplication among these programs, and whether there is sufficient oversight of monies spent on anti-trafficking activities. Ongoing international policy issues include how to measure the effectiveness of the U.S. and international responses to TIP, the U.S. Department of State's annual country rankings and the use of unilateral sanctions, and how to prevent known sex offenders from engaging in international child sex tourism. Domestic issues include whether there is equal treatment of all victims—both foreign nationals and U.S. citizens, as well as victims of labor and sex trafficking; and whether current law and services are adequate to deal with the emerging issue of domestic child sex trafficking (i.e., the prostitution of children in the United States). Other overarching issues include whether all forms of prostitution (i.e., children and adults) fit the definition of TIP, and whether sufficient efforts are applied to addressing all forms of TIP, including not only sexual exploitation, but also forced labor and child soldiers.

In June 2011, the State Department issued its annual, congressionally mandated TIP Report. In addition to outlining major trends and ongoing challenges in combating TIP, the report provides a country-by-country analysis and ranking, based on what progress countries have made in their efforts to prosecute traffickers, protect victims, and prevent TIP. The report categorizes countries according to the government's efforts to combat trafficking, with the worst-performing countries at risk of losing selected non-humanitarian, nontrade-related U.S. foreign assistance. For FY2012, TIP sanctions were fully imposed on three of the worst-performing countries: Eritrea, Madagascar, and North Korea.

OVERVIEW

Trafficking in persons (TIP) for the purposes of exploitation is both an international and a domestic crime that involves violations of labor, public health, and human rights standards. As such, the United States and the international community have committed to combating the various manifestations of human trafficking. Anti-TIP efforts have accelerated in the United States since the enactment of the Trafficking Victims Protection Act of 2000 (TVPA, Div. A of P.L. 106-386), and internationally since the passage of the U.N. Protocol to Prevent, Suppress, and Punish Trafficking in Persons, adopted in 2000. Congress has been active in enacting anti-TIP laws, appropriating funds, and authorizing and evaluating anti-trafficking programs. Since 2000, Congress reauthorized the TVPA three times, most recently in 2008. The 110th Congress passed the William Wilberforce Trafficking Victims Reauthorization Act of 2008 (TVPRA of 2008, P.L. 110-457), which, among other provisions, authorized appropriations for FY2008 through FY2011 and established a requirement for the President to develop a system to evaluate the effectiveness of TIP assistance. The 112th Congress has introduced several bills related to human trafficking, including bills to reauthorize the TVPA beyond FY2011.

This report focuses on international and domestic human trafficking and U.S. policy responses, with particular emphasis on the TVPA and its subsequent reauthorizations. The report begins with an overview of the human trafficking problem. It follows with an analysis of the TVPA's primary foreign policy responses to international human trafficking. The report then focuses on responses to trafficking into and within the United States, examining relief for trafficking victims in the United States and discussing U.S. law enforcement efforts to combat domestic trafficking. The report concludes with an overview of current anti-trafficking legislation and an analysis of policy issues. Notably, TIP is a modern form of slavery and does not have to include the movement of a person from one location to another.

Definitions

The United Nations and the United States generally characterize human trafficking in similar terms. Neither definition of human trafficking requires the movement of a person from one location to another for the situation to qualify as human trafficking. The United Nations defines human trafficking as:

> The recruitment, transportation, transfer, harboring, or receipt of persons, by means of the threat or use of force or other forms of coercion, of abduction, of fraud or deception, of the abuse of power or of a position of vulnerability or of the giving or receiving of payments or benefits to achieve the consent of a person having control over another person, for the purpose of exploitation. Exploitation includes, at a minimum, the exploitation or the prostitution of others or other forms of sexual exploitation, forced labor or services, slavery, servitude, or the removal of organs.1

Additional examples of human trafficking exploitation suggested by the United Nations include forced involvement in criminal activities; begging, including child begging; forced marriage; illicit adoption; and exploitation in the military, including child soldiers and forced participation in armed conflicts.[2]

The TVPA, as amended, does not define human trafficking per se. However, it does define "severe forms of human trafficking" as:

> Sex trafficking in which a commercial sex act is induced by force, fraud, or coercion, or in which the person induced to perform such act has not attained 18 years of age; or ... the recruitment, harboring, transportation, provision, or obtaining of a person for labor or services, through the use of force, fraud, or coercion for the purpose of subjection to involuntary servitude, peonage, debt bondage, or slavery.3

In the case of minors, there is general agreement in the United States and much of the international community that the trafficking term applies, regardless of whether a child was recruited, harbored, transported, provided, or obtained by force, fraud, coercion, or voluntarily. Illegal adoptions, however, do not necessarily involve human trafficking, particularly if the children are not taken for the purpose of some form of exploitation. In some, but not all, circumstances, child pornography may involve human trafficking; visual depictions and renderings of pornography appearing to involve children may not be considered human trafficking alone, though the exploitation of a child for a commercial sex act constitutes human trafficking. In both the U.N. and U.S. definitions, there is no distinction between trafficking domestically within the borders of a single country and international or cross-border trafficking. The U.S. definition omits the removal of organs as a severe form of human trafficking and makes a distinction between prostitution and sex trafficking. Notably, transnational trafficking may involve trafficking victims and traffickers crossing political boundaries overtly and covertly, legally and illegally.

Distinctions also exist between human trafficking and human smuggling. Human smuggling typically involves the provision of a service, generally procurement or transport, to people who knowingly consent to that service in order to gain illegal entry into a foreign country. In some instances, an individual who appears to have consented to being smuggled may actually be a trafficked person if, for example, force, fraud, or coercion are found to have played a role.

Scope of the Problem

Human trafficking is widely considered to be one of today's leading criminal enterprises and is believed to affect virtually all countries around the globe. Data on the nature and severity of the problem, however, are both limited and varied.[4] According to the International Labor Organization (ILO), for example, as many as 12.3 million adults and children around the world may be current victims of forced labor, bonded labor, and forced prostitution.[5] According to the United Nations, governments reported that from 1996 to 2003, human trafficking victims originated in 127 countries and were exploited in 137 countries.[6] The U.S. government estimates that approximately 600,000 to 800,000 people are trafficked across global borders each year—at least 56% of which involve female victims.[7] If trafficking within countries is included in the total world figures, official U.S. estimates are that 2 million to 4 million people are trafficked annually.

Other organizations also track data associated with human trafficking. The non-profit organization Free the Slaves estimates that there are 27 million "slaves" in the world today.[8] Another estimate suggests that there may be at least 2.4 million persons in the process of being trafficked for forced labor at any given moment and generating profits as high as $32 billion, according to ILO.[9] In Latin America alone, the International Organization for Migration (IOM) estimates that TIP in women and girls for sexual exploitation may be worth $16 billion annually. The Federal Bureau of Investigation (FBI) estimated in 2006 that human trafficking generates approximately $9.5 billion annually for organized crime.[10]

Despite such estimates of the global prevalence of human trafficking, there remain significant gaps in effective responses to the problem. According to the State Department's 2011 Trafficking in Persons Report (TIP Report), 62 countries have yet to convict a human trafficker under anti-trafficking laws in compliance with international standards.[11]

In most reported instances, TIP involves the movement of victims across national borders. Such international, or cross-border, trafficking may differ in the relative distances from a victim's country of origin and the location where the victimization takes place.

Most international TIP occurs between countries within the same geographic region or between neighboring countries. In other instances, international trafficking involves long-distance flows—across continents or across distinct geographic regions.

International patterns of victim flows also differ in terms of the frequency with which destination country authorities identify victims from a certain region of origin and the breadth of foreign countries in which victims of a certain region of origin are found. For example, East Asians have been reportedly found in more than 20 countries across at least five distinct geographic regions (Europe, the Americas, the Middle East, Central Asia, and Africa).

By contrast, victims from West Africa are detected mainly in just a few countries in Europe, but with a greater frequency of detection than East Asians.[12]

Throughout the world, sex trafficking victims have traditionally ended up in large cities, in vacation and tourist areas, or near military bases, where the demand for sex workers is high. In addition to the sex industry, forced labor trafficking victims are subjected to work in seasonal agriculture, manufacturing (particularly the garment industry), construction, and domestic service. These global trends may change, however, as traffickers adapt to new or emerging vulnerabilities and opportunities.A potentially significant but largely undocumented amount of trafficking also occurs within countries.

According to the United Nations Office on Drugs and Crime (UNODC), such domestic trafficking occurs in both geographically large and socioeconomically stratified countries, such as India and Brazil, but also among relatively small and wealthy countries, such as those in Europe. Recent research also indicates that domestic trafficking occurs within the United States.[13]

Continuing Human Trafficking Challenges

Human trafficking is not a new phenomenon, and many factors may account for its continued existence.

In general, the trafficking business feeds on conditions of vulnerability, including youth; gender; poverty or acute economic crisis; ignorance; social and cultural exclusion; political instability, social upheaval, war, and conflicts; and discriminatory social, cultural, and legal frameworks.

Ongoing demand for cheap labor and commercial sex also perpetuates the trafficking industry.

The globalization of the world economy has increased the movement of people across borders, legally and illegally, especially from poorer to wealthier countries.

International organized crime has taken advantage of the freer flow of people, money, goods, and services to extend its own international reach. Other contributing factors include

- The continuing subordination of women in many societies, as reflected in economic, educational, and employment disparities between men and women.[14] Poverty and a lack of educational and job opportunities in many countries may put children, especially girls, from families with multiple children at risk.
- The hardship and economic or physical dislocation caused by conflict, humanitarian disasters, and vulnerability of people in other situations of political crisis. Refugees, internally displaced persons, and those who are stateless (i.e., lacking identity documents) may also be particularly vulnerable to trafficking.[15]
- The tendency to treat trafficking victims as criminals, which has made many victims reluctant to cooperate with law enforcement.[16]
- The inadequacy of laws and law enforcement capacity in some origin, transit, and destination countries hampers efforts to fight trafficking. Even if countries have specific laws aimed at TIP, enforcement of such laws is sporadic, and penalties for

trafficking humans are often relatively minor compared with those for other criminal activities.

- The disinterest in investigating or prosecuting complex trafficking cases, particularly in which there might be government complicity, according to State Department officials.[17]

U.S. Response: Interagency Funding and Coordination

In response to the ongoing scourge of human trafficking and as part of its international commitments to eradicate the problem globally, the U.S. government supports many types of anti-TIP initiatives overseas and domestically. Most U.S. anti-trafficking activities are authorized by the TVPA, as amended, which also established the interagency coordination framework for U.S. government-wide programs to combat human trafficking.

Domestic and Overseas Obligated Funds

Overall, between FY2001 and FY2010, U.S. agencies have obligated an estimated $771 million on domestic and international anti-TIP assistance.[18] FY2011 obligations by agency are not yet available for all agencies. In FY2010, the U.S. government obligated an estimated $85.3 million for international anti-trafficking assistance programs, up from $83.7 million obligated in FY2009. In FY2010, the U.S. government obligated roughly $24.2 million for domestic anti-TIP programs, an increase from $19.7 million obligated in FY2009. The total for domestic obligations does not include the costs of administering TIP operations or TIP-related law enforcement investigations.

Interagency Coordination

As authorized by TVPA, U.S. anti-TIP programs are coordinated at the cabinet level by the President's Interagency Task Force to Monitor and Combat Trafficking in Persons (PITF), which is chaired by the Secretary of State.

The PITF's purpose is to de-conflict and prevent duplication of efforts across agencies involved in anti-TIP programming and ensure compliance with U.S. government policies on combating TIP. The PITF meets annually to coordinate broad U.S. anti-TIP policy, most recently on February 1, 2011.

The TVPA also established the Senior Policy Operating Group (SPOG), another interagency entity that meets quarterly to carry out PITF initiatives and to discuss anti-TIP policy issues. The SPOG, among other activities, facilitates a review by SPOG programming agencies and each other's grant proposals for anti-trafficking projects. Members of the PITF and SPOG include the Departments of State, Justice, Homeland Security, Labor, Defense, Education, Agriculture, and Health and Human Services; USAID; U.S. Equal Employment Opportunity Commission; the Office of Management and Budget (OMB); the Office of the Director of National Intelligence (O/DNI); the National Security Council; and the Domestic Policy Council.[19]

(in current U.S. $ millions)

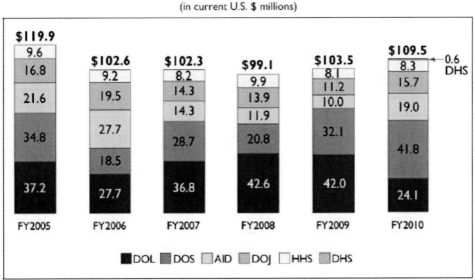

Figure 1. Anti-TIP Obligations by Agency: FY2005-FY2010.

Source: CRS presentation of data from the U.S. Department of State, Office to Monitor and Combat Trafficking in Persons.

Note: Numbers may not total due to rounding. Domestic obligations, which are included in this chart, do not include the costs of administering TIP operations or TIP-related law enforcement investigations. DOL's projects primarily address trafficking as one of the worst forms of child labor. Such projects include standalone TIP projects, but many include multi-faceted projects to address other worst forms of child labor in addition to trafficking. In these projects, the funds cannot be disaggregated.

INTERNATIONAL EFFORTS TO COMBAT TRAFFICKINGIN PERSONS

The international community has long condemned TIP and related elements of human trafficking through multilateral, regional, and bilateral declarations, treaties, agreements, or other instruments.

Some of the earliest commitments to combating TIP in various forms include the 1921 International Convention for the Suppression of the Traffic in Women and Children, the 1926 Slavery Convention, the 1949 Convention for the Suppression of the Traffic in Persons and of the Exploitation of the Prostitution of Others, and the 1957 Convention Concerning the Abolition of Forced Labour.

Although TIP is not a new phenomenon, it became an increasingly high-priority human rights issue of concern in the 1990s. As the decade progressed, the trafficking of women for sexual exploitation began to be seen as both a form of discrimination against women and as a major human rights violation.[20]

Given the international dimension of the problem, TIP also became viewed in the context of a transnational criminal enterprise for which unilateral and domestic anti-TIP efforts would be inadequate for successfully eliminating the threat.

U.N. Protocol to Prevent, Suppress, and Punish Trafficking in Persons

On November 15, 2000, the United Nations General Assembly adopted the Convention on Transnational Crime and several associated protocols, including the Protocol to Prevent, Suppress, and Punish Trafficking in Persons.

The convention and its protocols, formally signed in Palermo, Italy, in December 2000, were designed to enable countries to work together more closely against criminals engaged in cross-border crimes. The Protocol on Trafficking defines trafficking in persons and commits countries to take law enforcement actions against traffickers, to provide some assistance and protection for TIP victims, and to share intelligence and increase border security cooperation with other countries. The United States signed the U.N. Protocol on Trafficking in December 2000 and ratified and became party to the protocol on December 3, 2005, following Senate advice and consent on October 7, 2005.

Other Relevant International Agreements

The United States is party to several other international agreements that have been adopted to address aspects of human trafficking, including the 1999 International Labor Organization (ILO) Convention No. 182 concerning the Prohibition and Immediate Action for the Elimination of the Worst Forms of Child Labor (ratified by the United States in December 1999); the 1957 ILO Convention No. 105 concerning the Abolition of Forced Labor (ratified by the United States in 1991); the Optional Protocol to the U.N. Convention on the Rights of the Child on Sale of Children, Child Prostitution and Child Pornography (ratified by the United States in December 2002); and the Optional Protocol to the U.N. Convention on the Rights of the Child on the Rights of the Child in Armed Conflict (ratified by the United States in December 2002).

Key U.S. Foreign Policy Responses in the TVPA

The cornerstone legislative vehicle for current U.S. foreign policy on combating international human trafficking is the Trafficking Victims Protection Act of 2000 (TVPA, Division A of P.L. 106-386) and its three reauthorizations in 2003, 2005, and 2008 (TVPRAs).

Among its key provisions, the TVPA authorized foreign assistance for preventing trafficking, protecting victims, and prosecuting traffickers (the three "Ps"). It also established an annual requirement for the State Department to publish a report on progress made by the international community to eliminate severe forms of human trafficking. Pursuant to the TVPA, the State Department has issued this report, called the TIP Report, each year since 2001.

Countries described by the TIP Report are ranked, based on their efforts to combat TIP. To incentivize foreign countries to adhere to their international anti-TIP obligations, the TVPA established a mechanism whereby a low ranking in the TIP Report can trigger certain restrictions on U.S.-provided foreign assistance.

Foreign Aid

For FY2008 through FY2011, the William Wilberforce Trafficking Victims Reauthorization Act of 2008 (TVPRA of 2008) authorized the U.S. government to provide anti-trafficking assistance to foreign countries. While current anti-TIP funding breakdowns are not available for all agencies, international anti-TIP foreign assistance data appropriated through the combined Foreign Operations budget for the Department of State and U.S. Agency for International Development (USAID) are available by country and region.

According to the State Department, approximately $37.1 million for FY2012 through the Foreign Operations budget was requested for anti-TIP efforts in 24 countries as well as for programs that are regional or global in scope (see *Table 1*).

In FY2011, an estimated $24 million was provided for anti-TIP efforts through the Foreign Operations budget.

Table 1. Anti-TIP Assistance through the Foreign Operations Budget
(in current U.S. $ thousands)

	FY2009 Actual	FY2010 Actual	FY2011 Estimate	FY2012 Request
Africa	900	435	700	1,500
East Asia and Pacific	4,505	2,818	2,900	5,150
Europe and Eurasia	5,894	3,136	—	3,381
Near East	300	—	—	—
South and Central Asia	3,834	4,930	2,505	5,288
Western Hemisphere	1,565	1,150	896	—
USAID's Bureau for Economic Growth, Agriculture, and Trade	1,567	900	—	1,000
USAID's Bureau for Democracy, Conflict, and Humanitarian Assistance	—	—	800	—
State Department's Office to Monitor and Combat Trafficking in Persons	19,380	21,262	16,233	20,808
TOTAL	38,444.7	34,631	24,034	37,127.0

Source: U.S. Department of State, Response to CRS Request, December 21, 2011.

The bulk of U.S. anti-trafficking assistance programs abroad is administered by the U.S. Department of State, U.S. Agency for International Development (USAID), and the U.S. Department of Labor (DOL). With regard to foreign assistance administered by the State Department and USAID, anti-TIP aid has been disbursed through four program accounts: Development Assistance (DA); Economic Support Fund (ESF); Assistance for Europe, Eurasia, and Central Asia (AEECA); and International Narcotics Control and Law Enforcement (INCLE).

Within the State Department, multiple bureaus and offices address various aspects of human trafficking issues, including the Office to Monitor and Combat Trafficking in Persons (G/TIP); Bureau of Population, Refugees, and Migration (PRM); Bureau of Democracy, Human Rights and Labor (DRL); Bureau of Diplomatic Security (DS); Office of Global Women's Issues (S/GWI); and Bureau of Education and Cultural Exchanges (ECA). Regional bureaus, such as the Bureau of Europe and Eurasian Affairs (EUR), are also involved in human trafficking issues.

DOL's Bureau of International Labor Affairs (ILAB), particularly its Office of Child Labor, Forced Labor, and Human Trafficking (OCFT), supports programs that focus on providing assistance to child victims of trafficking and preventing trafficking and forced labor through policy and legislative reform, public awareness campaigns, and capacity-building for governments and service providers.

Separately, USAID funds international anti-trafficking programs with emphasis on victim protection and trafficking prevention, as well as some training for police and criminal justice personnel. The Department of Homeland Security (DHS) and the Department of Justice's (DOJ's) International Criminal Training Assistance Program (ICITAP) also provide some anti-TIP training to law enforcement and judicial officials overseas. Some U.S. funding supports the anti-TIP efforts of the United Nations and other international organizations.

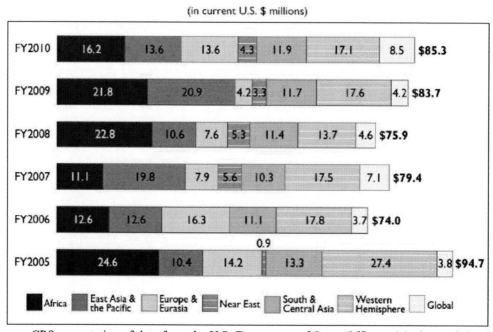

Source: CRS presentation of data from the U.S. Department of State, Office to Monitor and Combat Trafficking in Persons.

Note: Numbers may not total due to rounding. Domestic obligations are not included in this chart. DOL's projects primarily address trafficking as one of the worst forms of child labor. Such projects include standalone TIP projects, but many include multi-faceted projects to address other worst forms of child labor in addition to trafficking. In these projects, the funds cannot be disaggregated.

Figure 2. International Anti-TIP Obligations by Region: FY2005-FY2010.

Figure 2 provides a regional breakdown of U.S. international anti-TIP obligations from FY2005 through FY2010 by geographic region—including not only State Department and USAID contributions, but also assistance provided by DOL, DOJ, and HHS. In FY2010, U.S. funding for global anti-TIP activities supported roughly 175 international anti-trafficking programs in over 80 countries.[21]

The majority of international anti-TIP programs supported by the United States are either regional or aimed at helping countries resolve specific challenges they have had in addressing human trafficking.[22]

The 2011 TIP Report

On June 27, 2011, the State Department issued its 11th annual report on human trafficking, *Trafficking in Persons (TIP) Report, June 2011*, as mandated by the TVPA (P.L. 106-386, as amended). In addition to outlining major trends and ongoing challenges in combating TIP, the report provides a country-by-country analysis and ranking, based on what progress foreign countries have made, from April 2010 through March 2011, in their efforts to prosecute, protect, and prevent TIP. The 2011 TIP Report ranked more countries than any previous year, up from 82 countries in 2001 to 181 countries in 2011, including the United States.[23] In addition to the 181 countries that were ranked, the report discusses trafficking in three "special case" countries— Cote D'Ivoire, Haiti, and Somalia—where sufficient information was not available to provide a ranking.

The 2011 TIP Report presents a sobering view of the state of U.S. and international campaigns against human trafficking. While acknowledging that significant progress has been made in recent years, particularly in the realm of introducing new or amended legislation in more countries around the world that help prosecute, protect, and prevent TIP, progress in combating TIP globally appears to be mixed.

While the number of prosecutions reported per year worldwide against TIP offenders has improved in the past two years, it has declined on average 3.8% per year since 2003, when the State Department first collected this information globally—from 7,992 prosecutions in 2003 to 6,017 in 2010 (see *Table 2*).

A disproportionate minority of reported prosecutions are related to labor trafficking (607 of the 6,017 prosecutions in 2010, or 10.1% of prosecutions). Approximately 60% of all reported trafficking prosecutions in 2010 resulted in convictions.

Table 2. Global Prosecutions of TIP Offenders, 2003-2010

Year	Sub-Saharan Africa	Europe	East Asia & the Pacific	Middle East & North Africa	South & Central Asia	Western Hemisphere	Global	Global % change from previous year
2003	50	2,231	1,727	1,004	2,805	175	7,992	—
2004	134	3,270	438	134	2764	145	6,885	-13.9%
2005	194	2,521	2,580	112	1,041	170	6,618	-3.9%
2006	170	2,950	1,321	295	629	443	5,808	-12.2%
2007	123	2,820	1,047	415	824	426	5,655	-2.6%
2008	109	2,808	1,083	120	644	448	5,212	-7.8%
2009	325	2,208	357	80	1,989	647	5,606	7.1%
2010	272	2,803	427	323	1,460	732	6,017	6.8%

Source: CRS presentation of law enforcement data in the State Department's TIP Reports through 2011.

Notes: Global totals are the sum of the reported totals for all six regions. The Western Hemisphere does not include the United States in this analysis.

The 2011 TIP Report also discussed a variety of emerging issues and trends in TIP. Selected topics of interest in the 2011 Report included the recruitment of children in armed conflicts, recent research on local demand for commercial sexual exploitation of minors, techniques of psychological control used by sex traffickers and pimps, and bonded labor on deep sea fishing vessels in Southeast Asia. Other issues discussed in the 2011 TIP Report include recommendations for best practices to prevent labor trafficking, including procurement guidelines and options for improving the regulation of labor recruiters.

2011 TIP Report Country Designations and Trends

The centerpiece of the annual TIP Reports is their country-by-country analyses and rankings, which describe progress foreign countries have made in their efforts to prosecute, protect, and prevent human trafficking. Beginning with the 2010 TIP Report, the State Department has also ranked the United States and described U.S. efforts and ongoing challenges in combating human trafficking. In both the 2010 and 2011 TIP Reports, the United States received a "Tier 1" ranking, signifying that it is among the top-performing countries in the world and that it meets the legislatively defined "minimum standards" for eliminating severe forms of human trafficking.[24]

Pursuant to the TVPA, as amended, the 2011 TIP Report ranked countries in four categories on the basis of their efforts to combat human trafficking, with Tier 1 composed of the best-performing countries and Tier 3 composed of the worst-performing countries. Only Tier 1 countries are compliant with the TVPA's minimum standards for eliminating trafficking. The rest, totaling approximately 82% of all countries ranked in the 2011 TIP Report, are listed as noncompliant—variously receiving designations as Tier 2, Tier 2 Watch List, or Tier 3, depending on their level of effort in achieving the minimum standards.

In total, the number of non-compliant countries described in the 2011 TIP Report has increased slightly in absolute size since 2010, from 143 countries to 149. Tier 2 increased from 74 countries in 2010 to 85 countries in 2011. Tier 2 Watch List decreased from 58 in 2010 to 41 in 2011. Tier 3 increased from 13 in 2010 to 23 in 2011.

Tier 1 is composed of countries deemed by the State Department as having fully complied with the minimum standards for eliminating trafficking as outlined in the TVPA, as amended. Thirty-two countries, or approximately 17.4% of all countries listed, received a Tier 1 ranking in the 2011 TIP Report. Since last year, three countries improved their rankings from Tier 2 to Tier 1 (Macedonia, Portugal, and the Slovak Republic) and one country dropped from Tier 1 to Tier 2 (the Czech Republic). In general, countries in Western Europe have been among the most consistent top performers. For example, 14 countries have consistently been ranked Tier 1 for every year they have been listed on the TIP Report—and all but four of these countries (Australia, Colombia, New Zealand, United States) are located in Western Europe.[25] See *Table 3*.

The other three TIP Report categories include countries that are non-compliant with the TVPA's minimum standards for eliminating trafficking. These categories differ on the basis of perceived political effort and political will to become compliant—ranging from countries that are noncompliant, but making significant efforts to improve (Tier 2) to countries that are non-compliant and making no effort to improve (Tier 3). Approximately 82% of all countries ranked in the TIP Report are listed as Tier 2, Tier 2 Watch List, or Tier 3 countries. In total, the number of noncompliant countries described in the 2011 TIP report has increased slightly in absolute size since 2010, from 143 countries to 149. Tier 2 increased from 74 countries in

2010 to 85 countries in 2011. Tier 2 Watch List, composed of countries on the border between Tier 2 and Tier 3, decreased from 58 in 2010 to 41 in 2011. Tier 3, the worst, increased from 13 in 2010 to 23 in 2011.

Table 3. Tier 1 Countries in 2011 TIP Report, by Region

Region	Country Names
East Asia & the Pacific (4 of 29)	Australia, New Zealand, South Korea, and Taiwan
Europe (23 of 47)	Austria, Belgium, Bosnia, Croatia, Denmark, Finland, France, Georgia, Germany, Ireland, Italy, Lithuania, Luxembourg, Macedonia, the Netherlands, Norway, Poland, Portugal, the Slovak Republic, Slovenia, Spain, Sweden, and United Kingdom
Middle East & North Africa (0 of 18)	—
South & Central Asia (0 of 12)	—
Sub-Saharan Africa (2 of 46)	Mauritius and Nigeria
Western Hemisphere (3 of 32)	Canada, Colombia, and United States

Source: U.S. Department of State, 2011 TIP Report.

Table 4. Tier 2 Countries in the 2011 TIP Report, by Region

Region	Country Names
East Asia & the Pacific (14 of 29)	Cambodia, Fiji, Hong Kong, Indonesia, Japan, Laos, Macau, Marshall Islands, Mongolia, Palau, Philippines, Singapore, Timor-Leste, and Tonga
Europe (17 of 47)	Albania, Armenia, Aruba, Bulgaria, Czech Republic, Greece, Hungary, Iceland, Kosovo, Latvia, Moldova, Montenegro, Romania, Serbia, Switzerland, Turkey, and the Ukraine
Middle East & North Africa (7 of 18)	Bahrain, Egypt, Israel, Jordan, Morocco, Oman, and the United Arab Emirates
South & Central Asia (7 of 12)	India, Kazakhstan, Kyrgyz Republic, Nepal, Pakistan, Sri Lanka, and Tajikistan
Sub-Saharan Africa (21 of 46)	Benin, Botswana, Burkina Faso, Djibouti, Ethiopia, Gabon, Ghana, Kenya, Lesotho, Malawi, Mozambique, Namibia, Rwanda, Senegal, Seychelles, Sierra Leone, South Africa, Swaziland, Togo, Uganda, and Zambia
Western Hemisphere (19 of 32)	Antigua & Barbuda, Argentina, Belize, Bolivia, Brazil, Chile, El Salvador, Guatemala, Guyana, Honduras, Jamaica, Mexico, Nicaragua, Paraguay, Peru, St. Lucia, Suriname, Trinidad & Tobago, and Uruguay

Source: U.S. Department of State, 2011 TIP Report.

Tier 2 includes countries whose governments the State Department views as not fully complying with the minimum standards for eliminating trafficking, but which are seen as making "significant efforts to bring themselves into compliance." In 2011, 85 countries were listed as Tier 2, representing, as in past years, the largest category of countries. Since last year, 19 countries improved their rankings from Tier 2 Watch List to Tier 2[26] and 10 countries dropped from Tier 2 to Tier 2 Watch List.[27] See *Table 4.*

Tier 2 Watch List was first added as a category in the 2004 TIP Report. The 2011 TIP Report included 41 countries in this group, which represents a decline compared to the 58 countries ranked as Tier 2 Watch List in 2010. Since last year, one country improved its ranking from Tier 3 to Tier 2 Watch List (the Dominican Republic) and 11 countries dropped from Tier 2 Watch List to Tier 3.[28] See *Table 5*.

This category is composed of a subset of Tier 2 countries in which at least one of the following conditions apply:

- the absolute number of TIP victims is very significant or is significantly increasing;
- there is no evidence that increasing efforts to combat severe forms of trafficking in persons from the previous year; or
- the determination that a country is making significant efforts to bring themselves into compliance with minimum standards was based on commitments by the country to take additional future steps over the next year.

Table 5. Tier 2 Watch List Countries in the 2011 TIP Report, by Region

Region	Country Names
East Asia & the Pacific (7 of 29)	Brunei, China, Kiribati, Malaysia, Solomon Islands, Thailand, and Vietnam
Europe (7 of 47)	Azerbaijan, Belarus, Curacao, Cyprus, Estonia, Malta, and Russia
Middle East & North Africa (4 of 18)	Iraq, Qatar, Syria, and Tunisia
South & Central Asia (4 of 12)	Afghanistan, Bangladesh, Maldives, and Uzbekistan
Sub-Saharan Africa (12 of 46)	Angola, Burundi, Cameroon, Chad, Comoros, Guinea, Liberia, Mali, Niger, Republic of the Congo, Tanzania, and the Gambia
Western Hemisphere (7 of 32)	Barbados, Costa Rica, Dominican Republic, Ecuador, Panama, St. Vincent & the Grenadines, and the Bahamas

Source: U.S. Department of State, 2011 TIP Report.

Table 6. Tier 3 Countries in the 2011 TIP Report, by Region

Region	Country Names
East Asia & the Pacific (7 of 29)	Brunei, China, Kiribati, Malaysia, Solomon Islands, Thailand, and Vietnam
Europe (7 of 47)	Azerbaijan, Belarus, Curacao, Cyprus, Estonia, Malta, and Russia
Middle East & North Africa (4 of 18)	Iraq, Qatar, Syria, and Tunisia
South & Central Asia (4 of 12)	Afghanistan, Bangladesh, Maldives, and Uzbekistan
Sub-Saharan Africa (12 of 46)	Angola, Burundi, Cameroon, Chad, Comoros, Guinea, Liberia, Mali, Niger, Republic of the Congo, Tanzania, and the Gambia
Western Hemisphere (7 of 32)	Barbados, Costa Rica, Dominican Republic, Ecuador, Panama, St. Vincent & the Grenadines, and the Bahamas

Source: U.S. Department of State, 2011 TIP Report.

Tier 3 includes countries whose governments the State Department deems as not fully complying with those standards and not making significant efforts to do so. This group includes a total of 23 countries in 2011, up from 13 in 2010. See Table 6. Countries new to Tier 3 in 2011 include Algeria, Central African Republic, Equatorial Guinea, Guinea-Bissau,

Lebanon, Libya, Madagascar, Micronesia, Turkmenistan, Venezuela, and Yemen. The TVPA, as amended, subjects to sanctions those countries listed in Tier 3 in the following fiscal year, including termination of non-humanitarian, non-trade-related assistance and loss of U.S. support for loans from international financial institutions. Sanctions are to be imposed if such countries have not improved their performance within 90 days from the release of the TIP Report.

2008 Provision: Automatic Downgrade from Tier 2 Watch List

The William Wilberforce Trafficking Victims Protection Reauthorization Act of 2008 (TVPRA of 2008, P.L. 110-457) added a new requirement to the TIP country rankings process, in which Tier 2 Watch List countries are automatically downgraded to the Tier 3 category after two consecutive years on the Tier 2 Watch List (unless the President issues a waiver to block the autodowngrade).[29] The first year in which this new requirement came into effect was the 2009 TIP Report. Those countries on the Tier 2 Watch List countries in 2009 could only remain on the Tier 2 Watch List through the 2010 TIP Report. Subsequent to the 2010 TIP Report, these countries would be required to drop to Tier 3, unless they have improved their efforts to combat TIP or unless the President issues waivers. To this end, 22 countries were at risk in 2011 for an auto-downgrade to Tier 3 because they had been identified as Tier 2 Watch List in both the 2009 and 2010 TIP Reports (see *Table 2*). Of these, 10 countries were downgraded in the 2011 TIP report to Tier 3 while 12 remained listed as Tier 2 Watch List after the Obama Administration issued a waiver to prevent these countries from receiving the automatic downgrade to Tier 3.

According to the 2011 TIP Report, such waivers were issued in cases in which the government in question has a written plan that "would constitute making significant efforts to comply with the TVPA's minimum standards for the elimination of trafficking," if implemented, and that there is credible evidence that the government in question is "devoting sufficient resources to implement the plan." In addition to the 12 countries that remained Tier 2 Watch List in 2011 due to the granting of a waiver, 15 additional countries are at risk of an auto-downgrade in next year's TIP Report (see *Table 7*). Combined, these 27 countries will have been listed consecutively under the Tier 2 Watch List category in both the 2010 and 2011 TIP Reports.

Aid Restrictions to Tier 3 Countries for FY2012

Pursuant to the TVPA, it is the policy of the U.S. government to deny nonhumanitarian, nontraderelated foreign assistance—including both bilateral and multilateral assistance—to any foreign government that does not comply with the minimum standards for the elimination of trafficking and is not making significant efforts to bring itself into compliance with such standards.

Each year, the President is required to make a determination on whether to impose such aid restrictions on the Tier 3 countries annually identified by the State Department for the subsequent fiscal year. If Tier 3 countries did not receive nonhumanitarian, nontrade-related foreign assistance from the U.S. government in the prior fiscal year, then future U.S. funding for participation of noncompliant country government officials in educational and cultural exchange programs may be denied. Pursuant to the TVPA, the President reserves the discretion to waive part or all of the aid and funding restrictions on the basis of national interest reasons.

**Table 7. Countries at Risk of Auto-Downgrade to Tier 3 in the 2011
and 2012 TIP Reports**

2011 TIP Report Results		At Risk of Auto-Downgrade in 2012 TIP Report (in addition to those that remained Tier 2 Watch List due to a waiver in 2011)
Downgraded to Tier 3 After Two Years on Tier 2 Watch List	Remained Tier 2 Watch List Due to a Waiver	(in addition to those that remained Tier 2 Watch List due to a waiver in 2011)
Algeria Central African Republic Equatorial Guinea Guinea-Bissau Lebanon Libya Micronesia Turkmenistan Venezuela Yemen	Azerbaijan Bangladesh Cameroon China Guinea Iraq Mali Qatar Republic of Congo Russia St. Vincent & the Grenadines Uzbekistan	Afghanistan Barbados Brunei Chad Kiribati Malaysia Maldives Malta Niger Panama Syria Tanzania Thailand Tunisia Vietnam

Source: U.S. Department of State, 2011 TIP Report.

On September 30, 2011, President Obama issued his determination on whether to impose aid restrictions during FY2012 on the 23 listed Tier 3 countries from the 2011 TIP Report.[30] For FY2012 the President determined that sanctions would be *fully* imposed on three countries: Eritrea, Madagascar, and North Korea.

None of these three countries, however, received nonhumanitarian, nontrade-related foreign assistance in FY2011. As a result, the President determined to withhold U.S. funding for participation by officials or employees of these three governments in educational and cultural exchange programs for FY2012.

Seven countries were granted by the President *partial waivers* from the aid prohibitions: Burma, Cuba, the Democratic Republic of Congo (DRC), Equatorial Guinea, Iran, Venezuela, and Zimbabwe.

Thirteen countries—Algeria, the Central Africa Republic (CAR), Guinea-Bissau, Kuwait, Lebanon, Libya, Mauritania, Micronesia, Papua New Guinea, Saudi Arabia, Sudan, Turkmenistan, and Yemen—were granted *full waivers* from the aid prohibitions. The President determined that continued U.S. support in FY2012 to these 13 countries would be in the U.S. national interest.

Among the most notable changes in FY2012 with respect to TIP-related aid restrictions is the full restriction on nonhumanitarian, nontrade-related aid to Madagascar.

Madagascar received its first Tier 3 country ranking in the State Department's June 2011 TIP Report.[31] FY2012 will also be the first fiscal year in which the country is subject to the full TIP aid restrictions.

List of Countries Involved in Recruiting and Using Child Soldiers

While not directly connected to the TIP Report country tier rankings and related aid restrictions, the Child Soldiers Prevention Act of 2008 (CSPA, Title IV of P.L. 110-457) requires, beginning with the 2010 TIP Report, that the TIP Report annually publish a list of countries that recruit or use child soldiers in their armed forces, or that host non-government armed forces that recruit or use child soldiers.

Child soldiers are defined as individuals who are under 18 years of age and who (1) have taken direct part in hostilities as a member of a government's armed forces, (2) were recruited or used in hostilities by non-governmental armed forces, or (3) were compulsorily recruited to join a government's armed forces. Individuals who are under 15 years of age and who were voluntarily recruited to join a government's armed forces are also defined as child soldiers. Additionally, those who meet the above conditions but have not taken direct part in hostilities, instead serving in a support role for an armed group, such as a cook, porter, messenger, medic, guard, or sex slave, are also defined as child soldiers according to the CSPA.

Following these guidelines, the 2011 TIP Report identified six countries involved in recruiting and using child soldiers, whether directly in the government's armed forces or indirectly in non-governmental armed forces: Burma, Chad, Democratic Republic of Congo (DRC), Somalia, Sudan, and Yemen.[32] These six are the same six identified by the 2010 TIP Report.

Unless the President issues waivers, identified countries would be subject to foreign assistance restrictions in FY2012, including prohibitions on assistance for international military education and training (IMET); foreign military financing (FMF); excess defense articles; assistance provided pursuant to Section 1206 of the National Defense Authorization Act of FY2006, as amended and extended; and the issuance for direct commercial sales of military equipment. Pursuant to the CSPA, the President may also allow for the reinstatement of barred assistance if he certifies to Congress that such countries have taken the necessary steps to prevent and prohibit future use of child soldiers.

On October 25, 2010, President Obama waived sanctions for four of the six listed countries in the 2010 TIP report: Chad, DRC, Sudan, and Yemen. The other two, Burma and Somalia, were subject to sanctions in FY2011 pursuant to the CSPA.

On October 4, 2011, President Obama certified that Chad has taken necessary steps to allow for the reinstatement of barred assistance. He fully waived the sanctions for Yemen and partially waived the sanctions for DRC. The other three, Burma, Somalia, and Sudan, are subject to sanctions in FY2012 pursuant to the CSPA.

TRAFFICKING IN THE UNITED STATES

The United States is a source, transit, and destination country for men, women, and children subject to trafficking in persons.[33] Human trafficking happens in the United States to both U.S. citizens and noncitizens, and occurs in every state.[34] As many as 17,500 people are trafficked to the United States each year, according to U.S. government estimates.[35] The trafficking of individuals within U.S. borders is commonly referred to as domestic or "internal" human trafficking. Domestic human trafficking occurs primarily for labor and most commonly in domestic servitude, agriculture, manufacturing, janitorial services, hotel services, construction, health and elder care, hair and nail salons, and strip club dancing. However, more investigations and prosecutions have taken place for sex trafficking offenses than for labor trafficking offenses.[36]

Noncitizens are more susceptible than U.S. citizens to labor trafficking,[37] and more foreign victims[38] are found in labor trafficking than in sex trafficking. Conversely, although labor trafficking can happen to U.S. citizens, more adult and child U.S. citizens are found in sex trafficking than in labor trafficking.[39]

Research indicates that most of the victims of sex trafficking into and within the United States are women and children. In addition, migrant labor camps tend to be common settings for labor exploitation and domestic trafficking.[40]

Before 2000, U.S. laws were widely believed to be inadequate to deal with trafficking in women and children or to protect and assist victims. Anti-trafficking legislation and programs have been implemented with the hope of improving the situation.

Sex Trafficking of Children in the United States

Domestic sex trafficking of children is sex trafficking within the United States involving a commercial sex act in which the person induced to perform such act has not attained 18 years of age.[41] Most of the victims are U.S. citizens and Legal Permanent Residents (LPRs).[42]

As discussed above the TVPA does not define sex trafficking or human trafficking per se. However, it does define "severe forms of human trafficking" as:

> Sex trafficking in which a commercial sex act is induced by force, fraud, or coercion, or in which the person induced to perform such act has not attained 18 years of age; or ... the recruitment, harboring, transportation, provision, or obtaining of a person for labor or services, through the use of force, fraud, or coercion for the purpose of subjection to involuntary servitude, peonage, debt bondage, or slavery.

In the case of minors, there is general agreement that the severe form of trafficking term applies whether the child's actions were forced or voluntary. Under the TVPA, the term "commercial sex act" means "any sex act, on account of which anything of value is given to or received by any person." There appears to be a consensus that prostitution by minors fits the definition of "severe forms of human trafficking" as defined under the TVPA.

Official Estimates of Human Trafficking in the United States

Due to the nature of human trafficking, it is difficult to estimate the number of trafficking victims in the United States.[43] U.S. governmental estimates of trafficking victims focus on the number of foreign victims who are trafficked into the United States, while two other studies have focused on the number of minor victims of sex trafficking or foreign victims in specific geographic areas.

Estimates Into the United States

For FY2005, the Department of Justice (DOJ) estimated that there were between 14,500 and 17,500 victims trafficked into the United States each year.[44] As of January 2011, this remains the most recent U.S. government estimate of trafficking victims.[45]

This estimate of 14,500 to 17,500 victims first appeared in the 2004 report, *Assessment of U.S. Government Activities to Combat Trafficking in Persons*,[46] and subsequent reports have not included estimates of the number of trafficking victims.[47]

The *Attorney General's Report on U.S. Government Activities to Combat Trafficking in Persons Fiscal Year 2006*[48] stated that this estimate may be "overstated," and asserted that "[f]urther research is underway to determine a more accurate figure based on more advanced methodologies and more complete understanding of the nature of trafficking."

Notably, previous reports by the Central Intelligence Agency's Center for the Study of Intelligence and the Department of Justice produced higher estimates of the number of trafficking victims in the United States. In November 1999, a report issued by the Center for the Study of Intelligence estimated that 45,000 to 50,000 women and children are trafficked annually to the United States.[49]

In addition, the August 2003 version of the report, *Assessment of U.S. Government Activities to Combat Trafficking in Persons*, estimated that between 18,000 and 20,000 people are trafficked into the United States annually. Some researchers contend that the government estimates of human trafficking do not provide a full description of the data and methodologies used to arrive at the estimates. As a result, they argue that the lack of methodological information makes it difficult, if not impossible, to recreate, assess the validity of, or improve upon the estimates.[50]

Estimates of Sex Trafficking of Children in the United States

Comprehensive research on the number of children in the United States who are victims of sex trafficking does not exist, but there have been two recent studies that attempt to measure the problem in specific geographic areas.[51]

Shared Hope International

In 2006, Shared Hope International began working with 10 of the Department of Justice-funded human trafficking task forces to assess the scope of sex trafficking of children in the United States.[52] The study uses the term "Domestic Minor Sex Trafficking" (DMST) and defines DMST as the commercial exploitation of U.S. citizens and LPR children with U.S. borders. As part of their study, the researchers noted that an accurate count of the number of victims was not available due to many factors, including a lack of tracking protocols and misidentification of the victims.

Table 8 presents the findings from the 10 study sites. Notably, the data collected are not uniform and represent different time periods.

Ohio Trafficking in Persons Study Commission

Former Ohio Attorney General Richard Cordray tasked the Ohio Trafficking in Persons Study Commission to explore the scope of human trafficking within Ohio. Using methodologies developed in other studies, the commission estimated that of the American-born youth in Ohio, 2,879 are at risk for sex trafficking, and another 1,078 have been victims of sex trafficking over the course of a year.[53] The researchers also estimated that 3,437 foreign-born persons (adults and juveniles) in Ohio may be at risk for sex or labor trafficking, of which 783 are estimated to be trafficking victims.[54] Importantly, the report states, "due to the very nature of human trafficking, it is virtually impossible to determine the exact number of victims in Ohio at any given time and with any degree of certainty."[55]

Table 8. Number of Suspected Domestic Minor Sex Trafficking Victims by Location (Shared Hope International Study)

Research Site	State/Territory	Number of Suspected DMST Victims	Time Period
Dallas	Texas	150	2007
San Antonio/Bexar County	Texas	3-4	2005-2008
Fort Worth/Tarrant County	Texas	29	2000-2008
Las Vegas	Nevada	5,122	1994-2007
Independence/Kansas City Area	Missouri	227	2000-2008
Baton Rouge/New Orleans Area	Louisiana	105	2000-2007
Saipan/Rota/Tinian	Northern Mariana Islands	1	2008
Salt Lake City	Utah	83	1996-2008
Buffalo/Erie County	New York	74-84	2000-2008
Clearwater/Tampa Bay Area	Florida	36	2000-2008

Source: Linda A. Smith, Samantha Healy Vardaman, and Melissa A. Snow, "The National Report on Domestic Minor Sex Trafficking: America's Prostituted Children," Shared Hope International, May 2009, p. 11.

Notes: Due to a lack of formal tracking protocols, some victims may be duplicated within a city and some may not have been included in the counts. These numbers were obtained through an interview process in addition to official government records.

RESPONSE TO TRAFFICKING WITHIN THE UNITED STATES

The response to human trafficking within the United States has focused on (1) assistance to victims of trafficking and (2) law enforcement efforts to arrest and prosecute traffickers, and identify victims.

Immigration Relief for Trafficking Victims

Some of the trafficking victims in the United States are aliens (noncitizens) who are illegally present (i.e., unauthorized/illegal aliens). Some of these aliens entered legally, but overstayed their length of legal admittance. Other aliens were smuggled into or illegally entered the United States, and then became trafficking victims. In addition, some aliens have had their immigration documents confiscated by the traffickers as a form of control. The lack of immigration status may prevent victims from seeking help, and may interfere with the ability of the victim to provide testimony during a criminal trial. As such, under law, there are certain protections from removal (deportation) available to noncitizen victims of trafficking.

T Nonimmigrant Status

The Victims of Trafficking and Violence Protection Act of 2000 (TVPA) created a new nonimmigrant category, known as T status or T-visa, for aliens who are victims of severe forms of TIP.[56] Aliens who received T status are eligible to remain in the United States for four years and may apply for lawful permanent residence status (LPR) after being continually present in the United States for three years.

To qualify for the "T" category, in addition to being a victim of a severe form of TIP,[57] the alien must

- be physically present in the United States, American Samoa, the Commonwealth of the Northern Mariana Islands, or a U.S. port of entry because of such trafficking including physical presence on account of the alien having been allowed entry into the United States for participation in investigative or judicial processes associated with an act or a perpetrator of trafficking;[58]
- have complied with any reasonable request for assistance to law enforcement[59] in the investigation or prosecution of acts of trafficking unless unable to do so due to physical or psychological trauma,[60] or be under the age of 18;[61] and
- be likely to suffer extreme hardship involving unusual and severe harm upon removal.

To receive T status, the alien must also be admissible to the United States or obtain a waiver of inadmissibility. A waiver of inadmissibility is available for health related grounds, public charge grounds, or criminal grounds if the activities rendering the alien inadmissible were caused by or were incident to the alien's victimization.[62] Waivers are not automatically granted, and there is no appeal if the inadmissibility waiver is denied. This waiver is especially important for those involved in sexual trafficking since prostitution is one of the grounds of inadmissibility specified in the Immigration and Nationality Act (INA).[63] Additionally, aliens who are present without being admitted or paroled[64] into the United States are inadmissible and would need to obtain a waiver to be eligible for T status. For example, an alien who paid a smuggler to enter the country illegally and then was held in servitude would need to get an inadmissibility waiver to be eligible for T status.

T status is limited to 5,000 principal aliens each fiscal year. Additionally, the spouse, children, or parents of an alien under age 21, in order to avoid extreme hardship, may be given derivative T status which is not counted against the numerical limit.[65] Individuals who are eligible for T status may be granted work authorization.[66] T status is valid for four years, and may be extended if a federal, state, or local law enforcement official, prosecutor, judge, or other authority investigating or prosecuting activity relating to human trafficking certifies that the presence of the alien in the United States is necessary to assist in the investigation or prosecution of TIP.[67]

Under law, aliens who have bona fide T applications[68] are eligible to receive certain public benefits to the same extent as refugees.[69] Aliens who receive derivative T status (i.e., the family members of trafficking victims) are also eligible for benefits. In addition, regulations require that federal officials provide trafficking victims with specific information regarding their rights and services such as

- immigration benefits;
- federal and state benefits and services (e.g., certification by the Department of Health and Human Services [HHS] and assistance through HHS's Office of Refugee Resettlement [ORR]);
- medical services;
- pro-bono and low cost legal services;
- victim service organizations;
- victims compensation (trafficked aliens are often eligible for compensation from state and federal crime victims programs);[70]
- the right to restitution; and
- the rights of privacy and confidentiality.[71]

T Visas Issued

As *Table 9.* shows, between FY2002 and FY2011, there were 4,317 applications for T-1 status (i.e., trafficking victims), and 2,595 of these applications were approved.

During the same period, there were 3,406 applications for derivative T status (i.e., family members of trafficking victims), and 2,544 applications were approved. Of the adjudicated applications for T-1 status, 68% were approved. In addition, of the adjudicated applications for derivative T status, 82% were approved.

Table 9. T-visas Issued: FY2002 through FY2011

	FY02	FY03	FY04	FY05	FY06	FY07	FY08	FY09	FY10	FY11	Total
				Principal Aliens (Victims)							
Applied	163	587	352	229	346	230	394	475	574	967	4,317
Approved	17	285	156	112	182	279	247	313	447	557	2,595
Denied	12	72	303	213	46	70	64	77	138	223	1,218
				Derivative Aliens (Family)							
Applied	234	456	359	124	301	149	290	235	463	795	3,406
Approved	9	268	271	114	106	261	171	273	349	722	2,544
Denied	4	56	58	18	39	52	19	54	105	137	542

Source: Department of Homeland Security data provided to CRS.

Notes: Some approvals are from prior fiscal year(s) filings. Also, some applicants were denied more than once (e.g., filed once, denied, and filed again). For FY2004 and FY2005, 170 of the denials stemmed from one case where the applicants did not qualify as victims of trafficking under TVPA.

Since FY2007, the number of applications for T-1 status has increased, and in FY2011 there was a historically high number of applicants (967). In the past three years, there has been an increase in the number of aliens granted T-status (i.e., approved applications) but the increase is a function of the increase in applicants, not in the approval rate.[72]

Adjustment to Lawful Permanent Residence

T status, which is originally valid for four years, is not renewable after the alien's presence in the United States is not necessary to assist in the investigation or prosecution of TIP. Nonetheless, after three years, aliens with T status may petition for legal permanent residence (LPR) status (i.e., green card or immigrant status). To adjust to LPR status an alien must

- be admissible (i.e., that the alien is not ineligible for a visa or status adjustment under the so-called "grounds for inadmissibility" of the INA, which include having a criminal history, being a terrorist, and being a security risk to the United States);
- have been physically present in the United States for either (1) a continuous period of at least three years since the date of admission under T status, or (2) a continuous period during the investigation or prosecution of the acts of trafficking, provided that the Attorney General has certified that the investigation or prosecution is complete;
- since being granted T status, has been a person of good moral character; and
- establish that (1) they have complied with reasonable requests of assistance in the investigation or prosecution of acts of trafficking, or (2) that they would suffer extreme hardship upon removal from the United States.[73]

The regulations concerning adjustment to LPR status from T status were released on December 12, 2008, and became effective on January 12, 2009.[74] Under statute, 5,000 aliens in T-1 status can adjust to LPR status in a fiscal year. The cap does not apply to family members (e.g., T-2 visa holders).

Continued Presence

Federal law enforcement officials who encounter victims of severe forms of TIP and are potential witnesses to that trafficking may request that DHS grant the continued presence of the alien in the United States. Historically, the Attorney General has had the discretionary authority to use a variety of statutory and administrative mechanisms to ensure the alien's continued presence.[75] Most of the statutory and administrative mechanisms for continued presence required that the alien depart from the United States once her presence for the criminal investigation or prosecution is no longer required. In most cases, victims granted continued presence are eligible for work authorization.[76] Requests for continued presence are handled by the Law Enforcement Parole Branch of DHS's Immigration and Customs Enforcement (ICE).

In some cases, law enforcement prefer giving the alien continued presence rather than T status to prevent the appearance during the prosecution of the traffickers that the alien's testimony was "bought." In FY2010, continued presence was granted to 186 potential trafficking victims, a decrease from 299 in FY2009.[77]

U Nonimmigrant Status

Some victims of trafficking are eligible for U nonimmigrant status. The Violence Against Women Act of 2000, Division B of TVPA, created the U nonimmigrant status, often called the U-visa, for victims of physical or mental abuse.[78] To qualify for U status, the alien must file a petition and establish that

- he/she suffered substantial physical or mental abuse as a result of having been a victim of certain criminal activities;[79]
- as certified by a law enforcement or immigration official, he/she (or if the alien is a child under age 16, the child's parent, guardian or friend) possesses information about the criminal activity involved;
- he/she has been, is being or is likely to be helpful in the investigation and prosecution of the criminal activity by federal, state or local law enforcement authorities; and
- the criminal activity violated the laws of the United States or occurred in the United States.

The U category is limited to 10,000 principal aliens per fiscal year.[80] After three years, those in U status may apply for LPR status.[81]

The number of aliens granted U status because of trafficking is unknown. Unlike aliens with T status, those with U status are not eligible for assistance through the Office of Refugee Resettlement or for federal public benefits. Those who receive U status may be eligible for programs to assist crime victims though the Department of Justice's Office for Victims of Crime.

Table 10. U Visas Issued 2009-2011

Fiscal Year	Principal Aliens (Victims)			Derivative Aliens (Family)		
	Applied	Approved	Denied	Applied	Approved	Denied
2009	6,835	5,825	688	4,102	2,838	158
2010	10,742	10,073	4,347	6,418	9,315	2,576
2011	16,768	10,088	2.929	10,033	7,602	1,645
Total	34,345	25,986	7,964	20,553	19,755	4,379

Source: CRS presentation of unpublished data from the Department of Homeland Security (DHS).

From October 2008 through September 2011, there were 34,345 applications for U-1 status, and 25,986 were approved.82 During the same time period, there were 20,553 applications for derivative U status, and 19,755 were approved. Of the adjudicated applications for U-1 status, approximately 76% were approved, while almost 82% of the derivative U adjudicated applications were approved.

The 10,000 Cap for U Status

As discussed above, the U category is statutorily limited to 10,000 principal aliens per fiscal year.[83] The statutory cap of 10,000 was reached in both FY2010 and FY2011. Although the statutory cap was been reached, USCIS continued to accept and process new petitions for U status and issued a Notice of Conditional Approval to petitioners who were found eligible for but were unable to receive U status because the cap has been reached.[84]

Aid Available to Victims of Trafficking in the United States

Under the TVPA, the Departments of Justice (DOJ), Health and Human Services (HHS), and Labor (DOL) have programs or administer grants to other entities to provide services to trafficking victims. In From July 1, 2009, to June 30, 2010, at least 1,472 potential victims (foreign nationals and U.S. citizens) received services from non-governmental organizations (NGOs) supported by HHS and DOJ.[85] In addition, the Legal Services Corporation[86] has instructed its lawyers to provide legal assistance to trafficking victims.[87]

There is confusion over whether U.S. citizens, as well as noncitizens, are eligible for services under all the anti-trafficking grant programs in TVPA, and whether Congress has provided funding for programs that target U.S. citizen and LPR victims.[88] Notably, the *FY2009 Attorney General's Annual Report to Congress on U.S. Government Activities to Combat Trafficking in Persons* states, "the funds provided under the TVPA by the federal government for direct services to victims are dedicated to assist non-U.S. citizen victims and may not currently be used to assist U.S. citizen victims."[89] Nonetheless, each year since FY2008, Congress has appropriated approximately $10 million[90] to HHS to "carry out the Trafficking Victims Protection Act of 2000."[91] Thus, it appears likely that the funding would be available for benefits and programs specifically for U.S. citizens that were authorized under the reauthorization acts.

Regardless of funding, there seems to be disagreement over whether U.S. citizen and noncitizen victims of trafficking are eligible for each of the programs discussed below. Certification by HHS appears to be a necessary condition of receiving trafficking victims' services from HHS, DOL, and the Legal Services Corporation, under the programs created in the Victims of Trafficking and Violence Protection Act (P.L. 106-386, §107(b)(1), 22 U.S.C. §7105(b)(1)), as enacted in 2000.[92] Certification is a process that enables noncitizen trafficking victims to be classified as such, and therefore eligible for services. U.S. citizen and LPR trafficking victims are not required to be certified by HHS, and indeed would not meet the criteria to be certified because certification applies only to foreign nationals who need an immigration status (e.g., T status or continued presence) to remain in the United States. Nonetheless, a 2007 report by the Senior Policy Operating Group on Trafficking in Persons (SPOG) states that "there are not many differences in trafficking victims' eligibility for the services we reviewed when one looks at the relevant statutes." However, the report does note that U.S. citizen victims may have less intensive case management services compared to noncitizens.[93] In addition, only noncitizen trafficking victims are eligible for refugee-specific programs.[94]

Health and Human Services Grants

The TVPA required HHS to expand benefits and services to victims of severe forms of trafficking in the United States, without regard to the immigration status of such victims.[95] Under the law, to receive these benefits and services, victims of severe forms of trafficking who are at least 18 years of age must be certified by the Secretary of Health and Human Services, after consultation with the Secretary of Homeland Security,[96] as willing to assist in every reasonable way in the investigation and prosecution of severe forms of trafficking, having made a bona fide application for a T-visa that has not been denied, and being granted continued presence in the United States by the Secretary of Homeland Security to effectuate the prosecution of traffickers in persons.[97] Under the law, trafficking victims under the age of 18 do not have to be certified to receive benefits and services, but it is HHS policy to issue eligibility letters to such victims.[98] Although the law does not differentiate between U.S. citizen and noncitizen trafficking victims, according to HHS, U.S. citizen trafficking victims also do not have to be certified to receive services.[99] HHS's Office of Refugee Resettlement (ORR) provides certification and eligibility letters for victims.

From FY2001 through FY2009, HHS certified 2,076 people; 212 (9.6%) of the victims were minors.[100] In addition, in FY2010, 449 adult victims received certifications, and 92 children received eligibility letters. The certified victims represented 47 different countries; however, the countries with the largest percentage of certified victims were Thailand, India, Mexico, Honduras, Philippines, Haiti, El Salvador, and the Dominican Republic.[101]

ORR funds and facilitates a variety of programs to help refugees "economic and social self-sufficiency in their new homes in the United States," and noncitizen victims of severe forms of trafficking are eligible for these programs.[102] ORR-funded activities include cash and medical assistance, social services to help refugees become socially and economically self-sufficient, and targeted assistance for impacted areas. Special refugee cash assistance (RCA) and refugee medical assistance (RMA) are the heart of the refugee program. RCA and RMA, which are administered by the states, are intended to help needy refugees who are ineligible to receive benefits from mainstream federal assistance programs. In addition, minor noncitizen victims can participate in DHS's Unaccompanied Refugee Minor Program.[103] TVPA and the subsequent reauthorization acts, authorize funds for ORR to provide similar assistance to trafficking victims.

While both U.S. citizen and noncitizen trafficking victims are eligible for the general federal public benefits, only noncitizen trafficking victims are eligible for the benefits specifically designed for refugees.[104]

ORR also provides grants to organizations that render assistance specific to the needs of victims of trafficking, such as temporary housing, independent living skills, cultural orientation, transportation needs, access to appropriate educational programs, and legal assistance and referrals. It is unclear whether these services are available to U.S. citizen trafficking victims. ORR may also supply trafficking victims with intensive case management programs to help the victim find housing and employment, and provide mental health counseling and specialized foster care programs for children. ORR performs outreach to inform victims of services and educate the public about trafficking.[105]

In addition, HHS conducts outreach to inform victims of services and to educate the public about trafficking. HHS has established the Rescue and Restore Victims of Human Trafficking public awareness campaign, which promotes public awareness about trafficking and the protections available for trafficking victims. The goal of the campaign is to help communities identify and serve victims of trafficking, supporting them in coming forward to receive services and aid law enforcement. In addition to promoting public awareness about trafficking, HHS through the Rescue and Restore campaign has established anti-trafficking coalitions in 25 areas.[106] Another component of the campaign is the creation of a toll-free National Human Trafficking Resource Center available for advice 24 hours a day.[107] (For a discussion of authorizations and appropriations for the HHS grant program, see *Appendix B* and *Appendix C*.)

Department of Justice, Office for Victims of Crime

The TVPA created a grant program administered by the Attorney General to provide grants to states, Indian tribes, local governments, and nonprofit victims services organizations to develop, expand, or strengthen victims service programs for trafficking victims.[108] This grant program is administer through DOJ's Office for Victims of Crime (OVC) and provides emergency services, including temporary housing, medical care, crisis counseling and legal assistance, to victims as soon as they have been encountered, until certification by HHS (discussed above). The program also provides grants to build community capacity in addressing the needs of trafficking victims by enhancing interagency collaboration and supporting coordinated victim responses.[109] According to DOJ, OVC awards grants to non-governmental organizations to provide trafficking victims with comprehensive or specialized services, and training and technical assistance to grantees for program support and enhancement.[110] (For a discussion of authorizations and appropriations for this program, see *Appendix B* and *Appendix C*.)

Department of Labor

DOL's Employment and Training Administration (ETA) One-Stop Career Centers[111] provide job search assistance, career counseling, and occupational skills training to trafficking victims.[112] These services are provided directly by state and local grantees to trafficking victims. The ETA does not collect information on the extent to which such services are used by trafficking victims.[113]

In addition, victims between the ages of 16 and 24—both U.S. citizen victims and noncitizen victims who have work authorization—may be eligible to participate in Job Corps.[114] Job Corps does not collect information on the extent to which these services are offered to or utilized by trafficking victims.115 (For program authorizations, see *Appendix B.*)

Domestic Investigations of Trafficking Offenses

Human trafficking investigations are often complicated by language and humanitarian issues (e.g., the victim has been traumatized and is unable to aid in the investigation), as well as logistical challenges and difficulties (e.g., transporting, housing, and processing the victims, especially alien victims). In addition, certain types of investigative techniques, such as controlled delivery operations,[116] cannot be used. Moreover, unlike drug trafficking cases where the contraband itself is proof of the illegal activity, the successful prosecution of trafficking cases relies on the availability of witnesses who may refuse to testify because of fear of retribution against themselves or their families.[117]

Within the United States, the Departments of Justice (DOJ), Homeland Security (DHS), and Labor (DOL) have primary responsibility for investigating and prosecuting traffickers.[118] The majority of the cases are investigated by agents in DOJ's Federal Bureau of Investigation (FBI) and DHS's U.S. Immigration and Customs Enforcement (ICE), who coordinate as appropriate,[119] and are prosecuted by DOJ.[120] Agents in the FBI's Civil Rights Unit (CRU) investigate trafficking in the United States. In addition, under the FBI's Human Trafficking Initiative, FBI field offices use threat assessment to determine the existence and scope of trafficking in their region, participate in the anti-trafficking task force, conduct investigations, and report significant case developments to the CRU. In FY2010, federal law enforcement charged 181 individuals, and obtained 141 convictions in 103 human trafficking prosecutions.[121]

In addition, DOJ funds 39 anti-trafficking task forces nationwide. These task forces are composed of federal, state, and local law enforcement investigators and prosecutors, labor enforcement and NGO victims service providers. These task forces coordinate cases as well as conduct law enforcement training on the identification, investigation, and prosecution of human trafficking cases. Reportedly, research has shown that locales with task forces are more likely to identify and prosecute trafficking cases.[122] These taskforces reported 750 trafficking investigations during FY2010.[123]

ICE uses a global enforcement strategy to disrupt and dismantle domestic and international criminal organizations that engage in human trafficking. In FY2009, ICE opened 566 cases with a nexus to human trafficking[124] In addition, DOL is involved in cases of trafficking through enforcement of labor standards laws such as the Fair Labor Standards Act[125] and the Migrant and Seasonal Agricultural Worker Protection Act.[126]

Human Smuggling and Trafficking Center

In July 2004, the Secretaries of DOS and DHS and the Attorney General signed a charter to establish the Human Smuggling and Trafficking Center (HSTC), and The Intelligence Reform and Terrorism Protection Act of 2004 (P.L. 108-458, §7202), signed into law on December 17, 2004, formalized the HSTC. The HSTC severs as the federal government's information clearinghouse and intelligence fusion center for all federal agencies addressing human smuggling, human trafficking, and the potential use of smuggling routes by terrorists. Specifically, the HSTC is tasked with

- serving as the focal point for interagency efforts to address terrorist travel;
- serving as a clearinghouse with respect to all relevant information from all federal agencies in support of the United States strategy to prevent clandestine terrorist travel, migrant smuggling, and trafficking of persons;
- ensuring cooperation among all relevant policy, law enforcement, diplomatic, and intelligence agencies of the federal government to improve effectiveness and to convert all information relating to clandestine terrorist travel, the facilitation of migrant smuggling, and trafficking of persons into tactical, operational, and strategic intelligence that can be used to combat such illegal activities; and
- submitting to Congress, on an annual basis, a strategic assessment regarding vulnerabilities that may be exploited by international terrorists, human smugglers, and traffickers.

The HSTC has had issues with cooperation between the different agencies and departments, related to funding, staffing, and information sharing.[127] In The Implementing the 9/11 Commission Recommendations Act of 2007 (P.L. 110-53, discussed in *Appendix A*), Congress attempted to address these issues.

TVPA REAUTHORIZATION ACTIVITY IN THE 112TH CONGRESS

The William Wilberforce Trafficking Victims Protection Reauthorization Act of 2008 (P.L. 110- 457) reauthorized the TVPA through FY2011. There have been bills introduced in the 112th Congress to reauthorize the TVPA, possibly making changes to the act and extending authorizations for some current programs. In addition, there have been several other bills introduced in the 112th Congress that contain provisions related to human trafficking.

Two bills that would reauthorize the TVPA have received action. S. 1301[128] was reported by the Senate Judiciary Committee on October 13, 2011, and H.R. 2830[129] was ordered reported by the House Foreign Affairs Committee on October 5, 2011. The reported versions of both bills, due in part to the current state of the economy,[130] are less expansive than the introduced versions of the bills.

H.R. 2830 as reported by the House Foreign Affairs Committee: The Trafficking Victims Protection Reauthorization Act of 2011[131]

H.R. 2830 would authorize the Secretary of State to limit the time that a U.S. passport issued to a sex offender is valid, and to revoke the passport of an individual convicted in a foreign country of a sex offense. The revocation would not prevent the U.S. citizen from reentering the United States, and the citizen could reapply for a passport at any time after he returned to the United States (§101). The bill would also change the title of the State Department's Office to Monitor and Combat Human Trafficking to the Office to Monitor and Combat Modern Slavery and Other Forms of Human Trafficking (§102).

Section 103 of H.R. 2830 would expand existing authorities to provide economic alternatives to human trafficking, including public-private partnerships for youth employment opportunities. Section 103 identifies specific vulnerable populations for which to prioritize trafficking prevention efforts and would also authorize the State Department to provide assistance specifically in post-conflict and humanitarian emergencies. Section 104 would require the Department of State in its annual TIP Report to include sections on (1) best practices in slavery eradication; (2) the connection between refuges and human trafficking; and (3) an assessment of actions by the Departments of State and Justice to investigate allegations of trafficking or abuse of aliens holding A-3 or G-5 visas.[132] Section 105 of the House bill would also extend the additional $1 issuance fee for machine-readable visas till September 30, 2015. The Department of Labor would be mandated to monitor and report on forced and child labor practices in foreign countries as well as the United States (§106).

H.R. 2830 would expand the existing federal prohibition, which forbids U.S. citizens and LPRs from traveling in the foreign commerce of the United States and engaging in such sexual contact with a child as would be unlawful had it occurred in U.S. territorial jurisdiction, to include travel that affects the U.S. foreign commerce and to make it clear that the proscription applies to those who reside overseas and regardless of the fact the contact may be generally accepted or even lawful under the laws of the place where it occurs (§107).

In addition, Section 201 of H.R. 2830 would require the annual reports to Congress on U.S. anti-trafficking activities to include expanded data collection on U.S. contractors or subcontractors engaging in trafficking in persons. The report would also have to include information from each DOJ human trafficking task-force on T and U visa certifications requested and granted, and requests and grants of continued presence. It would also require information on such trafficking victims such as age, gender, citizenship, type of trafficking (i.e., labor or sex). The bill would also require that requests for continued presence made to federal law enforcement officers be responded to no later than 15 days after the request was made to whether the official filed an application with the DHS Secretary, and if not, when or if the official expects to do so. The DHS Secretary would have to approve or deny the application within one month (§202). Section 203 would mandate the State Department to report in its annual TIP Report to Congress on the efforts of the U.S. government to comply with minimum standards for the elimination of trafficking, which the State Department has been doing for the past two years.

In the introduced version of H.R. 2830, Title II included a provision to establish a Director of Anti-Trafficking Policies within the Office of the Secretary of Defense with a rank of Assistant Secretary. The Director would be responsible for overseeing Defense Department policies on combating human trafficking, including the enforcement of contractor requirements to prevent human trafficking in the performance of defense contracts, both in the United States and at overseas installations. In the House Foreign Affairs Committee mark-up session, this language was removed, reportedly due to concerns related to cost.[133]

Section 214 of H.R. 2830 would make it a criminal offense to knowingly destroy, or for a period of more than 48 hours, conceal, remove, confiscate, or possess another person's passport or immigration or personal identification documents in the course of committing or attempting to commit the offense of fraud in foreign labor contracting or alien smuggling. It would also be a criminal offence to destroy, conceal, remove, confiscate, or possess such documents in order to unlawfully maintain, prevent, or restrict the labor or services of the individual. Violators would be subject to a fine and/or imprisonment of not more than one year. The bill would also add foreign labor contracting fraud (18 U.S.C. 1351) to the list of racketeering (RICO) predicate offenses with the additional result that such fraud would automatically become a money laundering predicate offense as well; foreign labor contracting fraud is a 5-year felony; RICO and money laundering are 20-year felonies, and both trigger asset forfeiture provisions (§215).

The House bill (§221) would also require the Secretary of Homeland Security, in consultation with the Secretaries of the Departments of Health and Human Services and State, to report annually to Congress on alien children encountered and screened for being trafficking victims by CPB, including the outcomes of the screenings. H.R. 2830 would also lower from 48 hours to 24 hours the required time that a federal agency must notify HHS when they encountered an unaccompanied alien child. Would make several changes to the provisions related to the custody and care of unaccompanied alien children (these provisions were included in P.L. 110-457, §235) including specifying that the Secretary of DHS should release or place in the least restrictive setting unaccompanied alien children who are not a danger to the community or a flight risk, and any unaccompanied alien child who turns 18 while in custody. H.R. 2830 would also amend the law so that a home study is not necessary before placing an unaccompanied minor with his/her parents unless there were past allegation of abuse or neglect.

In addition, H.R. 2830 would require states as part of their plans for adoption and foster care assistance to include information on existing practices and future plans to prevent and provide victim assistance to foreign, U.S. citizen, and LPR victims children who are victims of human trafficking (§222). The House bill (§223) also contains provisions that would attempt to increase public awareness of the National Human Trafficking Resource Center hotline, by among other requirements, mandating that posters advertising the hotline be posted in certain establishments (e.g., massage parlors, train stations, strip clubs).

H.R. 2830 would reauthorize appropriations for grant programs in the TVPA of 2000, as amended, and the TVPRA of 2005 for FY2012 and FY2013 (§§301-302). The House bill would maintain most programs at current authorization levels.[134] (See *Table 11* for a detailed list of authorization levels.) Section 303 of H.R. 2830 would also require a report to Congress on the amount of appropriations each department or agency received and a list of activities funded by the appropriations and the appropriations account from which they were funded. H.R. 2830 would also require the Senior Policy Operating Group in coordination with the Department of State to submit a report to Congress on internet-facilitated human trafficking.

The House Foreign Affairs Committee adopted, en bloc, four amendments to H.R. 2830. Representative Fortenberry offered an amendment that would prohibit foreign assistance from the peacekeeping operations account to countries that the Secretary of State annually designates as conscripting or harboring child soldiers in armed conflict. Representative Murphy offered an amendment that would require the Secretary of State to encourage to any publicly traded or private entity with worldwide receipts in excess of $100 million to disclose on an annual basis on the company's website and to the Secretary of State any efforts that have been taken to identify and address human trafficking within the supply chains. Representative Royce offered an amendment that described the Sense of Congress on human trafficking in Cambodia, stating that it should be designated a Tier 3 country. And Representative Bass offered an amendment to require the Senior Policy Operating Group to submit a report to Congress on internet-facilitated human trafficking.

S. 1301 as reported by the Senate Judiciary Committee: The Trafficking Victims Protection Reauthorization Act of 2011[135]

Sections 101 and 102 of the Senate bill (S. 1301) would require the State Department's regional bureaus to create bilateral plans and objectives for combating trafficking and would authorize the appointment of anti-trafficking officers to promote anti-trafficking diplomacy and initiatives. The bill would also attempt to promote partnerships among the U.S. government, foreign governments, and private sector entities to ensure that U.S. citizens do not use items produced by victims of trafficking and that the entities do not contribute to trafficking in persons (§103). Section 103 would mandate the President and the Secretary of State to establish additional anti-trafficking assistance programs, including programs related to anti-labor trafficking, human trafficking in emergency situations, and child trafficking. Section 104 of S. 1301 would direct DOJ anti-trafficking taskforces to make all reasonable efforts to distribute information to enable government agencies to publicize the Nation Human Trafficking Resource Center Hotline. The bill would also require the State Department's TIP Report to include a section on best practices in the eradication of human trafficking (§106). Section 105 would update the criteria used to determine whether governments are achieving congressionally designated "minimum standards for the elimination of trafficking."

Section 107 of S. 1301 would require that a video to be shown in consular waiting rooms to provide information on the rights and responsibilities of the employee under U.S. immigration, labor, and employment law. The video would have to be developed and available within one year after enactment. The Senate bill would also require the Secretary of State to develop a multi-year, multi-sectoral strategy to prevent child marriage, and the Secretary of State would be required to report on countries where child marriage is prevalent (§108). Section 109 would prohibit, except in certain circumstances, foreign assistance from the peacekeeping operations account to countries that the Secretary of State annually designates as conscripting or harboring child soldiers in armed conflict. Section 110 would create a presidential award for technological innovations to combat trafficking in persons. The Senate bill would create additional requirements to provide oversight that contractors and subcontactors were not engaging in human trafficking (§111). Section 112 of S. 1301 would require that all known trafficking in persons cases are reported to the Under Secretary of Defense for Personnel and Readiness (U.S. defense personnel) or the Under Secretary of Defense for Acquisition of Technology and Logistics (contractors).

As with H.R. 2830, S. 1301 (§202) would make it a criminal offense to knowingly destroy, or for a period of more than 48 hours, conceal, remove, confiscate, or possess another person's passport, or immigration or personal identification documents in the course of committing or attempting to commit the offense of fraud in foreign labor contracting or alien smuggling. It would also be a criminal offence to destroy, conceal, remove, confiscate, or possess such documents in order to unlawfully maintain, prevent, or restrict the labor or services of the individual. Violators would be subject to a fine and/or imprisonment of not more than one year. Moreover, S. 1301 would allow for civil remedies for personal injuries caused during the commission of most criminal trafficking offenses (§202).

S. 1301 (§221) would require that additional information be included in the AG's report on anti-trafficking activities such as information on the number of persons who have applied for, been granted, and been denied T and U status; the mean time it takes to adjudicate an application; efforts being taken to reduce adjudication time; activities taken by federal agencies to train state, tribal, and local governments and law enforcement officials to identify trafficking victims and prosecute trafficking offenses, including the number of victims; and activities taken by DOJ and HHS to meet the needs of minor victims of domestic trafficking. The Senate bill (§222) would also require the Secretary of Labor to report to Congress biennially goods from countries that the Bureau of International Labor Affairs has reason to believe are produced by forced labor or child labor in violation of international standards. The bill would also require the Secretary of State to provide the Secretary of Labor with information on the use of child and forced labor in the production of goods (§223). The Senate bill would also require GAO to produce a report on the use of foreign labor contractors and abuses by such contractors. Section 226 of the Senate bill would require that all DOJ grants awarded under the TVPA be subject to audits, and would bar grantees from receiving grants for two years if violations were found. The bill would also require non-federal grantees to secure a 25% non-federal match of funds before the federal funds could be expended. S. 1301 would also set procedures and prohibitions related to using grant monies for administrative expenses, conferences, and lobbying.

Section 231 of S. 1301 would replace the HHS grant program for states, Indian tribes, units of local government, and nonprofit, nongovernmental victims' service organizations to provide assistance programs for U.S. citizens or LPR trafficking victims created in P.L. 109-164, Section 202, with a new grant program for child sex trafficking victims. The new grant program would authorize the Assistant Attorney General for DOJ's Office of Justice Programs, in consultation with the Assistant Secretary for Children and Families in HHS, to award one-year grants to six eligible to combat sex trafficking of children in the United States. Each grant could range from $2 million to $2.5 million. Of the grant amounts, at least 67% would have to be allocated to nongovernmental organizations (NGOs) to provide counseling, legal services, shelter, clothing, and other social services to victims, while not less than 10% would have to be allocated provide services to victims or training for service providers on sex trafficking of children. Funds could also be used for training for law enforcement; investigative and prosecution expenses; case management; salaries for law enforcement officers and state and local prosecutors; and outreach, education, and treatment programs.[136]

In addition, S. 1301 would specify that the model state anti-trafficking laws created by the AG should include safe harbor provisions that treat an individual under 18 years of age who has been arrested for prostitution as a victim of a severe form of trafficking, prohibit the prosecution of such as person, and refer them to the service providers who provide assistance to victims of commercial sexual exploitation (§233).

The Senate bill would reauthorize appropriations for the Trafficking Victims Protection Act of 2000 for FY2012 through FY2015, decreasing some authorization levels and increasing others.[137] (See *Table 11* for a detailed list of authorization levels.)

As in H.R. 2830, S. 1301 contains provisions dealing with the care and custody of unaccompanied alien children. The provisions in the Senate bill are similar but not identical. As in H.R. 2830, Section 401 would specify that the DHS Secretary should release or place in the least restrictive setting any unaccompanied alien child who turns 18 while in custody. Unlike H.R. 2830, the Senate bill (§402) would require the DHS Secretary to create a pilot program in three states to proved independent child advocates at immigration detention sites for child trafficking victims and other vulnerable unaccompanied alien children.

In addition, the Senate bill would specify that children who receive U status and are in the custody of HHS are eligible for programs and services to the same extent as refugees, and the federal government will reimburse states for foster care provided these children (§403), and would require GAO to do a study on the effectiveness of CBP screening of children to determine if they are or are at risk for becoming victims of trafficking (§404).

Table 11. H.R. 2830 and S. 1301: Comparison of Authorizations of Appropriations (in $ U.S. millions)

Authorized Programs	FY11	FY12		FY13		FY14		FY15	
	P.L. 110-457	H.R. 2830	S. 1301	H.R. 2830	S. 1301	H.R. 2830	S. 1301	H.R. 2830	S. 1301
International Programs									
U.S. Agency for International Development (USAID)									
USAID: Pilot Program for Rehabilitation Facilities (22 U.S.C. 7105 note)	$2.5	$1.5	Struck	$1.5	Struck	—	Struck	—	Struck
U.S. Department of State (DOS)									
DOS: Interagency Task Force (22 U.S.C. 7110(a))	$5.5	$5.5	$2.0	$5.5	$2.0	—	$2.0	—	$2.0
DOS: Interagency Task Force: Reception Expenses (22 U.S.C. 7110(a))	$.003	$.003	Struck	$.003	Struck	—	Struck	—	Struck
DOS: Interagency Task Force: Additional Personnel (22 U.S.C. 7110(a))	$1.5	$1.5	N/A	$1.5	N/A	—	N/A	—	N/A
DOS: Prevention (22 U.S.C. 7110(c)(1)(A))	$10.0	$10.0	$10.0	$10.0	$10.0	—	$10.0	—	$10.0

Table 11. (Continued)

Authorized Programs	FY11	FY12		FY13		FY14		FY15	
	P.L. 110-457	H.R. 2830	S. 1301	H.R. 2830	S. 1301	H.R. 2830	S. 1301	H.R. 2830	S. 1301
DOS: Protection (22 U.S.C. 7110(c)(1)(B))	$10.0	$10.0	$10.0	$10.0	$10.0	—	$10.0	—	$10.0
DOS: Prosecution and Meeting Minimum Standards (22 U.S.C. 7110(c)(1)(C))	$10.0	$10.0	$10.0	$10.0	$10.0	—	$10.0	—	$10.0
DOS: Refugees and Internally Displaced Persons (22 U.S.C. 7110(c)(1)(B))	$1.0	$1.0	$1.0	$1.0	$1.0	—	$1.0	—	$1.0
president									
President: Foreign Assistance for Law Enforcement Training (22 U.S.C. 7110(d)(B))	$0.25	$0.25	N/A	$0.25	N/A	—	N/A	—	N/A
President: Foreign Victim Assistance (22 U.S.C. 7110(e)(1))	$15.0	$15.0	$7.5	$15.0	$7.5	—	$7.5	—	$7.5
President: Foreign Assistance to Meet Minimum Standards (22 U.S.C. 7110(e)(2))	$15.0	$15.0	$7.5	$15.0	$7.5	—	$7.5	—	$7.5
President: Research (22 U.S.C. 7110(e)(3))	$2.0	$2.0	N/A	$2.0	N/A	—	N/A	—	N/A
President: Award for Extraordinary Efforts (22 U.S.C. 7109b(d))	—a	$0.5	N/A	$0.5	N/A	—	N/A	—	N/A
Domestic Programs									
U.S. Department of Health and Human Services (HHS)									
HHS: Assistance for Trafficking Victims (22 U.S.C. 7110(b)(1))	12.5	12.5	14.5	12.5	14.5	—	14.5	—	14.5
HHS: Assistance for U.S. Citizens (USCs) and Legal Permanent Residents (LPRs) (22 U.S.C. 7110(b)(2))	7.0	7.0	7.0	7.0	7.0	—	7.0	—	7.0
HHS: Local Grant for USC/LPR Sex Trafficking Victims (42 U.S.C. 14044a(d))	8.0	8.0	8.0	8.0	8.0	—	8.0	—	8.0
HHS: Pilot Program for Juveniles (42 U.S.C. 14044b(g))	5.0	3.0	—	3.0	—	—	—	—	—
HHS: Child Advocates for Unaccompanied Minors	—	—	1.0	—	1.0	—	2.0	—	2.0
U.S. Department of Homeland Security (DHS)									
DHS: Immigration and Customs Enforcement (ICE) Investigations (22 U.S.C. 7110(i))	18.0	18.0	10.0	18.0	10.0	—	10.0	—	10.0
DHS: Human Smuggling and Trafficking Center (HSTC) (22 U.S.C. 7109a(b)(4))	2.0	2.0	1.0	1.0	1.0	—	1.0	—	1.0
U.S. Department of Justice (DOJ)									
DOJ: Assistance for Tracking Victims (22 U.S.C. 7110(d)(A))	10.0	10.0	11.0	10.0	11.0	—	11.0	—	11.0
DOJ: Assistance for USCs and LPRs (22 U.S.C. 7110(d)(C))	7.0	7.0	8.0	7.0	8.0	—	8.0	—	8.0

Authorized Programs	FY11	FY12		FY13		FY14		FY15	
	P.L. 110-457	H.R. 2830	S. 1301	H.R. 2830	S. 1301	H.R. 2830	S. 1301	H.R. 2830	S. 1301
DOJ: Prevent Domestic Sex Trafficking (DST)—Study on Trafficking (42 U.S.C. 14044(c)(1)) DOJ: Prevent DST—Study on	1.5	1.5	1.5	1.5	1.5	—	1.5	—	1.5
Sex Trafficking (42 U.S.C. 14044(c)(1)) DOJ: Prevent DST—	1.5	1.5	1.5	1.5	1.5	—	1.5	—	1.5
Conference (42 U.S.C. 14044(c)(2)) DOJ: Local Grant for Law	1.0	1.0	1.0	1.0	1.0	—	1.0	—	1.0
Enforcement (42 U.S.C. 14044c(d)) DOJ: Federal Bureau of	20.0	10.0	11.0	10.0	11.0	—	11.0	—	11.0
Investigation (FBI) (22 U.S.C. 7110(h))	15.0	15.0	15.0	15.0	15.0	—	15.0	—	15.0
U.S. Department of Labor (DOL)									
DOL: Assistance for Trafficking Victims (22 U.S.C. 7110(f))	10.0	10.0	5.0	10.0	5.0	—	5.0	—	5.0

Source: CRS analysis of P.L. 106-386, P.L. 108-193, P.L. 109-164, P.L. 110-457, H.R. 2830, as ordered reported by the House Foreign Affairs Committee, and S. 1301, as reported by the Senate Judiciary Committee.

Notes: N/A = Authorized program not referenced in bill. Struck = the program would be struck from law by the bill. H.R. 2830 seeks to reauthorize TVPA programs through FY2013, whereas S. 1301 seeks to reauthorize TVPA programs through FY2015. The TVPA and its subsequent reauthorizations include several additional provisions without specific funding amounts. Such provisions include §107A(f) of P.L. 106-386, as amended (22 U.S.C. 7104a), which authorizes not more than 5% of the amounts made available to carry out the TVPA, as amended, in each fiscal year 2008 through 2011 to the President to evaluate anti-trafficking programs and projects. §114(c)(2) of P.L. 106-386, as amended (22 U.S.C. 7110(c)(2)), also authorizes such sums as may be necessary for each fiscal year 2008 through 2011 to the Department of State for the preparation of congressionally mandated human rights reports with reference to human trafficking issues. Note also that additional funding outside the scope of the TVPA and its reauthorizations has been authorized in separate legislative vehicles. See for example, §111 of P.L. 109-162, which authorizes $10 million for each fiscal year 2008 through 2011 to the Department of Justice for state and local law enforcement grants for human trafficking victim identification.

a. With respect to the presidential award for extraordinary efforts to combat trafficking in persons, §112B of P.L. 106-386, as amended (22 U.S.C. 7109b(d)), authorizes to be appropriated for fiscal years 2008 through 2011 "such sums as may be necessary to carry out this section."

POLICY ISSUES

A broad consensus appears to be shared in Congress and the policy community on the need for decisive action to curb human trafficking. However, there are some fundamental questions related to how broadly human trafficking should be defined. In addition, questions have been raised about the effective implementation of anti-trafficking programs.

Credibility of TIP Rankings

Many analysts have asserted that the overall impact of the TIP report and sanctions process depends upon the credibility of the State Department's annual country TIP rankings. Some would argue that, although the TIP reports have improved with each year, "inconsistent application of the minimum standards [mandated by TVPA] and superficial country assessments have compromised their credibility."[138]

Some argue that it is difficult to determine what standards make a country eligible for Tier 1. They assert that the Tier 2 and Tier 2 Watch List have become "catch-all" categories that include countries which should really be placed on Tier 3.

According to the GAO, in addition to a lack of clarity in the tier ranking process, the TIP report's "incomplete narratives reduce the report's utility." The State Department, while acknowledging the need to continue to increase the comprehensiveness of the report, has stated that "keeping the report concise is paramount."[139]

U.S. Sanctions: A Useful Tool?

Most agree that extensive international cooperation is required in order to stop international trafficking and that both "carrots" and "sticks" may be needed to influence the policies of other governments, including financial and technical assistance, as well as the threat of sanctions.

Some assert that unilateral sanctions, when designed in accordance with international norms, can incite countries to internalize those norms.[140] Sanctions seem to be most effective when they are clearly defined and evenly applied, criteria which some say U.S. trafficking sanctions have not yet met.[141] Some argue that sanctions will probably only be applied to countries already subject to other sanctions—such as Burma and North Korea—and that threatening other countries with sanctions may actually encourage them to become less open to working with the United States.

Others argue that while that may be true in a few cases, most countries depend on good political and economic relations with the United States and fear the public humiliation that comes with a Tier 3 designation as much as actual sanctions.

Equal Focus on all Types of Trafficking?

Although the TVPA defines trafficking broadly to include problems such as forced labor, sex slavery, and domestic servitude, and although the U.S. government funds programs to combat all types of TIP, some argue that U.S. government anti-trafficking efforts disproportionately focus on sexual exploitation at the expense of other forms of trafficking. They argue that too high a percentage of the U.S. anti-trafficking budget has been directed to NGOs focused on rescuing women and children from the commercial sex industry. Inventories of U.S. anti-trafficking programs since 2004 appear to counter these claims as they show U.S. support for a wide variety of NGOs that strive to protect victims and prosecute traffickers engaged in all types of human trafficking.[142]

Forced Labor: A Growing TIP Problem?

Research suggests that while TIP for sexual exploitation is both a highly prevalent and particularly visible form of human trafficking, TIP for forced labor exploitation may account for a large, often unreported, and possibly growing share of TIP globally.

According to the UNODC, sexual exploitation is by far the most commonly reported form of human trafficking, accounting for 79% of incidents globally. Forced labor, however, follows as the second-most reported form of human trafficking, at 18%.[143]

Other groups arrive at different estimates of the prevalence of various forms of human trafficking. The ILO, for example, found that 43% of all trafficking victims were trafficked into sexual exploitation, 32% into labor exploitation, and 25% a combination of both forced labor and sexual exploitation.[144]

Recent interest in forced labor as a form of TIP has sparked calls for greater research in analyzing the prevalence of forced labor, increased international efforts to combat this form of TIP, and more awareness to prevent and educate potential victims. The State Department's TIP reports since 2005 have placed an added emphasis on evaluating country efforts to combat trafficking for forced labor, and several other programmatic efforts to combat TIP for forced labor are underway at the State Department. Other international groups, particularly the ILO, also play a large role in efforts to combat forced labor.

Debates Regarding Prostitution and Sex Trafficking

The current U.N. definition of TIP assumes that there are at least two different types of prostitution, one of which is the result of free choice to participate in the prostitution business while the other is the result of coercion, vulnerability, deception, or other pressures. Of these, only the latter type is considered TIP under the U.N. definition. Based on the TVPA, as amended, sex trafficking is not considered a "severe form of TIP" unless it is associated with commercial sex acts induced by force, fraud, or coercion, or in which the person induced to perform such acts is a minor.[145]

Several groups in the United States have sought to redefine TIP to include all prostitution, but many countries have thus far rejected those attempts. Proponents of this broader definition of TIP argue that prostitution is "not 'sex work;' it is violence against women [that] exists because ... men are given social, moral and legal permission to buy women on demand."[146] Countries such as Germany, the Netherlands, Austria, France, and Italy, which have legal or government-regulated prostitution, reject such a definitional change and argue that this broader definition would impede the capacity of the international community to achieve consensus and work together to combat trafficking.[147]

The U.S. State Department asserts that prostitution and TIP are inextricably linked. In the 2008 TIP Report to Congress, for example, the State Department states that "sex trafficking would not exist without the demand for commercial sex flourishing around the world" and that prostitution and any related activities "should not be regulated as a legitimate form of work for any human being."[148] The Trafficking Victims Protection Reauthorization Act of 2003 (P.L. 108-193) restricts anti-trafficking funds to groups that oppose prostitution. Critics have argued that this policy excludes the people who are most able to report and combat abuses within the sex industry— prostitutes themselves—and may hinder the success of well-established anti-TIP programs. They believe that giving prostitutes some measure of legitimacy short of legalization reduces the risk that they will be exposed to the dangers of trafficking.[149]

Distinctions between Trafficking and Alien Smuggling

The concept of and responses to TIP are often confused with those of alien or human smuggling, irregular migration, and the movement of asylum seekers. In 2000, the United Nations drafted two protocols, known as the Palermo Protocols, to address TIP and human smuggling.[150] According to the U.N. Trafficking Protocol, people who have been *trafficked* are considered "victims" and are entitled to government protection and a broad range of social services.

In contrast, the U.N. Protocol against the Smuggling of Migrants by Land, Sea, and Air considers people who have been *smuggled* as willing participants in a criminal activity who should be given "humane treatment and full protection of their rights" while being returned to their country of origin.[151]

Some observers contend that smuggling is a "crime against the state" and that smuggled migrants should be immediately deported, while trafficking is a "crime against a person" whose victims deserve to be given government assistance and protection.[152] Others maintain that there are few clear-cut distinctions between trafficking and smuggling and that many people who are considered "smuggled" should actually be viewed as trafficking victims, and, at times, vice versa.

Some argue that as immigration and border restrictions have tightened, smuggling costs have increased and migration routes have become more dangerous, putting migrants at a high risk of trafficking. In some cases, smugglers have sold undocumented migrants into situations of forced labor or prostitution in order to recover their costs or obtain greater profits.[153]

Despite the U.N. protocols on trafficking and smuggling, many countries in practice conflate the two differing, but sometimes overlapping, phenomena. As a result, some observers argue that TIP policies can directly or indirectly shape migration (and vice versa) in both countries of origin and destination.[154]

How to Measure the Effectiveness of Global Anti-TIP Programs

It is often difficult to evaluate the impact of U.S. anti-trafficking efforts on curbing TIP. So far, few reliable indicators have been identified. For example, the new estimates of numbers of trafficking victims in the United States seem considerably lower than some of the previous high-end estimates. Whether these figures reflect the success of U.S. policies and programs or more accurate data gathering is unclear. Hard evidence with regard to the results of the more vigorous international campaign against trafficking is also lacking. Information is often anecdotal.

Worldwide estimates of the numbers of victims seemingly have not changed much, when cross-border trafficking and trafficking within countries are taken together. A 2006 GAO study seriously questions the adequacy of any of the estimates.[155]

Issues Concerning Immigration Relief for Trafficking Victims

Most of the trafficking victims' advocacy community and groups working to end trafficking are supportive of the T status. Nonetheless, these groups have raised concerns about aspects of the application process that may impede victims from applying for T status or create difficulties for the victims to meet the standards of T status.[156] Some advocacy groups have questioned whether the T status protects the victims or is primarily a tool for law enforcement.

The opponents to the creation of the T status, on the other hand, contend that the status rewards criminal behavior. Immigrant benefits are scarce and some argued that there are more meritorious people who deserve the benefits such as those who have been waiting to come into the country though legal methods. Some argue that there is a need to protect the victims, but that they are being given more access to public benefits than are relatives of United States citizens. Additionally, others expressed concern about the possibility of abuse of T status. For example, some aliens who had knowingly and willfully violated the law, may claim that they were coerced after they were arrested by DHS.

As discussed above, between FY2002 and FY2011, DHS approved 2,595 applications for T-1 status, while it is estimated that at least 14,500 aliens are trafficked into the United States each year. The comparatively small number of T visas issued relative to the estimates of trafficking into the United States raises some questions. Is the number of noncitizen trafficking victims in the United States overestimated? Is the United States government doing a poor job locating and identifying victims?[157] Indeed, DOS's 2010 Trafficking in Persons Report states: "[v]ictim identification, given the amount of resources put into the effort, is considered to be low."[158]

Stringency of T Determination

The regulations state that "In view of the annual limit imposed by Congress for T-1 status, and the standard of extreme hardship involving unusual and severe harm, [DHS] acknowledges that the T1 status will not be an appropriate response with respect to many cases involving aliens who are victims of severe forms of trafficking."[159] Some contend that the extreme hardship threshold makes it difficult for victims to receive T status.[160] Nonetheless, some in law enforcement have raised concerns that advocacy organizations are able to ask ICE headquarters without the input of the local ICE agents to have an alien certified as a trafficking victim, contending that some of these aliens are not truly trafficking victims.[161]

Tool of Law Enforcement or Aid to Victims

According to the policy memorandum on T status, "the T classification provides an immigration mechanism for cooperating victims to remain temporarily in the United States to assist in investigations and prosecutions and provide humanitarian protection to the victims." Some are concerned that the emphasis on aiding law enforcement is more important than aiding the victims, and note that a controversial aspect of the continued presence provision is that federal agents may supersede a victim's wishes and require the victim to remain in the United States, if the victim's "departure is deemed prejudicial to the interests of the United States."[162] NGOs have reported isolated incidents of law enforcement officers telling victims that they risk losing their benefits if they do not cooperate, and note that it is challenging getting law enforcement to recognize reluctant victims for protection purposes.[163] Others argue, however, that the only mechanism for ending trafficking is by encouraging the victims' cooperation in the prosecution and investigation.

Victims' Safety

Some victims' service providers who aid trafficking victims have also expressed concerns that outside of federal protective custody, there are few safe housing options for victims of trafficking. Shelters in many areas are full or inaccessible, and domestic violence shelters are ill-equipped to meet the safety needs of trafficking victims.[164] In addition, according to the DOS report, law officials are sometimes untrained or unwilling to undertake victim protection measures.[165] Other advocacy groups such as the Collation to Abolish Slavery and Trafficking (CAST) contend that forcing victims to aid in the investigation and prosecution of traffickers may endanger the victims' families who remain in the home country especially when the trafficker is deported back to the country.

They argue that there needs to be some mechanism to either ensure the victims' families' safety in their home country or reunite the families with the victims in the United States.[166] Dianne Post, an attorney for the Arizona Coalition Against Domestic Violence, argues that the TVPA may create problems for victims, because victims can not receive services and benefits until they apply for T status, and if they do not speak English, they can not fill out the application without help. Often they will need to turn to the local immigrant community, and the traffickers may have ties in the same community.[167]

Funding and Authority to Assist U.S. Citizen and LPR Victims of Trafficking

An overriding issue is the extent to which the agencies can provide services to U.S. citizen and LPR trafficking victims who do not receive certification.[168] As discussed above, a 2007 report by the Senior Policy Operating Group on Trafficking in Persons (SPOG) states that "there are not many differences in trafficking victims' eligibility for the services we reviewed when one looks at the relevant statutes." However, the report does note that U.S. citizen victims may have less intensive case management services compared to noncitizens.[169] Conversely, the AG's FY2009 report on anti-trafficking efforts states, "the funds provided under the TVPA by the federal government for direct services to victims are dedicated to assist non-U.S. citizen victims and may not currently be used to assist U.S. citizen victims."[170] More recently, ORR has stated that they do not provide services to U.S. citizen trafficking victims.[171] Nonetheless, the language in the appropriation acts may give the HHS the authority to provide some services to U.S. citizen trafficking victims. The appropriation acts since FY2008 state that the money appropriated to HHS is to "carry out the Trafficking Victims Protection Act of 2000."[172]

In addition, as discussed above, beginning in FY2009, OVC is funding a grant, Services for Domestic Minor Victims of Human Trafficking, that includes U.S. citizen and LPR victims.[173] According to DOJ, this grant is authorized under 22 U.S.C Section 7105(b)(2)(A), which was included in the TVPA as enacted in 2000.[174] The authorizing language of this grant program does not appear to differentiate between U.S. citizen and noncitizen victims. 22 U.S.C Section 7105(b)(2)(A) states:

IN GENERAL.—Subject to the availability of appropriations, the Attorney General may make grants to States, Indian tribes, units of local government, and nonprofit, nongovernmental victims' service organizations to develop, expand, or strengthen victim service programs for victims of trafficking.175

Additionally, in 2010, DOJ provided grant funding to six NGO service providers to assist U.S. citizen and lawful permanent resident victims, and released a new funding opportunity that included a focus on adult U.S. citizen victims, including Native Americans.[176] The funding of these grants appears to be inconsistent with the statement in the FY2009 AG's report that the funds appropriated under TVPA can be used only for noncitizen victims. Thus, it appears that there is ongoing confusion over the authority and funding available under TVPA to provide services to U.S. citizen trafficking victims.

Resources for Trafficking Victims' Services

A corollary issue is the overall amount of funding for victim services, especially as the focus on sex trafficking is broadening to include minor sex trafficking victims in the United States who are U.S. citizens. In FY2011, Congress appropriated approximately $20 million for services to trafficking victims. Since FY2009, HHS has spent all of its appropriated money on services for trafficking victims before the end of the fiscal year. In addition, there is no targeted federal funding to support state child welfare agencies anti-trafficking efforts.[177]

It is estimated that there are approximately 14,500 noncitizens trafficked into the United States each year.[178] Some have estimated that the number of minor sex trafficking victims could be in the hundreds of thousands.[179] This raises several questions: Are the resources for trafficking victims, both citizen and noncitizens, adequate? If funds were allocated based on estimated citizen populations and noncitizen populations, would certain victims have more trouble getting services? To what extent are the needs of U.S. citizen and noncitizen victims similar and to what extent do they differ? For example, are noncitizen victims more likely than U.S. citizen victims to identify themselves as victims?180 Are there other public benefit entitlement programs that noncitizen victims are ineligible for that could serve the needs of U.S. citizen trafficking victims?[181]

Oversight of Domestic Grants

In the current economic situation, Congress has been actively questioning whether there is effective and efficient management of the grants under TVPA.[182] Notably, one of the roles of the Senior Policy Operating Group (SPOG, discussed above) is to coordinate the work of multiple agencies to make sure that there is not a duplication of efforts. There has been one published report, a 2008 report from the DOJ Inspector General (IG), that provides oversight of DOJ's victims service and anti-trafficking task-forces grant recipients. The report found systemic weakness in DOJ's grant implementation,[183] and noted that while the agency has built significant capacities to serve victims, they had not been effective at identifying and serving a significant number of victims.[184]

More recently, a 2011 IG report that examined grant management by DOJ noted that since 2007 the agency had made significant improvement in the monitoring and oversight of grant recipients.[185] However, this report did not specifically examine grants awarded under the TVPA.

APPENDIX A. ANTI-TRAFFICKING ADMINISTRATIVE DIRECTIVES AND LEGISLATION

The human trafficking problem has gained increased attention in the United States and worldwide since the late 1990s. It has been addressed as a priority by Congress, as well as the Clinton, Bush, and Obama Administrations. As part of former President Clinton's announced International Crime Control Strategy, an interagency working group was set up to address international crime implications of trafficking. On March 11, 1998, President Clinton issued a directive establishing a government-wide anti-trafficking strategy of (1) prevention, (2) protection and support for victims, and (3) prosecution of traffickers.[186] The strategy, as announced, had strong domestic and international policy components:

- In the area of prevention, the Administration outlined the need for programs to increase economic opportunities for potential victims and dissemination of information in other countries to increase public awareness of trafficking dangers and funding for more research on trafficking.
- In terms of victim protection and assistance, the Administration argued for legislation to provide shelter and support services to victims who are in the country unlawfully and therefore presently ineligible for assistance. It pressed for the creation of a humanitarian, non-immigrant visa classification to allow victims to receive temporary resident status so they could receive assistance and help to prosecute traffickers. Also, support was sought for developing countries to protect and reintegrate trafficking victims once they were returned.
- As far as prosecution and enforcement, the Administration pressed for laws to more effectively go after traffickers and increase the penalties they can face. In addition, restitution for trafficked victims was sought in part by creating the possibility of bringing private civil lawsuits against traffickers. The Department of Justice (DOJ) called for laws that would expand the definition of involuntary servitude, criminalize a broader range of actions constituting involuntary servitude, and increase the penalties for placing people in involuntary servitude. Justice Department spokesmen also urged that prosecutors be give the capability to go after those who profit from trafficking, not just those directly involved in trafficking.[187] They also called for amending immigration statutes to punish traffickers who entrap victims by taking their passports and identification from them.

On the domestic side, a Workers' Exploitation Task Force, chaired by DOJ's Civil Rights Division and the Solicitor's Office in the Department of Labor (DOL), was charged with investigating and prosecuting cases of exploitation and trafficking. In addition, DOJ reviewed existing U.S. criminal laws and their enforcement to see if they adequately dealt with the crime of trafficking.

On the international front, the State Department sponsored the creation of a database on U.S. and international legislation on trafficking. An Interagency Council on Women formed by the Clinton Administration established a senior governmental working group on trafficking. The Administration urged the enactment of legislation to encourage and support strong action by foreign governments and help the work of non-governmental organizations (NGOs) in this area.

Victims of Trafficking and Violence Protection Act of 2000

Several bills were introduced in the 106th Congress on human trafficking. In conference, the bills were combined with the Violence against Women Act of 2000 and repackaged as the Victims of Trafficking and Violence Protection Act of 2000, along with miscellaneous anti-crime and antiterrorism provisions. President Clinton signed the bill into law on October 28, 2000 (P.L. 106- 386). The act's key provisions on human trafficking:

- Directed the Secretary of State to provide an annual report by June 1, listing countries that do and do not comply with minimum standards for the elimination of trafficking, and to provide information on the nature and extent of severe forms of trafficking in persons (TIP) in each country and an assessment of the efforts by each government to combat trafficking in the State Department's annual human rights report;
- Called for establishing an Interagency Task Force to Monitor and Combat Trafficking, chaired by the Secretary of State, and authorized the Secretary to establish within the Department of State an Office to Monitor and Combat Trafficking to assist the Task Force;
- Called for measures to enhance economic opportunity for potential victims of trafficking as a method to deter trafficking, to increase public awareness, particularly among potential victims, of the dangers of trafficking and the protections that are available for victims, and for the government to work with NGOs to combat trafficking;
- Established programs and initiatives in foreign countries to assist in the safe integration, reintegration, or resettlement of victims of trafficking and their children, as well as programs to provide assistance to victims of severe forms of TIP within the United States, without regard to such victims' immigration status and to make such victims eligible for any benefits that are otherwise available under the Crime Victims Fund;[188]
- Provided protection and assistance for victims of severe forms of trafficking while in the United States;
- Amended the Federal Criminal code to make funds derived from the sale of assets seized from and forfeited by traffickers available for victims assistance programs under this act;
- Amended the Immigration and Nationality Act (INA) to allow the Attorney General to grant up to 5,000 nonimmigrant visas (T visas) per year to certain victims of severe forms of trafficking who are in the United States and who would face unusual

and severe harm if they were removed from the United States. In addition, amended the INA to allow up to 5,000 T visas holders per year to adjust to lawful permanent resident status if the aliens have been in the United States continuously for three years since admission, have remained of good moral character, have not unreasonably refused to assist in trafficking investigations or prosecutions, and would suffer extreme hardship if removed from the United States;

- Established minimum standards to combat human trafficking applicable to countries that have a significant trafficking problem. Urged such countries to prohibit severe forms of TIP, to punish such acts, and to make serious and sustained efforts to eliminate such trafficking;

- Provided for assistance to foreign countries for programs and activities designed to meet the minimum international standards for the elimination of trafficking;

- Called for the United States to withhold non-humanitarian assistance and instructed the U.S. executive director of each multilateral development bank and the International Monetary Fund to vote against non-humanitarian assistance to such countries that do not meet minimum standards against trafficking and are not making efforts to meet minimum standards, unless continued assistance is deemed to be in the U.S. national interest;

- Encouraged the President to compile and publish a list of foreign persons who play a significant role in a severe form of TIP. Also encouraged the President to impose sanctions under the International Emergency Economic Powers Act, including the freezing of assets located in the United States, and to exclude significant traffickers, and those who knowingly assist them, from entry into the United States; and

- Amended the Federal Criminal Code (18 U.S.C.) to double the current maximum penalties for peonage, enticement into slavery, and sale into involuntary servitude from 10 years to 20 years imprisonment and to add the possibility of life imprisonment for such violations resulting in death or involving kidnapping, aggravated sexual abuse, or an attempt to kill.

The Bush Administration, as well as Congress, continued the anti-trafficking effort. Then-Attorney General John Ashcroft announced in March 2001 that the fight against trafficking would be a top priority for the Administration and that U.S. law enforcement agencies, including the Federal Bureau of Investigation (FBI), the former Immigration and Naturalization Service, and the Justice Department's Civil Rights Division would cooperate closely to upgrade their efforts to combat trafficking. The Justice Department also announced new guidelines for federal prosecutors to pursue trafficking cases.[189] The State Department issued its first congressionally mandated report on worldwide trafficking in July 2001.

On January 24, 2002, Ashcroft announced the implementation of a special "T" visa, as called for in P.L. 106-386, for victims of trafficking in the United States who cooperate with law enforcement officials. Under the statute, victims who cooperate with law enforcement against their traffickers and would be likely to suffer severe harm if returned to their home countries may be granted permission to stay in the United States. After three years in T status, the victims are eligible to apply for permanent residency and for non-immigrant status for their spouses and children.[190]

On February 13, 2002, President Bush signed an Executive Order establishing an Interagency Task Force to Monitor and Combat TIP. The Task Force, mandated by the Trafficking Victims Protection Act of 2000 (P.L. 106-386), includes the Secretary of State, the Attorney General, the Secretary of Labor, the Secretary of Health and Human Services (HHS), the Director of the Central Intelligence Agency, the Administrator of the Agency for International Development, the Director of the Office of Management and Budget, and Office of the National Security Advisor. The Task Force is charged with strengthening coordination among key agencies by identifying what more needs to be done to protect potential victims, to punish traffickers, and to prevent future trafficking. The State Department Office to Monitor and Combat Trafficking in Persons (G-TIP) was tasked with assisting the Interagency Task Force in implementing P.L. 106-386 and Task Force initiatives.

The Foreign Relations Authorization Act of 2003

In 2002, Congress amended the Victims of Trafficking and Violence Protection Act of 2000 in Section 682 of the Foreign Relations Authorization Act, FY2003 (P.L. 107-228) to provide

- support for local in-country nongovernmental organization to operated hotlines, culturally and linguistically appropriate protective shelters, and regional and international nongovernmental organizational networks and databases on trafficking;
- support for nongovernmental organizations and advocates to provide legal, social, and other services and assistance to trafficked individuals, particularly those individuals in detention;
- education and training for trafficked women and girls;
- the safe integration or reintegration of trafficked individuals into an appropriate community or family, while respecting the wishes, dignity, and safety of the trafficked individual; and
- support for developing or increasing programs to assist families of victims in locating, repatriating, and treating their trafficked family members.

The amendment also authorized an increase in appropriations for FY2003 to fund such programs.

Trafficking Victims Protection Reauthorization Act of 2003

In 2003, Congress approved the Trafficking Victims Protection Reauthorization Act (TVPRA) of 2003. The President signed the act into law on December 19, 2003 (P.L. 108-193). The act authorized substantial increases in funding for anti-trafficking programs in FY2004 and FY2005 (over $100 million for each fiscal year). P.L. 108-193 refined and expanded the Minimum standards for the elimination of trafficking that governments must meet and placed on such governments the responsibility to provide the information and data by which their compliance with the standards could be judged. The legislation created a "special watch list" of countries that the Secretary of State determined were to get special scrutiny in the coming year. The list was to include countries where (1) the absolute number of victims of severe forms of trafficking is very significant or is significantly increasing; (2) there is a failure to provide evidence of increasing efforts to combat severe forms of TIP from the previous year; or (3) the determination that a country is making significant efforts to bring itself into compliance with minimum standards is based on its commitments to take additional steps over the next year. In the case of such countries, not later than February 1 of each year, the Secretary of State is to provide to the appropriate congressional committees an assessment of the progress that the country had made since the last annual report.

Intelligence Reform and Terrorism Protection Act of 2004

In December 2004, Congress approved the Intelligence Reform and Terrorism Protection Act of 2004, signed into law on December 17, 2004 (P.L. 108-458). The law established a Human Smuggling and Trafficking Center (HSTC) to be jointly operated by the Department of Homeland Security (DHS), the State Department, and DOJ. It required that the Center serve as a clearinghouse for Federal agency information in support of U.S. efforts to combat terrorist travel, migrant smuggling, and human trafficking.

Trafficking Victims Protection Reauthorization Act of 2005

On February 17, 2005, Representative Christopher Smith and nine co-sponsors introduced the Trafficking Victims Protection Reauthorization Act of 2005 to authorize appropriations for FY2006 and FY2007 and close loopholes in previous anti-trafficking legislation. The bill was signed into law by the President on January 10, 2006 (P.L. 109-164). Among other things, the legislation had provisions to increase U.S. assistance to foreign trafficking victims in the United States, including access to legal counsel and better information on programs to aid victims. It attempted to address the special needs of child victims, as well as the plight of Americans trafficked within the United States. It directed relevant U.S. government agencies to develop anti-trafficking strategies for post-conflict situations and humanitarian emergencies abroad. It sought to extend U.S. criminal jurisdiction over government personnel and contractors who are involved in acts of trafficking abroad while doing work for the government. It addressed the problem of peacekeepers and aid workers who are complicit in trafficking.

The Implementing the 9/11 Commission Recommendations Act of 2007

The Implementing the 9/11 Commission Recommendations Act of 2007, P.L. 110-53 (H.R. 1), signed into law on August 3, 2007, directs the Secretary of Homeland Security (Secretary of DHS) to provide specified funding and administrative support to strengthen the HSTC. The act directs the Secretary of DHS to nominate a U.S. government employee to direct the HSTC, and specifics that the HSTC be staffed by at least 40 full-time staff, including detailees.191 In addition, the act mandates the hiring of not less than 40 full-time equivalent staff for the HSTC, and would specify the agencies and departments from which the personnel should be detailed (e.g., Transportation and Security Administration, U.S. Coast Guard, ICE, Central Intelligence Agency), and their areas of expertise (e.g., consular affairs, counter terrorism). It also directs the Secretary of DHS to provide the administrative support and funding for the HSTC.

William Wilberforce Trafficking Victims Protection Reauthorization Act of 2008

The William Wilberforce Trafficking Victims Protection Reauthorization Act of 2008 (TVPRA 2008, P.L. 110-457; H.R. 7311) was signed into law on December 23, 2008.[192] The act authorizes appropriations for FY2008 through FY2011 for the TVPA as amended and establishes a system to monitor and evaluate all assistance under the act. P.L. 110-457 requires the establishment of an integrated database to be used by U.S. government departments and agencies to collect data for analysis on TIP. In addition, the act creates a Presidential award for extraordinary efforts to combat TIP.

Measures to Address Human Trafficking in Foreign Countries
P.L. 110-457 increases the technical assistance and other support to help foreign governments inspect locations where forced labor occurs, register vulnerable populations, and provide more protection to foreign migrant workers. The act requires that specific actions be taken against governments of countries that have been on the Tier 2 Watch-List for two consecutive years. P.L. 110-457 also requires U.S. Department of State to translate the TIP Report into the principal languages of as many countries as possible. In addition, among other measures to address the issue of child soldiers, the act prohibits military assistance to foreign governments that recruit and use child soldiers.

Preventing Trafficking to the United States
TVPRA 2008 requires pamphlets on the rights and responsibilities of the employee to be produced and given to employment-based and educational-based nonimmigrants,[193] P.L. 110-457 also requires consular officers to make sure that certain aliens interviewing for nonimmigrant visas have received, read, and understood the pamphlet. During the interview, the consular officer is also required to discuss the alien's legal rights under U.S. immigration, labor and employment law. The act contains several provisions aimed to protect A-3 and G-5 visas holders[194] including directing the Secretary of State to deny A-3 and G-5 visas to aliens who would be working at a diplomatic mission or international institution where an alien had been subject to trafficking or exploitation at the mission or institution. In addition, the Secretary of State has maintained records on the presence of A-3 and G-5 visa holders in the United States, including information regarding any allegations of abuse.

Measures to Address Trafficking in the United States
P.L. 110-457 amends the requirements for the T visa, so that an alien would be eligible for a T visa if the alien was unable to comply with requests for assistance in the investigation and prosecution of acts of trafficking due to physical or psychological trauma. TVPRA 2008

also requires when determining whether the alien meets the extreme hardship requirement for T status that the Secretary of DHS consider whether the country to which the alien would be removed can adequately address the alien's security and mental and physical health needs.

In addition, P.L. 110-457 amends the requirements for the T visa so that an alien would be eligible if she was present in the United States after being allowed entry to aid in the prosecution of traffickers.

The act also broadens the requirements for an alien to receive continued presence in the United States, and makes it easier for families of trafficking victims to be paroled into the United States. In addition, P.L. 110-457 amends the law to allow the Secretary of DHS to waive the good moral character requirement for those adjusting from T to LPR status, and allows the Secretary of DHS to provide a stay of removal for aliens with pending T applications (with a prima facie case for approval), until the application has been adjudicated.

The act also makes aliens with pending applications for T status eligible for public benefits, and makes T visa holders, including derivatives, eligible for public benefits.[195] Furthermore, P.L. 110-457 requires the Secretary of HHS to make a prompt determination of eligibility for assistance for child trafficking victims.

TVPRA 2008 has provisions relating to enhancing protections for child victims of trafficking. Among these provision include requiring the United States to enter into agreements with contiguous countries regarding the return of unaccompanied minors designed to protect children from severe forms of TIP,[196] and specifying screening procedures for children suspected of being trafficking victims.

In addition, the act directs the Secretary of HHS to the extent possible to provide legal counsel and appoint child advocates to child trafficking victims and other vulnerable unaccompanied alien children.

Moreover, P.L. 110-457 creates new grant programs for U.S. citizen victims of severe forms of trafficking and authorizes appropriations for such programs. The act also requires the Secretary of HHS and the Attorney General, within one year of enactment, to submit a report to Congress identifying any gaps between services provided to U.S. citizen and noncitizen victims of trafficking.

It also prohibits DOS from issuing passports to those convicted of sex tourism until the person has completed their sentence. Furthermore, the act creates new criminal offenses related to human trafficking, including criminalizing retaliation in foreign labor contracting. P.L. 110-457 creates additional jurisdiction in U.S. courts for trafficking offenses occurring in other countries if the alleged offender is present in the United States.

APPENDIX B. TRAFFICKING FUNDING ISSUES

The U.S. government supports many types of anti-trafficking (anti-TIP) activities overseas and domestically. U.S. anti-trafficking activities are authorized by the Trafficking Victims Protection Act (TVPA) of 2000 (P.L. 106-386), as amended. *Table B-1* lists trafficking authorization levels for FY2008-FY2011. Those authorizations are for TIP operations (including law enforcement investigations) and TIP programs. Since many U.S. government agencies do not have a line item in their budget requests for trafficking programs and/or TIP-related operations, it is often difficult to calculate the exact level of funding that

Congress appropriated for trafficking activities (programs and operations/law enforcement activities) by agency. Despite the challenges, the Office of Management and Budget (OMB) tracks estimated TIP appropriations levels by gathering agency estimations of TIP-related spending for each fiscal year. See *Table B-2* for TIP authorizations versus appropriations for FY2001-FY2011.

According to OMB, funding for TVPA programs comes from appropriations to a number of U.S. departments and agencies, including the Department of State (Economic Support Fund, Migration and Refugee Assistance, International Narcotics Control and Law Enforcement (INCLE) Assistance); the Department of Justice (Victims of Trafficking Grants, Criminal and Civil Rights programs, and the Federal Bureau of Investigations); the Department of Labor (Bureau of International Labor Affairs); the Department of Health and Human Services; and the Department of Homeland Security (Immigration and Customs Enforcement).

Table B-1. Current Authorizations to Implement Victims of Trafficking Act (in $ U.S. millions)

Authorized Programs	Original Authorizing Source	FY08	FY09	FY10	FY11
International Programs					
U.S. Agency for International Development (USAID)					
USAID: Pilot Program for Rehabilitation Facilities	P.L. 109-164, §102(b)(7)	$2.5	$2.5	$2.5	$2.5
U.S. Department of State (DOS)					
DOS: Interagency Task Force	P.L. 106-386, §§104, 105(e), 105(f), 110	$5.5	$5.5	$5.5	$5.5
DOS: Interagency Task Force: Reception Expenses	P.L. 109-164, §301	$.003	$.003	$.003	$.003
DOS: Interagency Task Force: Additional Personnel	P.L. 110-457, §301(1)(B)(i)	$1.5	$1.5	$1.5	$1.5
DOS: Prevention	P.L. 106-386 §106	$10.0	$10.0	$10.0	$10.0
DOS: Protection	P.L. 106-386 §107(a)	$10.0	$10.0	$10.0	$10.0
DOS: Prosecution and Meeting Minimum Standards	P.L. 106-386 §§108-109	$10.0	$10.0	$10.0	$10.0
DOS: Refugees and Internally Displaced Persons	P.L. 110-457, §104	$1.0	$1.0	$1.0	$1.0
	President				
President: Foreign Assistance for Law Enforcement Training	P.L. 106-386, §109	$.25	$.25	$.25	$.25
President: Foreign Victim Assistance	P.L. 106-386, §106	$15.0	$15.0	$15.0	$15.0
President: Foreign Assistance to Meet Minimum Standards	P.L. 106-386, §109	$15.0	$15.0	$15.0	$15.0
President: Research	P.L. 108-193, §7(5)(B)	$2.0	$2.0	$2.0	$2.0
Domestic Programs					
Department of Health and Human Services (HHS)					
HHS: Victims' assistance	P.L. 106-386, §107(b)(1)	$12.5	$12.5	$12.5	$12.5
HHS: Grants to U.S. citizen and LPR victims of trafficking within U.S.	P.L. 109-164, §202	$8.0	$8.0	$8.0	$8.0
HHS: Pilot program residential treatment facilities juvenile victims in U.S.	P.L. 109-164, §203	$5.0	$5.0	$5.0	$5.0
HHS: Victims assistance for U.S. citizens and Legal Permanent Residents (LPRs)	P.L. 110-457, §213	$2.5	$5.0	$7.0	$7.0
Department of Homeland Security (DHS)					
DHS (Immigration and Customs Enforcement):	P.L. 109-164, §301(h)	$18.0	$18.0	$18.0	$18.0

Table B-1. (Continued)

Authorized Programs	Original Authorizing Source	FY08	FY09	FY10	FY11
International Programs					
trafficking investigations					
DHS: Human Smuggling and Trafficking Center	P.L. 110-457, §108(a)(2)	$2.0	$2.0	$2.0	$2.0
Department of Justice (DOJ)					
DOJ: Grants to strengthen victims services	P.L. 106-386, §107(b)(2)	$10.0	$10.0	$10.0	$10.0
DOJ: Study on severe forms of trafficking in persons in U.S.	P.L. 109-164, §201(a)(1)(B)(i)	$1.5	$1.5	$1.5	$1.5
DOJ: Study on sex trafficking in U.S.	P.L. 109-164, §201(a)(1)(B)(ii)	$1.5	$1.5	$1.5	$1.5
DOJ: Annual trafficking conference	P.L. 109-164, §201(a)(2)	$1.0	$1.0	$1.0	$1.0
DOJ: grants to state and local law enforcement for anti-trafficking programs	P.L. 109-164, §204	$20.0	$20.0	$20.0	$20.0
DOJ Federal Bureau of Investigation: trafficking investigations	P.L. 109-164, §301(h)	$15.0	$15.0	$15.0	$15.0
DOJ: Victims assistance for U.S. citizens and Legal Permanent Residents (LPRs)	P.L. 110-457, §213	$2.5	$5.0	$7.0	$7.0
Department of Labor (DOL)					
DOL: Expand services to trafficking victims	P.L. 106-386, §107(b)(1)(B)	$10.0	$10.0	$10.0	$10.

Note: The TVPA and its subsequent reauthorizations include several additional provisions without specific funding amounts. Such provisions include §107A(f) of P.L. 106-386, as amended, which authorizes not more than 5% of the amounts made available to carry out the TVPA, as amended, in each fiscal year 2008 through 2011 to the President to evaluate anti-trafficking programs and projects. §112B of P.L. 106-386, as amended, authorizes such sums as may be necessary for each fiscal year 2008 through 2011 to the President to provide an award for "Extraordinary Efforts to Combat Trafficking in Persons." §114(c)(2) of P.L. 106-386, as amended, also authorizes such sums as may be necessary for each fiscal year 2008 through 2011 to the Department of State for the preparation of congressionally mandated human rights reports with reference to human trafficking issues. Note also that additional funding outside the scope of the TVPA and its reauthorizations has been authorized in separate legislative vehicles. See for example, §111 of P.L. 109-162, which authorizes $10 million for each fiscal year 2008 through 2011 to the Department of Justice for state and local law enforcement grants for human trafficking victim identification.

Table B-2. Trafficking Victims Protection Act (TVPA) of 2000, as Amended Authorizations and Appropriations, FY2001-2011
(in $ U.S. millions)

Fiscal Year	Authorizing Public Law	Title	Authorizations (Millions $)	Appropriations (Millions $)
2001	P.L. 106-386(Part A)	Victims of Trafficking and Violence Protection Act of 2000	$31.8	N/A
2002	P.L. 106-386 (Part A)	Victims of Trafficking and Violence Protection Act of 2000	$63.3	N/A
2003	P.L. 106-386 (Part A)[a]	Victims of Trafficking and Violence Protection Act of 2000	$48.3	N/A
2004	P.L. 108-193	Trafficking Victims Protection Reauthorization Act of 2003	$105.6	$109.8
2005			$105.6	$109.6
2006	P.L. 109-164	Trafficking Victims Protection Reauthorization Act of 2005	$177.3	$152.4
2007			$162.3	$153.1
2008	P.L. 110-457	William Wilberforce Trafficking	$182.3	$167.4

Fiscal Year	Authorizing Public Law	Title	Authorizations (Millions $)	Appropriations (Millions $)
2009		Victims Reauthorization Act of 2008	$187.3	$182.7
2010			$191.3	$162.2
2011			$191.3	N/A

Source: Estimated appropriations levels as calculated by the Office of Management and Budget (multiple responses to CRS, most recently on May 17, 2011). Estimates not collected prior to FY2004. Authorizations estimates are rounded to the first decimal and do not include provisions without specific dollar amounts authorized.

[a]. As amended by Section 682 of the Foreign Assistance Act for FY2003 (P.L. 107-228).

APPENDIX C. APPROPRIATIONS FOR GRANT PROGRAMS FOR DOMESTIC TIP VICTIMS

Table C-1. Authorizations and Appropriations for Grant Programs to Assist Victims of Trafficking in the United States: FY2001-FY2012 ($ in millions)

Fiscal Year	Victims Services—DOJ		Office of Refugee Resettlement[a]	
	Authorized	Appropriated	Authorized	Appropriated
FY2001	$5	$0	$5	$5
FY2002	$10	$10	$10	$10
FY2003	N.A.	$10	N.A.	$9.9
FY2004	$15	$10	$15	$9.9
FY2005	$15	$10	$15	$9.9
FY2006	$15	$9.9	$15	$9.8
FY2007	$15	$9.9	$15	$9.8
FY2008	$10[b]	$9.4[c]	$12.5[b]	$10[d]
FY2009	$10	$10	$12.5	$9.8[d]
FY2010	$10	$12.5[c]	$12.5	$9.8[d]
FY2011	$10	$10.4[ce]	$12.5	$9.8[d]
FY2012	N.A.	$10.5	N.A.	$9.8

Sources: P.L. 106-386, P.L. 108-193, P.L. 109-164, P.L. 107-77, P.L. 107-116, P.L. 108-7, P.L. 108-90, P.L. 108- 199, P.L. 108-334, P.L. 108-447, P.L. 109-90, P.L. 109-149, P.L. 109-164, P.L. 110-5, P.L. 110-161, P.L. 110-457, P.L. 111-8, P.L. 111-117, P.L. 112-10.

[a] This only includes authorizations for the HHS grant program, authorized originally in P.L. 106-386, to provide assistance to victims. Three other HHS victims service programs have been authorized but according to HHS none have received appropriations. For a listing of these programs, see Table B-1.

[b] Authorizations for FY2008 were enacted during FY2009.

[c] This includes funding for victims services programs under The Victims of Trafficking Act of 2000 (P.L. 106- 386) and DOJ programs authorized under Trafficking Victims Protection Reauthorization Act of 2005 (P.L. 109-164).

[d] The language in act states that the money should be available to carry out The Victims of Trafficking Act of 2000.

[e] On April 15, 2011, President Obama signed into law the Department of Defense and Full-Year Continuing Appropriations Act, 2011 (P.L. 112-10). P.L. 112-10 required a reduction in funding to be applied proportionately to each program funded under the account which contains this appropriation in FY2010. Thus, CRS calculates that each grant program funded under this account will be reduced 17.0% and from that amount the 0.2% across-the-board rescission is applied. For more on this reduction, see CRS Report R41161, Commerce, Justice, Science, and Related Agencies: FY2011 Appropriations, coordinated by Nathan James, Oscar R. Gonzales, and Jennifer D. Williams.

Domestic anti-TIP activities include both services to victims, as well as law enforcement operations. Investigations into human trafficking are complex and as a result often require significant resources. See *Table C-1* for authorizations and appropriations for grant programs to assist trafficking victims in the United States for FY2001-FY2010.

APPENDIX D. LEGISLATION IN THE 111TH CONGRESS

Several bills were introduced in the 111th Congress that would have addressed issues related to human trafficking. The discussion in the following section is limited to legislation in the 111th Congress (excluding appropriations) that received congressional action. Notably, none of the bills were passed by Congress.

S. 2925: Domestic Minor Sex Trafficking Deterrence and Victims Support Act of 2010

The Senate passed S. 2925 on December 13, 2010, and the House passed an amended but similar version of S. 2925 on December 21, 2010.[197] The House and Senate versions of the bill would have authorized the Assistant Attorney General for DOJ's Office of Justice Programs, in consultation with the Assistant Secretary for Children and Families in HHS, to award one-year grants to six eligible entities[198] in different regions of the United States to combat domestic minor sex trafficking (DMST). At least one of the grants would have to have been awarded to a state with a population less than 5 million people. The grants would have been renewable twice, for one year for each renewal (for a total grant length of three years). Each grant could have ranged from $2 million to $2.5 million. Under the House and Senate versions of the bill, at least 67% of the grants would have to have been allocated to non-governmental organizations (NGOs) to provide counseling, legal services, shelter, clothing, and other social services to victims of DMST. Not less than 10% of the funds would have been allocated by the eligible entity to NGOs to provide services to DMST victims or training for service providers on DMST. Funds could have also been used for training for law enforcement; investigative and prosecution expenses; case management; salaries for law enforcement officers and state and local prosecutors; and outreach, education, and treatment programs, all related to cases of DMST. The House and Senate versions of S. 2925 would have authorized $15 million each year, for FY2012 through FY2014, for this program. The grantees would have been required to match at least 25% of the grant in the first year, 40% in the second year, and 50% in the third year.[199]

H.R. 5138: International Megan's Law of 2010

H.R. 5138 was introduced on April 26, 2010, and passed the House on July 27, 2010. The bill's stated purpose was to protect children from sexual exploitation by preventing or monitoring the international travel of sex traffickers and other sex offenders who pose a risk of committing a sex offense against a minor while traveling abroad. Among other provisions,

H.R. 5138 would have amended the TVPA to expand criteria that determine whether foreign countries were meeting the minimum standards for the elimination of severe forms of trafficking in persons to include whether a country was investigating and prosecuting nationals suspected of engaging in severe forms of trafficking in persons abroad. The bill would have required that the Secretary of State, in consultation with the Attorney General, submit a report to Congress on international mechanisms related to traveling child sex offenders. The bill also would have encouraged the President to use existing foreign assistance authorities for combating trafficking in persons to additionally provide assistance to strengthen foreign country efforts to target child sex offenders.

H.R. 2410 and S. 2971: Foreign Relations Authorization Act, Fiscal Years 2010 and 2011

H.R. 2410 was introduced on May 14, 2009, and passed the House on June 10, 2009. Among other provisions unrelated to trafficking in persons, Section 1016 of Title X would have required that the Secretary of State report to Congress on the best use of U.S. foreign assistance to reduce smuggling and trafficking in persons.

S. 2971, a corresponding but separate Senate bill with the same title, was introduced on January 29, 2010, and was reported out of the Senate Foreign Relations Committee on September 23, 2010, with an amendment in the nature of a substitute.

The bill as reported included a provision to amend Section 660 of the Foreign Assistance Act of 1961 (FAA, 22 U.S.C. 2420), which generally prohibits training of foreign police forces.

Section 402 of Title IV of S. 2971 would have made an exception to Section 660 of the FAA and would have authorized foreign police assistance for combating trafficking in persons.

S. 3184: Child Protection Compact Act of 2010

S. 3184 was introduced on March 25, 2010, and was reported out of the Senate Foreign Relations Committee on September 28, 2010, without amendment. According to the committee report, S.Rept. 111-337, the purpose of S. 3184 was to "provide incentives to protect and rescue children subjected to severe forms of trafficking in persons or sexual exploitation through the establishment of Child Protection Compacts between the United States and select, eligible countries." Related to S. 3184 is H.R. 2737, the Child Protection Compact Act of 2009. H.R. 2737 was referred to the House Foreign Affairs Committee on June 4, 2009, and did not receive action.

S. 3184 would have authorized each Compact to provide up to $15 million in assistance and would have recommended that appropriators provide the State Department up to $30 million for FY2011 through FY2013 for the Compacts. As part of a Compact, eligible countries would have to have committed to a three-year plan to improve efforts to combat child trafficking. To be eligible to receive a Compact, a country would have to have been on the Tier II or Tier II Watch List and would have to have been low-income and eligible for assistance from the International Development Association. In addition, countries must not have been ineligible to receive U.S. economic assistance under part I of the FAA (22 U.S.C. 2151 et seq.).

End Notes

[1] United Nations, United Nations Convention against Transnational Organized Crime and the Protocols Thereto, Protocol to Prevent, Suppress, and Punish Trafficking in Persons, Especially Women and Children, Supplementing the United Nations Convention against Transnational Organized Crime, http://www.unodc.org/documents/treaties/ UNTOC/ Publications/TOC%20Convention/TOCebook-e.pdf.

[2] United Nations Office on Drugs and Crime (UNODC), Human Trafficking: An Overview, 2008.

[3] §103(8) of Div. A of P.L. 106-386.

[4] Note that the accuracy of estimates on the scope of TIP has been questioned. For example, the U.S. Government Accountability Office (GAO) released a report in 2006 casting doubt on the methodology and reliability of official U.S. government figures. It concluded that the "U.S. government has not yet established an effective mechanism for estimating the number of victims or for conducting ongoing analysis of trafficking related data that resides within various government agencies." See GAO, Human Trafficking: Better Data, Strategy, and Reporting Needed to Enhance U.S. Antitrafficking Efforts Abroad, GAO-06-825, July 2006.

[5] International Labor Organization (ILO), ILO Minimum Estimate of Forced Labour in the World, April 2005.

[6] United Nations Office on Drugs and Crime (UNODC), Trafficking in Persons: Global Patterns, April 2006.

[7] Most recently cited in U.S. Department of State, Trafficking in Persons Report, June 2010.

[8] Kevin Bales, President of Free the Slaves, Disposable People: New Slavery in the Global Economy, Berkeley: University of California Press, 2004 (revised edition).

[9] International Labor Organization (ILO), ILO Action against Trafficking in Human Beings, 2008.

[10] This figure was cited in the U.S. Department of State, Trafficking in Persons Report, June 2006.

[11] U.S. Department of State, Trafficking in Persons Report, 2011.

[12] United Nations Office on Drugs and Crime (UNODC) and the United Nations Global Initiative to Fight Human Trafficking (UNGIFT), Global Report on Trafficking in Persons, February 2009.

[13] United Nations Office on Drugs and Crime (UNODC) and the United Nations Global Initiative to Fight Human Trafficking (UNGIFT), Global Report on Trafficking in Persons, February 2009.

[14] United Nations Development Fund for Women (UNIFEM), " Trafficking in Persons, A Gender & Rights Perspective Briefing Kit," 2002.

[15] A variety of studies are discussed in Sally Cameron and Edward Newman, "Trafficking in Humans: Structural Factors," in Trafficking in Humans: Social Cultural and Political Dimensions, New York: U.N. University Press, 2008.

[16] Janie Chuang, "Beyond a Snapshot: Preventing Human Trafficking in the Global Economy," Indiana Journal of Global Legal Studies, Vol. 13, No. 1, Winter 2006.

[17] Ambassador Mark P. Lagon, Former Director, State Department Office to Monitor and Combat Trafficking in Persons (G-TIP), Remarks at "Human Trafficking and Freedom Event," December 3, 2007.

[18] For FY2001 through FY2005, GAO, "Human Trafficking: Monitoring and Evaluation of International Projects Are Limited, but Experts Suggest Improvements," GAO-07-1034, July 2007; for FY2006 through FY2010, U.S. Department of State, responses to CRS requests. Due to the methodological difficulties involved in calculating TIP appropriations and the fact that TIP programs are supported by foreign aid accounts that can be appropriated to remain available for two years, the State Department calculates TIP program obligations by agency per fiscal year. According to the Office to Monitor and Combat Trafficking in Persons (G/TIP), this generates the best estimate of the amount of funding spent on TIP programs by agency for each fiscal year.

[19] U.S. Department of State, Office to Combat and Monitor Trafficking in Persons, "U.S. Government Entities Combating Human Trafficking," June 14, 2010.

[20] United Nations General Assembly, "In-Depth Study on All Forms of Violence Against Women," July 6, 2006.

[21] U.S. Department of State, Office to Monitor and Combat Trafficking in Persons, Fact Sheet: U.S. Government Anti-Trafficking in Persons Project Funding (Fiscal Year 2010), June 2011.

[22] The countries with the largest numbers of programs obligated in recent years include several of the countries selected in 2004 by President George W. Bush as eligible to receive a combined total of $50 million in strategic anti-TIP assistance. The $50 million consists of projects, the bulk of which were obligated in FY2004 and FY2005, that were approved by an inter-agency Senior Policy Operating Group (SPOG) on human

trafficking and the Deputy Secretary of State for each region. Funding for the President's initiative came from channeling funds from existing aid programs to the countries identified to participate in the initiative. The funds came from roughly $25 million in FY2003 Child Survival and Health monies, $12.5 million in FY2004 Economic Support Funds, and $12.5 million in FY2005 Economic Support Funds. The President chose countries based on the severity of their trafficking programs, as well as their willingness to cooperate with U.S. agencies to combat the problem. They included Brazil, Cambodia, India, Indonesia, Mexico, Moldova, Sierra Leone, and Tanzania. As a result of this initiative, U.S. anti-TIP assistance to foreign governments spiked in FY2004 and FY2005, but is now on a downward trajectory.

[23] One reason for the increase in countries in the TIP report, particularly since 2009, is because of a change in the TVPA reporting requirement, as amended by the William Wilberforce Trafficking Victims Protection Reauthorization Act of 2008 (§106(1) of P.L. 110-457). Prior TIP reports were required to include countries that are a point of origin, transit, or destination for "a significant number of" victims of severe forms of trafficking. This was interpreted by the State Department to mean at least 100 cases per year. P.L. 110-457 struck out the phrase "a significant number of," resulting in a lower threshold requirement for reporting on countries in the 2009 TIP report and thereafter.

[24] Section 108 of the TVPA, as amended, defines the minimum standards for eliminating severe forms of human trafficking to include prohibiting severe forms of trafficking in persons and punishing such acts; prescribing punishment that is sufficiently stringent to deter future acts and commensurate with punishments for other grave crimes; and evidence of serious and sustained efforts to eliminate severe forms of trafficking in persons.

[25] Those with consistent Tier 1 rankings from Western Europe include Austria, Belgium, Denmark, Germany, Italy, Luxembourg, the Netherlands, Norway, Spain, and United Kingdom.

[26] Those countries that improved from Tier 2 Watch List in 2010 to Tier 2 in 2011 include Belize, Fiji, Gabon, Guatemala, Guyana, India, Kazakhstan, Laos, Lesotho, Moldova, Mozambique, Nicaragua, Philippines, Senegal, Singapore, Sri Lanka, Swaziland, Tajikistan, and Trinidad and Tobago.

[27] Those countries that dropped from Tier 2 in 2010 to Tier 2 Watch List in 2011 include Angola, the Bahamas, Belarus, Burundi, Costa Rica, Cyprus, Ecuador, Estonia, the Gambia, and Liberia.

[28] Those countries that dropped from Tier 2 Watch List in 2010 to Tier 3 in 2011 include Algeria, Central African Republic, Equatorial Guinea, Guinea-Bissau, Lebanon, Libya, Madagascar, Micronesia, Turkmenistan, Venezuela, and Yemen.

[29] Such a waiver permits the President to waive the Tier 3 listing for up to two years. In exercising this waiver authority, the President must determine that such a waiver is justified because the country has a "written plan" to start making "significant efforts" to comply with the TVPA's minimum standards to combat TIP, and because the country has committed "sufficient resources" to implement the plan.

[30] President Obama, "Presidential Determination With Respect To Foreign Governments' Efforts Regarding Trafficking In Persons," Presidential Determination 2011-18, September 30, 2011.

[31] The first year in which Madagascar was rated in the State Department's annual TIP Report was 2004. Since then, it has variously received designations as a Tier 1, Tier 2, and Tier 2 Watch List country.

[32] U.S. Department of State, TIP Report, June 2011.

[33] U.S. Department of State, Trafficking in Persons Report, June 2010, p. 338.

[34] Human Smuggling and Trafficking Center, Domestic Human Trafficking: An Internal Issue, Washington, DC, December 2008, p. 2, http://www.state.gov/documents/ organization /113612.pdf.

[35] For more on these estimates see the section of this report entitled, "Official Estimates of Human Trafficking into the United States." Department of Justice, Department of Health and Human Services, Department of State, Department of Labor, Department of Homeland Security, and U.S. Agency of International Development, Assessment of U.S. Government Efforts to Combat Trafficking in Persons, June 2004, p. 4.

[36] U.S. Department of State, Trafficking in Persons Report, June 2010, p. 338.

[37] Human Smuggling and Trafficking Center, Domestic Human Trafficking: An Internal Issue, Washington, DC, December 2008, pp. 3-6, http://www.state.gov/documents/ organization/ 113612.pdf.

[38] Foreign victims do not include Legal Permanent Residents (LPRs). For the purposes of discussing trafficking victims in the United States, LPRs are grouped with U.S. citizens.

[39] U.S. Department of State, Trafficking in Persons Report, June 2010, p. 338.

[40] Internal human trafficking of migrant labor is primarily occurring in the Southeast and Central regions of the United States, although such conduct has been identified in other places. Human Smuggling and Trafficking Center, Domestic Human Trafficking: An Internal Issue, Washington, DC, December 2008, pp. 3-6, http://www.state.gov/documents/ organization/ 113612.pdf.

41 For more information on sex trafficking of children in the United States, see CRS Report R41878, Sex Trafficking of Children in the United States: Overview and Issues for Congress, by Kristin M. Finklea, Adrienne L. FernandesAlcantara, and Alison Siskin.

42 Linda A. Smith, Samantha Headly Vardaman, and Mellissa A. Snow, The National Report on Domestic Minor Sex Trafficking: America's Prostituted Children, Shared Hope International, Arlington, VA, May 2009, http://www.sharedhope.org/files/SHI_ National_ Report_on_DMST_2009.pdf.

43 Despite mandates in the TVPA, uniform data collection for trafficking crimes or number of victims by federal, state, and local law enforcement agencies is not occurring. U.S. Department of State, Trafficking in Persons Report, June 2010, p. 340..

44 Department of Justice, Attorney General's Annual Report to Congress on U.S. Government Activities to Combat Trafficking in Persons: Fiscal Year 2005, June 2006. (Hereafter DOJ, Attorney General's Annual Report to Congress on U.S. Government Activities to Combat Trafficking in Persons: Fiscal Year 2005.)

45 The number of U.S. citizen trafficking victims in the United States is unknown. In addition, there does not seem to be a clear definition of what it means to be a U.S. citizen trafficked within the United States. For example, some would argue that all prostitutes who have pimps are victims of trafficking. In addition, Dr. Louise Shelly, the Director of the Terrorism, Transnational Crime, and Corruption Center at George Mason University, argues that the largest number of trafficking victims in the United States are U.S. citizen children, and estimates the number of these victims to be between 100,000 and 300,000. Conference, The Profits of Pimping: Abolishing Sex Trafficking in the United States, at the Hudson Institute, Washington D.C., July 10, 2008.

46 Department of Justice, Department of Health and Human Services, Department of State, Department of Labor, Department of Homeland Security, and U.S. Agency of International Development, Assessment of U.S. Government Efforts to Combat Trafficking in Persons, June 2004, p. 4.

47 Notably, the Attorney General's Report for FY2008, released in June 2009, does not contain an estimate of the number of victims trafficked into the United States annually. Department of Justice, Attorney General's Annual Report to Congress on U.S. Government Activities to Combat Trafficking in Persons: Fiscal Year 2008, June 2009.

48 DOJ, Attorney General's Annual Report to Congress on U.S. Government Activities to Combat Trafficking in Persons: Fiscal Year 2005.

49 Amy O'Neill Richard, International Trafficking in Women to the United States: A Contemporary Manifestation of Slavery and Organized Crime, Center for the Study of Intelligence, November 1999, p. iii.

50 Free the Slaves and the Human Rights Center, Hidden Slaves: Forced Labor in the United States, September 2004, available at http://digitalcommons.ilr.cornell.edu/cgi/ viewcontent. cgi?article=1007&context=forced labor.

51 P.L. 109-164 (§201) requires biennial reporting on human trafficking, using available data from state and local authorities. In response to this requirement, DOJ funded the creation of the Human Trafficking Reporting System (HTRS). The data in the HTRS come from investigations opened by approximately 40 federally funded human trafficking task forces, and do not represent all incidences of human trafficking nationwide. In January 2008, the task forces began entering data into HTRS. Between January 1, 2007 and September 30, 2008, the task forces reported 34 confirmed cases of sex trafficking of children in the United States and 341 cases where a determination was pending or that there was not enough information to confirm the trafficking. Tracey Kyckelhahn, Allen J. Beck, and Thomas Cohen, Characteristics of Suspected Human Trafficking Incidents, 2007-08, Department of Justice, Office of Justice Programs, Bureau of Justice Statistics Special Report, Washington, DC, January 2009, pp. 1-2, http://bjs.ojp.usdoj.gov/ content/pub/ pdf/cshti08.pdf.

52 There are 42 task forces in total. The Department of Justice makes awards to law enforcement agencies to form victim centered human trafficking task forces. Department of Justice, Attorney General's Annual Report to Congress on U.S. Government Activities to Combat Trafficking in Persons: Fiscal Year 2009, June 2010, p. 95. Testimony of Mary Lou Leary, Principle Deputy Assistant Attorney General, Department of Justice, at U.S. Congress, Senate Committee on the Judiciary, The Trafficking Victims Protection Reauthorization Act: Renewing the Commitment to Victims of Human Trafficking, 112th Cong., 1st sess., September 14, 2011.

53 Celia Williamson, Sharvari Karandikar-Chheda, and Jeff Barrows, et al., Report on the Prevalence of Human Trafficking in Ohio To Attorney General Richard Cordray, Ohio Trafficking in Persons Study Commission, Research and Analysis Sub-Committee, Toledo, OH, February 10, 2010, http://www.ohioattorneygeneral.gov/ TraffickingReport.

54 The researchers identified four factors that may increase the risk of becoming a minor victim of sex trafficking: (1) Ohio's weak response to minor trafficking victims; (2) evidence that first responders to sex trafficking incidents involving minors in Ohio are unaware and unprepared; (3) customers who purchase youth receive

minimal charges and are rarely prosecuted, while traffickers suffer minimal consequences; and (4) the high rates of vulnerable youth in Ohio. Ibid, p. 5.

[55] Ibid, p. 7.

[56] Section 107 of Division A of P.L. 106-386. "T" refers to the letter denoting the subsection of the Immigration and Nationality Act (INA) that provides the authority for the alien's admission into the United States (i.e., INA §101(a)(15)(T)). Although T nonimmigrant status is often referred to as the T-visa, it is not technically a visa if it is given to aliens present in the United States because status is conferred by the Department of Homeland Security (DHS) who does not have the authority to issue visas. Only the Department of State (DOS) though consular offices may issue visas. Thus, only aliens present outside of the United States can receive T visas while aliens present in the United States receive T status. For more information on nonimmigrant visa issuance see CRS Report RL31381, U.S. Immigration Policy on Temporary Admissions, by Ruth Ellen Wasem.

[57] As discussed previously, TVPA defines a "severe form of traffic king in persons" as either: (1) sex trafficking in which a commercial sex act is induced by force, fraud or coercion or in which the person induced to perform such act has not attained 18 years of age, or (2) the recruitment, harboring, transportation, provision, or obtaining of a person for labor or services, through the use of force, fraud, or coercion for the purpose of subjection to involuntary servitude, peonage, debt bondage, or slavery. It is the applicant's responsibility to demonstrate both elements of a severe form of trafficking in persons.

[58] Prior to P.L. 110-457, this was interpreted in the regulations to apply to those aliens who (1) are present because they are being held in some sort of severe form of trafficking situation; (2) were recently liberated from a severe form of trafficking; or (3) were subject to a severe form of trafficking in the past and remain present in the United States for reasons directly related to the original trafficking. P.L. 110-457 expanded the definition of physical presence to include trafficking victims admitted to the United States for trafficking investigations and legal proceedings.

[59] Applicants for T status may submit a Law Enforcement Agency (LEA) Enforcement to prove that they are complying with the investigation. The regulations require that the LEA enforcement come from a federal law enforcement agency since severe forms of trafficking in person are federal crimes under TVPA; however, the TVPRA of 2003 amended the law to allow state and local law enforcement to certify that the trafficking victim is aiding law enforcement.

[60] Although to be eligible for T status, most aliens must comply with reasonable requests for assistance from law enforcement, it is not necessary for the alien to be sponsored for status from a law enforcement agency as is required by those applying for S nonimmigrant status for alien witnesses and informants.

[61] Children under the age of 18 at the time that the application for T status is filed, are exempt from the requirement to comply with law enforcement requests for assistance. In the original law (TVPA of 2000) the age of mandatory compliance was under 15 years, but the TVPRA of 2003 increased the age of mandatory compliance to 18 years.

[62] INA §212(d)(13).

[63] INA §212(a)(2)(D).

[64] "Parole" is a term in immigration law which means that the alien has been granted temporary permission to be in the United States. Parole does not constitute formal admission to the United States and parolees are required to leave when the parole expires, or if eligible, to be admitted in a lawful status.

[65] In some cases, immediate family members of trafficking victims may receive a T visa to join the victim in the United States. This may be necessary if the traffickers are threatening the victim's family.

[66] From the perspective of trafficking victims' advocates, work authorization is viewed as an important tool in helping the victims become self sufficient and retake control of their lives.

[67] The four year period of validity for T-visas was codified by The Violence Against Women and Department of Justice Reauthorization Act of 2006 (P.L. 109-162, §821). Prior to P.L. 109-162, the validity period was three years and was specified, not by statute, but by regulation (8 C.F.R. 214.11).

[68] Bona fide application means an application for T status which after initial review has been determined that the application is complete, there is no evidence of fraud, and presents prima facie evidence of eligibility for T status including admissibility.

[69] Refugees are generally eligible for federal, state and local public benefits. In addition, refugees are eligible for Food Stamps and Supplemental Security Income (SSI) for seven years after entry, and for Medicaid and Temporary Assistance for Needy Families for seven years after entrance and then at state option. CRS Report RL33809, Noncitizen Eligibility for Federal Public Assistance: Policy Overview and Trends, by Ruth Ellen Wasem.

[70] Victims may also be repatriated to their home country if they desire with assistance from the Department of State, government of their country of origin, or nongovernmental organizations. The United States Conference of

Catholic Bishops et al., A Guide for Legal Advocates Providing Services to Victims of Human Trafficking, prepared with a grant from the Department of Health and Human Services, Office of Refugee Resettlement, November 2004, p. Appendix 1- 3. (Hereafter cited as Catholic Bishops, A Guide for Legal Advocates Providing Services to Victims of Human Trafficking.)

[71] 28 C.F.R. §1100.3-§1100.33.

[72] Between FY2006 and FY2009 the approval rate for T-1 status was approximately 80% and then declined slightly in FY2010 (76%) and FY2011 (71%). CRS analysis of unpublished data from DHS.

[73] INA §245(l)

[74] Department of Homeland Security, "Adjustment of Status to Lawful Permanent Resident for Aliens in T or U Nonimmigrant Status," 73 Federal Register 75540-75564, December 12, 2008.

[75] 28 C.F.R. Part 1000.35. The mechanisms for continued presence may include parole, voluntary departure, stay of final removal orders, or any other authorized form of continued presence in the United States, including adjustment to an applicable nonimmigrant status. Some of these authorities were transferred to the Secretary of DHS in the Homeland Security Act of 2002 (P.L. 107-296). Others remain with or are shared by the Attorney General.

[76] Viet D. Dinh, Department of Justice. Testimony before the Senate Subcommittee on Near Eastern and South Asian Affairs concerning Monitoring and Combating Trafficking in Persons: How Are We Doing?, March 7, 2002.

[77] In FY2009, there were 301 requests for continued presence relating to human trafficking cases; 299 were approved while 2 were withdrawn by the law enforcement agency due to insufficient evidence. In addition, there were 148 requests for extensions of existing continued presence grants, all of which were approved. In FY2009, aliens from 35 countries were granted continued presence due to human trafficking. Most victims were from Thailand, the Philippines, Haiti, and Mexico. In addition, Honolulu, Chicago, Miami and Tampa were the cites with the most requests for continued presence. Department of Justice, Attorney General's Annual Report to Congress on U.S. Government Activities to Combat Trafficking in Persons: Fiscal Year 2009, July 2010: pp. 35-36.

[78] INA 101(a)(15)(U).

[79] Certain criminal activity refers to one or more of the following or any similar activity in violation of federal or state criminal law: rape; torture; trafficking; incest; domestic violence; sexual assault; abusive sexual contact; prostitution; sexual exploitation; female genital mutilation; being held hostage; peonage; involuntary servitude; slave trade; kidnapping; abduction; unlawful criminal restraint; false imprisonment; blackmail; extortion; manslaughter, murder; felonious assault; witness tampering; obstruction of justice; perjury; or attempt, conspiracy, or solicitation to commit any of the above mentioned crimes.

[80] INA §214(o)(2). Although the interim final regulations on U status were released in September 2007, prior to that aliens who met the criteria for U status were given immigration benefits similar to U status. In 2005, for example, 287 aliens were given "quasi-U" status. Unpublished data from DHS.

[81] Department of Homeland Security, "Adjustment of Status to Lawful Permanent Resident for Aliens in T or U Nonimmigrant Status," 73 Federal Register 75540-75564, December 12, 2008.

[82] On July 15, 2010, the 10,000 application for U-1 status of approved for FY2010. Department of Homeland Security, U.S. Citizenship and Immigration Services, "USCIS Reaches Milestone: 10,000 U Visas Approved in Fiscal Year 2010: U Visa Protects Victims of Crime and Strengthens Law Enforcement Efforts," press release, July 15, 2010.

[83] P.L. 106-386, §1513(c). 8 U.S.C. 1184(o)(2).

[84] U.S. Citizenship and Immigration Services, "Questions and Answers, USCIS Reaches Milestone: 10,000 U Visas Approved in Fiscal Year 2010," press release, July 15, 2010; and U.S. Citizenship and Immigration Services, "Relief Provided to Thousands of Victims of Crimes, USCIS Achieves Significant Milestone—Approves 10,000 U-Visa Petitions for Second Straight Year," press release. September 19, 2011.

[85] The number of victims was more than double the number served during the previous year. U.S. Department of State, Trafficking in Persons Report, June 2011, p. 375.

[86] The Legal Services Corporation (LSC), established by Congress, is a private, nonprofit, federally funded corporation that helps provide legal assistance to low-income people in civil (i.e., non-criminal) matters.

[87] In FY2009, seven LSC grantees assisted 92 trafficking victims. DOJ, Assessment of U.S. Activities to Combat Trafficking in Persons: FY2009, p.34.

[88] Under the TVPA, "noncitizen victims" refer to victims of human trafficking in the United States who are either on temporary visas or are illegally present (i.e., unauthorized aliens). It does not include LPRs, i.e., aliens who are in the United States permanently, often referred to as immigrants. References to U.S. citizen trafficking victims include LPR victims.

[89] Department of Justice, Attorney General's Annual Report to Congress on U.S. Government Activities to Combat Trafficking in Persons: Fiscal Year 2009, July 2010: p. 75. (Hereafter DOJ, Attorney General's Annual Report to Congress on U.S. Government Activities to Combat Trafficking in Persons: Fiscal Year 2009.)

[90] FY2010 appropriations were $12.5 million.

[91] (P.L. 111-117, P.L. 111-8, P.L. 110-161). For FY2005 through FY2007, money was appropriated to "carry out the Trafficking Victims Protection Act of 2003 (P.L. 108-193)" (P.L. 110-5, P.L. 109-149, P.L. 108-447).

[92] "[in] the case of nonentitlement programs, subject to the availability of appropriations, the Secretary of Health and Human Services, the Secretary of Labor, the Board of Directors of the Legal Services Corporation, and the heads of other Federal agencies shall expand benefits and services to victims of severe forms of trafficking in persons in the United States,... without regard to the immigration status of such victims....For the purposes of this paragraph, the term "victim of a severe form of trafficking in persons" means only a person—(i) who has been subjected to an act or practice described in section 103(8) as in effect on the date of the enactment of this Act; and (ii)(I) who has not attained 18 years of age; or (II) who is the subject of a certification.... [C]ertification... is a certification by the Secretary of Health and Human Services...that the person...(I) is willing to assist in every reasonable way in the investigation and prosecution of severe forms of trafficking in persons or is unable to cooperate with such a request due to physical or psychological trauma; and (II)(aa) has made a bona fide application for a visa under section 101(a)(15)(T) of the Immigration and Nationality Act... that has not been denied; or (bb) is a person whose continued presence in the United States the Secretary of Homeland Security is ensuring in order to effectuate prosecution of traffickers in persons."

[93] Senior Policy Operating Group on Trafficking in Persons: Subcommittee on Domestic Trafficking, Final Report and Recommendations, Washington, DC, August 2007, http:// www.acf.hhs.gov/trafficking/SPOGReport-Final9-5-07.pdf.

[94] Personal conversation with the Department of Health and Human Services, Administration for Children and Families, Congressional Affairs, April 2, 2007.

[95] TVPA §107(b)(1)(B); 22 U.S.C. §7105(b)(1)(B). The act also created a grant program in DOJ for state, local, tribal governments, and nonprofit victims' service organizations to develop, strengthen, or expand service programs for trafficking victims. (22 U.S.C. §7105(b)(2)).

[96] The Homeland Security Act of 2002 (HSA; P.L. 107-296) abolished the Immigration and Naturalization Service (INS) and transferred most of its functions to various bureaus in the new Department of Homeland Security (DHS) effective March 1, 2003. In addition, due to HSA, much of the Attorney General's authority in immigration law is currently vested in or shared with the Secretary of Homeland Security. For more information on the role of the Attorney General and Secretary of Homeland Security over immigration law, see CRS Report RL31997, Authority to Enforce the Immigration and Nationality Act (INA) in the Wake of the Homeland Security Act: Legal Issues.

[97] If the alien pursues long-term immigration relief other than T status, services under the HHS programs are discontinued. TVPA §107(b)(1)(E); 22 U.S.C. §7105(b)(1)(E). U.S. Department of State, Trafficking in Persons Report, June 2011, p. 375.

[98] HHS has the exclusive authority to determine if a child is eligible on an interim basis (up to 120 days) for assistance. During the interim period, the Secretary of HHS consults with the AG, Secretary of HHS and NGOs to determine the child's eligibility for long-term assistance.. DOJ, Attorney General's Annual Report to Congress on U.S. Government Activities to Combat Trafficking in Persons: Fiscal Year 2009, pp 18-19.

[99] Personal conversation with the Department of Health and Human Services, Administration for Children and Families, Congressional Affairs, April 2, 2007.

[100] Certification letters are for adult victims, while minor victims receive eligibility letters since, under law, they do not have to be certified as trafficking victims for services.

[101] Fifty-five percent of adult victims certified in FY2010 were victims of labor trafficking. U.S. Department of State, Trafficking in Persons Report, June 2011, p. 375.

[102] P.L. 106-386, §107(b)(1)(A). The eligibility of noncitizens for public assistance programs is based on a complex set of rules that are determined largely by the type of noncitizen in question and the nature of services being offered. For example, refugees are eligible for Medicaid for five years after entry/grant of status, then made ineligible (unless they became citizens or qualified under another status). For a discussion of the eligibility of trafficking victims for state and federal means tested benefits see CRS Report RL33809, Noncitizen Eligibility for Federal Public Assistance: Policy Overview and Trends, by Ruth Ellen Wasem.

[103] P.L. 110-457, §235(b)(2).

[104] For additional information on programs for refugees see CRS Report R41570, U.S. Refugee Resettlement Assistance, by Andorra Bruno.

[105] Department of Justice, Attorney General's Annual Report to Congress on U.S. Government Activities to Combat Trafficking in Persons: Fiscal Year 2007, May 2008: p. 10.

[106] These areas are: Houston, Texas; Las Vegas, Nevada; New York, New York; Milwaukee, Wisconsin; Newark, New Jersey; Philadelphia, Pennsylvania; Phoenix, Arizona; Portland, Oregon; St. Louis, Missouri; San Francisco, California; Sacramento, California; Louisville, Kentucky; Nashville, Tennessee; Columbus, Ohio; Cincinnati, Ohio; San Diego, Los Angeles, and Orange Counties in California; and statewide in Colorado, Idaho, Florida, Georgia, Illinois, Minnesota, and North Carolina. Department of Justice, Attorney General's Annual Report to Congress on U.S. Government Activities to Combat Trafficking in Persons: Fiscal Year 2008, June 2009: p. 14.

[107] Department of Health and Human Services, "About Human Trafficking," available at http://www.acf.hhs.gov/trafficking/about/index.html#wwd.

[108] P.L. 106-386, §107(b)(2).

[109] From the inception of the program in January 2003 through June 30, 2009, OVC provided services to 2,699 pre-certified potential victims of trafficking. In all but one reporting period during that time (January to June 2006) grantees served more labor trafficking victims than sex trafficking victims. Notably, in some cases, services may be stopped if the victim refuses to work with law enforcement. U.S. Department of State, Trafficking in Persons Report, June 2010, p. 341, and Department of Justice, Attorney General's Annual Report to Congress on U.S. Government Activities to Combat Trafficking in Persons: Fiscal Year 2009, July 2010: pp. 26-30. (Hereafter DOJ, Attorney General's Annual Report to Congress on U.S. Government Activities to Combat Trafficking in Persons: Fiscal Year 2009.)

[110] DOJ, Assessment of U.S. Activities to Combat Trafficking in Persons: FY2008, p.6.

[111] For more information on One-Stop Career Centers, see CRS Report RL34251, Federal Programs Available to Unemployed Workers, coordinated by Katelin P. Isaacs.

[112] These services are provided in accordance with the Training and Employment Guidance Letter No. 19-01, change 1, which was reissued by DOL's Employment and Training Administration (ETA) in 2008. In addition to informing the state and local workforce systems about federal resources for victims of trafficking, the guidance letter notes that services may not be denied to victims of severe forms of trafficking because of their immigration status. DOJ, Attorney General's Annual Report to Congress on U.S. Government Activities to Combat Trafficking in Persons: Fiscal Year 2009, p. 32.

[113] DOJ, Attorney General's Annual Report to Congress on U.S. Government Activities to Combat Trafficking in Persons: Fiscal Year 2009, pp. 32-33.

[114] The Job Corps program is carried out by the Office of Job Corps within the Office of the DOL Secretary, and consists of residential centers throughout the country. The purpose of the program is to provide disadvantaged youth with the skills needed to obtain and hold a job, enter the Armed Forces, or enroll in advanced training or higher education. In addition to receiving academic and employment training, youth also engage in social and other services to promote their overall well-being. For more information on Job Corps, see CRS Report R40929, Vulnerable Youth: Employment and Job Training Programs, by Adrienne L. Fernandes-Alcantara.

[115] Catholic Bishops, A Guide for Legal Advocates Providing Services to Victims of Human Trafficking, p. Appendix 1-6. DOJ, Attorney General's Annual Report to Congress on U.S. Government Activities to Combat Trafficking in Persons: Fiscal Year 2009, p. 33.

[116] Controlled delivery is an investigative technique in which law enforcement knowingly allows a shipment to travel to its destination so that law enforcement can learn more about a criminal enterprise and the people involved.

[117] U.S. Government Accountability Office, Combating Alien Smuggling, Opportunities Exist to Improve the Federal Response, GAO-05-305, May 2005, p. 10. (Hereafter cited as GAO, Combating Alien Smuggling, Opportunities Exist to Improve the Federal Response.)

[118] This section is based on the information in Department of Justice, Department of Health and Human Services, Department of State, Department of Labor, Department of Homeland Security, and U.S. Agency of International Development, Assessment of U.S. Government Efforts to Combat Trafficking in Persons, September 2007.

[119] The division of responsibilities between these two agencies is not clearly delineated which may lead to a lack of coordination between the agencies as well as possibly some duplicative efforts. In addition, according to an ICE Office of Investigations (OI) official, the Border Patrol only has a minor role in alien smuggling and trafficking investigations and is required to coordinate with OI before initiating anti-smuggling investigations. GAO, Immigration Enforcement: DHS Has Incorporated Immigration Enforcement Objectives and Is Addressing Future Planning Requirements (2004), p. 9.

[120] Both agencies also provide training to federal and state law enforcement on trafficking victim identification. U.S. Department of State, Trafficking in Persons Report, June 2010, p. 339, and U.S. Department of State, Trafficking in Persons Report, June 2011, p. 374.

[121] Of the cases, 32 were for labor trafficking and 71 were for sex trafficking. Note that these numbers do not reflect cases involving the commercial sexual exploitation of children that were brought under states other than TVPA's sex trafficking provisions. U.S. Department of State, Trafficking in Persons Report, June 2011, p. 373.

[122] The number of investigations and prosecutions among the task forces varies widely. More investigations are for sex trafficking than labor trafficking, which may be a result of law enforcement being able to rely upon pre-existing vice units devoted to prosecution enforcement. There are no comparable preexisting structures for involuntary servitude in the labor sector. Reportedly, DOJ is aware of these critiques and is implementing measures to address them. U.S. Department of State, Trafficking in Persons Report, June 2010, p. 340; and U.S. Department of State, Trafficking in Persons Report, June 2011, p. 373.

[123] As of the end of FY2009, the task-forces had identified 3,687 potential trafficking victims. U.S. Department of State, Trafficking in Persons Report, June 2011, p. 373, and DOJ, AG's Annual Report to Congress on U.S. Government Activities to Combat Trafficking in Persons: Fiscal Year 2009, p. 36.

[124] DOJ, AG's Annual Report to Congress on U.S. Government Activities to Combat Trafficking in Persons: Fiscal Year 2007, p. 23; DOJ, AG's Annual Report to Congress on U.S. Government Activities to Combat Trafficking in Persons: Fiscal Year 2008, p. 36; and DOJ, AG's Annual Report to Congress on U.S. Government Activities to Combat Trafficking in Persons: Fiscal Year 2009, p. 44 .

[125] 29 U.S.C. §§201-219.

[126] 29 U.S.C. Chapter 20.

[127] U.S. Congress, House Committee on Homeland Security, Subcommittee on Management, Integration, and Oversight, 9/11 Reform Act: Examining the Implementation of the Human Smuggling and Trafficking Center, hearings, 109th Cong., 2nd sess., March 8, 2006.

[128] S. 1301 was introduced on June 29, 2011 by Senator Patrick J. Leahy, Chairman of the Judiciary Committee. Senator Leahy offered a amendment in the nature of a substitute during the mark-up of S. 1301. The amendment was agreed to by voice-vote.

[129] H.R. 2830 was introduced on August 30, 2011 by Representative Christopher H. Smith. Representative Smith offered a amendment in the nature of a substitute during the mark-up of H.R. 2830, and the amendment was agreed to by voice-vote. For more information on the mark-up see Joanna Anderson, "House Panel Approves U.N. Population Fund, Anti-Trafficking Measures," CQ.Com, October 5, 2011, http://www.cq.com/doc/committees2011100500291818?wr=Nng4dW84NzhVdzBsRlJZSTlQZUVkUQ.

[130] U.S. Congress, House Foreign Affairs, Mark-Up of H.R. 2830, 112th Cong., 1st sess., October 5, 2011. U.S. Congress, Senate Judiciary Committee, Mark-Up of S. 1301, 112th Cong., 1st sess., October 13, 2011. U.S. Congress, Senate Judiciary Committee, Trafficking Victims Protection Reauthorization Act of 2011, report to accompany S. 1301, 112th Cong., 1st sess., November 17, 2011, S.Rept. 112-96.

[131] U.S. Congress, House Foreign Affairs, Mark-Up of H.R. 2830, 112th Cong., 1st sess., October 5, 2011.

[132] A-3 visa holders refer to workers admitted under INA §101(a)(15)(A)(iii), who are the attendants, servants or personal employees of Ambassadors, public ministers, career diplomats, consuls, other foreign government officials and employees or the immediate family of such workers. G-5 visa holders (admitted under INA §101(a)(15)(G)(v)) are the attendants, servants, or personal employees and their immediate family of foreign government representatives or foreign employees of international organizations.

[133] Joanna Anderson, "House Panel Approves U.N. Population Fund, Anti-Trafficking Measures," Congressional Quarterly, October 5, 2011.

[134] The authorization levels would be reduced for three grant programs that have yet to receive funding: HHS grants for U.S. citizen and LPR victims; grants for a pilot program for residential treatment for juvenile trafficking victims; and grants to local/state law enforcement for anti-trafficking activities.

[135] U.S. Congress, Senate Judiciary Committee, Mark-Up of S. 1301, 112th Cong., 1st sess., October 13, 2011. U.S. Congress, Senate Judiciary Committee, Trafficking Victims Protection Reauthorization Act of 2011, report to accompany S. 1301, 112th Cong., 1st sess., November 17, 2011, S.Rept. 112-96.

[136] The proposed grant program is identical to S. 596 in the 112th Congress, and S. 2925 in the 111th Congress.

[137] The authorization levels would be reduced for three grant programs that have yet to receive funding: HHS grants for U.S. citizen and LPR victims; grants for a pilot program for residential treatment for juvenile trafficking victims; and grants to local/state law enforcement for anti-trafficking activities.

[138] Chuang, 2006.

[139] GAO, July 2006, p. 3. (GAO-06-825).

[140] Sarah H. Cleveland, "Norm Internationalization and U.S. Economic Sanctions," Yale Journal of International Law, 2001, 1, 31.

[141] Chuang, 2006.

[142] Jennifer Block, "Sex Trafficking: Why the Faith Trade is Interested in the Sex Trade," Conscience, Summer/Autumn 2004; Debbie Nathan, "Oversexed," The Nation, August 29 - September 5, 2005, vol. 281; Janie Chuang, Winter 2006, 13, 1, G-TIP Fact Sheets, Available at http://www.state.gov/g/tip/rls/fs/index.htm.

[143] The study authors contend that using reported incidences creates a bias and most likely does not represent the actual frequency of different types of trafficking (e.g. sex versus labor trafficking). They note that the exploitation of women tends to be visible, in city centers, or along highways. Thus, because it is more frequently reported, sexual exploitation has become the most documented type of trafficking in aggregate statistics. They argue that in comparison, other forms of exploitation are under-reported: forced or bonded labor; domestic servitude and forced marriage; and the exploitation of children in begging, the sex trade, and warfare. UNODC and UNGIFT, Global Report on Trafficking in Persons, February 2009..

[144] International Labor Organization (ILO), ILO Action against Trafficking in Human Beings, 2008.

[145] §103 (8-9) of P.L. 106-386, as amended.

[146] Janice G. Raymond, "Sex Trafficking is Not 'Sex Work,'" Conscience, Spring 2005.

[147] Notably, some European countries, including Sweden, Norway, and Iceland, have sought to address this policy debate by criminalizing the purchase of sex, while leaving prostitution as legal. See for example, "Norway Set to Make Buying Sex Illegal," The Guardian, April 23, 2007.

[148] U.S. Department of State, 2008 TIP Report.

[149] U.S. Department of State website, http://www.state.gov/g/tip/index.htm; Feingold, September/October 2005.

[150] The United Nations Convention Against Organized Crime and Its Protocols, available at http://www.unodc.org/unodc/en/crime_cicp_convention.html.

[151] Ibid.

[152] Statement by Claire Antonelli of Global Rights, Center for Strategic and International Studies Event on Human Trafficking in Latin America, July 9, 2004.

[153] Kinsey Aldan Dinan, "Globalization and National Sovereignty: From Migration to Trafficking," In Trafficking in Humans: Social, Cultural, and Political Dimensions, Sally Cameron and Edward Newman, eds. New York: U.N. University Press, 2008. "Mexico-U.S.-Caribbean: Tighter Borders Spur People Traffickers," Latin America Weekly Report, April 11, 2006.

[154] UNODC and UNGIFT, An Introduction to Human Trafficking: Vulnerability, Impact, and Action, 2008, p. 88.

[155] GAO, July 2006, p. 3. (GAO-06-825).

[156] Some of these concerns were also raised in the minority views expressed in the House Judiciary Committee Report on H.R. 3244 which became the TVPA. See, U.S. Congress, House Committee on the Judiciary, Trafficking Victims Protection Act of 2000, Report to accompany H.R. 3244, 106th Cong., 2nd sess., April 13, 2000, H.Rept. 106-487.

[157] These issues are discussed in detail in: Jerry Markon, "Human Trafficking Evokes Outrage, Little Evidence; U.S. Estimates Thousands of Victims, But Efforts to Find Them Fall Short," Washington Post, September 23, 2007.

[158] U.S. Department of State, Trafficking in Persons Report, June 2010, p. 338.

[159] Federal Register vol. 67, no. 21: p. 4785. January 31, 2002.

[160] Testimony of Derek J. Marsh, Co-Director Orange County Human Trafficking Task Force, in U.S. Congress, House Committee on Homeland Security, Crossing the Border: Immigrants in Detention and Victims of Trafficking, Part II, 110th Cong., 1 sess., March 20, 2007.

[161] Personal communication with ICE special agents in Los Angeles, California, August 16, 2005.

[162] Raffonelli, "INS Final Rule to Assist Victims of Trafficking." p.4.

[163] U.S. Department of State, Trafficking in Persons Report, June 2011, p. 375.

[164] Lisa Raffonelli. "INS Final Rule to Assist Victims of Trafficking." Refugee Reports, vol. 23, no. 3 (April 2002): p.9. Hereafter referred to as Raffonelli, "INS Final Rule to Assist Victims of Trafficking." U.S. Department of State, Trafficking in Persons Report, June 2010, p. 340.

[165] U.S. Department of State, Trafficking in Persons Report, June 2010, p. 338.

[166] Testimony of Cho. Testimony of Wendy Patten, U.S. Advocacy Director, Human Rights Watch, in U.S. Congress, Senate Committee on Judiciary, Subcommittee on Constitution, Civil Rights and Property Rights, Examining U.S. Efforts to Combat Human Trafficking and Slavery, hearings, 108th Cong., 2nd sess., (July 7, 2004). (Hereafter, Testimony Wendy Patten.)

[167] Raffonelli, "INS Final Rule to Assist Victims of Trafficking." p. 9.

[168] Recommendation in the FY2009 Attorney General's Annual Report to Congress on U.S. Government Activities to Combat Trafficking in Persons include "examine and enhance the efficacy and parity of services provided

to U.S. citizen, LPR, and foreign national victims of trafficking." DOJ, Attorney General's Annual Report to Congress on U.S. Government Activities to Combat Trafficking in Persons: Fiscal Year 2009, p. 15.

[169] Senior Policy Operating Group on Trafficking in Persons: Subcommittee on Domestic Trafficking, Final Report and Recommendations, Washington, DC, August 2007, http://www.acf.hhs.gov/trafficking/SPOGReport-Final9-5-07.pdf.

[170] DOJ, Attorney General's Annual Report to Congress on U.S. Government Activities to Combat Trafficking in Persons: Fiscal Year 2009, p. 17.

[171] Personal Communication with U.S. Department of Health and Human Services, Administration for Children and Families, Office of Refugee Resettlement, Director, Anti-Trafficking in Persons Division, April 14, 2010.

[172] P.L. 111-117, P.L. 111-8, P.L. 110-161.

[173] The grant is authorized under 22 U.S.C 7105(b)(2)(A), pertaining to grants made by the Attorney General to develop, expand or strengthen victim service programs for victims of trafficking in the United States. It is a program that was in TVPA as enacted in 2000. U.S. Department of Justice, Office of Justice Programs, Office for Victims of Crime, "Announcing the Awardees from OVC's Services for Domestic Minor Victims," press release, 2009.

[174] The funding for this grant was also awarded using funding from the American Recovery and Reinvestment Act of 2009 (P.L. 111-5). DOJ, Attorney General's Annual Report to Congress on U.S. Government Activities to Combat Trafficking in Persons: Fiscal Year 2009, p. 7.

[175] 22 U.S.C §7105(b)(2)(A).

[176] U.S. Department of State, Trafficking in Persons Report, June 2011, p. 375.

[177] U.S. Department of State, Trafficking in Persons Report, June 2011, p. 375.

[178] Department of Justice, Department of Health and Human Services, Department of State, Department of Labor, Department of Homeland Security, and U.S. Agency of International Development, Assessment of U.S. Government Efforts to Combat Trafficking in Persons, June 2004, p. 4.

[179] For a full discussion of these estimates, see CRS Report R41878, Sex Trafficking of Children in the United States: Overview and Issues for Congress, by Kristin M. Finklea, Adrienne L. Fernandes-Alcantara, and Alison Siskin.

[180] Victims of domestic sex trafficking often do not self-identify as victims due to fear of the physical and psychological abuse inflicted by the trafficker, or due to the trauma bonds developed through the victimization process. Smith, Vardaman, and Snow, Domestic Minor Sex Trafficking: America's Prostituted Children, p. 41.

[181] The programs in TVPA for noncitizen victims were created in part because under the law noncitizen victims are statutorily ineligible for many public benefits (e.g., Medicaid, housing assistance). Nonetheless, while U.S. citizen victims are eligible for federal crime victims benefits and public benefit entitlement programs, there is little data to assess the extent to which U.S. citizen trafficking victims are accessing these benefits. DOJ, Attorney General's Annual Report to Congress on U.S. Government Activities to Combat Trafficking in Persons: Fiscal Year 2009, pp. 17-18. For a discussion of noncitizen eligibility for public benefits, see CRS Report RL33809, Noncitizen Eligibility for Federal Public Assistance: Policy Overview and Trends, by Ruth Ellen Wasem.

[182] At a recent hearing on the TVPA reauthorization, the ranking member of the Senate Judiciary Committee, Senator Charles Grassley stated: "[I] feel that the bill ought to be reauthorized. But I make a point of saying that we have a terrible budget situation and it requires that we take a close look at how some of this money is spent..." U.S. Congress, Senate Committee on the Judiciary, The Trafficking Victims Protection Reauthorization Act: Renewing the Commitment to Victims of Human Trafficking, 112th Cong., 1st sess., September 14, 2011.

[183] The audits found weaknesses in the areas of the established goals and accomplishments for grantees, grant reporting, fund drawdowns, local matching funds, expenditures, indirect costs, and monitoring of subrecipients. Department of Justice, Office of the Inspector General, Management of the Office of Justice Programs' Grant Programs for Trafficking Victims, Audit Report 08-26, Washington, DC, July 2008, http://www.justice.gov/oig/ reports/OJP/a0826/ final.pdf.

[184] Ibid.

[185] This report did not specifically examine the grants under TVPA, but concluded that OJP's management of grants in general had improved. Department of Justice, Office of the Inspector General, Audit of the Office of Justice Programs' Monitoring and Oversight of Recovery Act and Non-Recovery Act Grants, Audit Report 11-19, Washington, DC, March 2011, http://www.justice.gov/oig/reports/OJP/a1119.pdf.

[186] For a discussion of this directive, see Department of State, Office of the Historian, History of the Department of State During the Clinton Presidency (1993-2001), available at http://www.state.gov/r/pa/ho/pubs/8523.htm.

[187] Testimony of William R. Yeomans, Chief of Staff of the Civil Rights Division, Department of Justice, before the Subcommittee on Near Eastern and South Asian Affairs, Senate Foreign Relations Committee, April 4, 2000.

[188] For more information on the Crime Victims Fund, see CRS Report RL32579, Victims of Crime Compensation and Assistance: Background and Funding, by Celinda Franco.

[189] Attorney General John Ashcroft's news conference on March 27, 2001.

[190] U.S. Department of State, Washington File, January 24, 2002.

[191] The act specifies a number of agencies from which, as appropriate, staff may be detailed to the HSTC, including but not limited to U.S. Customs and Border Protection, Transportation Security Administration, Coast Guard, Central Intelligence Agency, National Security Agency, and the Departments of Defense, Justice, and State. The act also specifies that the detailees include an adequate number with specified expertise, and that agencies shall create policies and incentives for the detailees to serve terms of at least two years.

[192] The House and the Senate had each taken up their own versions of the 2008 reauthorization bill. H.R. 3887, The William Wilberforce Trafficking Victims Protection Reauthorization Act of 2007 (Lantos), was passed by the House under suspension of the rules on December 4, 2007. The vote was 405-2. S. 3061, The William Wilberforce Trafficking Victims Protection Reauthorization Act of 2008 (Biden/Brownback), was reported by the Senate Judiciary Committee on September 8, 2008. H.R. 3887 and S. 3061 included many identical provisions, and most of the differences between the two bills were from provisions that existed in only one of the bills rather than substantial differences between similar provisions in both bills. For a more detailed discussion of the differences between the two bills, see CRS Congressional Distribution Memorandum, Select Differences Between S. 3061 as Reported, and H.R. 3887 as Passed by the House, by Alison Siskin and Clare Ribando Seelke, available from the authors.

[193] Nonimmigrant visas are commonly referred to by the letter and numeral that denotes their subsection in the Immigration and Nationality Act (INA) §101(a)(15). Nonimmigrant visas are commonly referred to by the letter and numeral that denotes their subsection in the Immigration and Nationality Act (INA) §101(a)(15). Under the act, employment-based and educational-based visas refer to: A-3 visa holders (admitted under INA §101(a)(15)(A)(iii)), who are the attendants, servants or personal employees of Ambassadors, public ministers, career diplomats, consuls, other foreign government officials and employees or the immediate family of such workers; G-5 visa holders (admitted under INA §101(a)(15)(G)(v)) are the attendants, servants, or personal employees and their immediate family of foreign government representatives or foreign employees of international organizations; H visa holders (admitted under INA §101(a)(15)(H)) which is the main category for different types of temporary workers; and J visa holders (admitted under INA §101(a)(15)(J)) which are foreign exchange visitors and include diverse occupations as au pairs, foreign physicians, camp counselors, professors and teachers.

[194] A-3 visa holders refer to workers admitted under INA §101(a)(15)(A)(iii), who are the attendants, servants or personal employees of Ambassadors, public ministers, career diplomats, consuls, other foreign government officials and employees or the immediate family of such workers. G-5 visa holders (admitted under INA §101(a)(15)(G)(v)) are the attendants, servants, or personal employees and their immediate family of foreign government representatives or foreign employees of international organizations.

[195] Previously, T visa holders and their derivative were eligible for public benefits because of a provision in Victims of Trafficking and Violence Protection Act of 2000 (P.L. 106-386) stating for the purpose of benefits T visa holders are eligible to receive certain public benefits to the same extent as refugees. TVPRA 2008 amends the Personal Responsibility and Work Opportunity Act (P.L. 104-193, PWORA also known as Welfare Reform) to make T visa holders and their derivatives "qualified aliens" (i.e., eligible for public benefits under PWORA).

[196] Unaccompanied minors are aliens who are in the United States without a parent or guardian.

[197] S. 2925 was introduced by Senator Wyden on December 22, 2009, and ordered reported, amended, by the Senate Judiciary Committee on August 5, 2010. A similar bill, H.R. 5575, was introduced by Representative Maloney on June 23, 2010.

[198] An eligible entity is a state or local government that (1) has significant criminal activity involving DMST; (2) has demonstrated cooperation between state, local, and tribal law enforcement agencies (if applicable), prosecutors, and social service providers in addressing DMST; (3) has developed a workable, multidisciplinary plan to combat DMST; and (4) provides assurances that DMST victims would not be required to collaborate with law enforcement to have access to shelters or services.

[199] The main difference between the House and Senate versions of S. 2925 was that House-passed S. 2925 contained a provision prohibiting any of the monies from being used for medical care (as defined in 42 U.S.C. §300gg-91). This provision was not included in Senate-passed S. 2925.

In: The Persistence of Human Trafficking
Editors: Perry Simmons Foster and Kayla Brady

ISBN: 978-1-62257-773-6

Chapter 3

TRAFFICKING IN PERSONS IN LATIN AMERICA AND THE CARIBBEAN[*]

Clare Ribando Seelke

SUMMARY

Trafficking in persons (TIP) for the purpose of exploitation is a lucrative criminal activity that is of major concern to the United States and the international community. According to the most recent U.S. State Department estimates, roughly 800,000 people are trafficked across borders each year. If trafficking within countries is included in the total world figures, official U.S. estimates are that some 2 million to 4 million people are trafficked annually. While most trafficking victims still appear to originate from South and Southeast Asia or the former Soviet Union, human trafficking is also a growing problem in Latin America.

Countries in Latin America serve as source, transit, and destination countries for trafficking victims. Latin America is a primary source region for people trafficked to the United States. In FY2010, for example, primary countries of origin for the 449 foreign trafficking victims certified as eligible to receive U.S. assistance included Mexico, Honduras, Haiti, El Salvador, and the Dominican Republic (along with India and Thailand).

Since enactment of the Victims of Trafficking and Violence Protection Act of 2000 (TVPA, P.L. 106-386), Congress has taken steps to address human trafficking by authorizing new programs and reauthorizing existing ones, appropriating funds, creating new criminal laws, and conducting oversight on the effectiveness and implications of U.S. anti-TIP policy. Most recently, the TVPA was reauthorized through FY2011 in the William Wilberforce Trafficking Victims Protection Reauthorization Act of 2008 (P.L. 110-457). Obligations for U.S.-funded anti-TIP programs in Latin America totaled roughly $17.1 million in FY2010.

On June 27, 2011, the State Department issued its 11th annual, congressionally mandated report on human trafficking. The report categorizes countries into four "tiers" according to the government's efforts to combat trafficking. Those countries that do not cooperate in the fight against trafficking (Tier 3) have been made subject to U.S. foreign

---

[*] This is an edited, reformatted and augmented version of Congressional Research Service, Publication No. RL33200, dated January 23, 2012.

assistance sanctions. While Cuba and Venezuela are the only Latin American countries ranked on Tier 3 in this year's TIP report, seven other countries in the region—Barbados, Costa Rica, Dominican Republic, Ecuador, Panama, St. Vincent and the Grenadines, and the Bahamas—are on the Tier 2 Watch List. Unless those countries make significant progress, they could receive a Tier 3 ranking in the 2012 report.

Activity on combating TIP has continued into the 112th Congress, particularly related to efforts to reauthorize the TVPA and oversee TIP programs and operations, including U.S.-funded programs in Latin America. Congress may also consider increasing funding for anti-TIP programs in the region, possibly through the Mérida Initiative for Mexico, the Central America Regional Security Initiative (CARSI) or through other assistance programs. Congress is likely to monitor new trends in human trafficking in the region, such as the increasing involvement of Mexican drug trafficking organizations in TIP and the problem of child trafficking in Haiti, which has worsened since that country experienced a devastating earthquake on January 12, 2010.

BACKGROUND

Trafficking in persons (TIP) is a growing problem in Latin America and the Caribbean, a region that contains major source, transit, and destination countries for trafficking victims. Major forms of TIP in the region now include commercial sexual exploitation of women and girls, labor trafficking within national borders (including child labor), and the trafficking of illegal immigrants in Mexico and Central America. Latin America is a primary source region for people that are trafficked to the United States, as well as for victims trafficked to Western Europe and Japan. Latin America is also a transit region for Asian victims destined for the United States, Canada, and Europe. Some of the wealthier countries in the region (such as Brazil, Costa Rica, Chile, Argentina, Panama, and Mexico) also serve as TIP destinations.

This report describes the nature and scope of the problem of trafficking in persons in Latin America and the Caribbean.[1] It then describes U.S. efforts to deal with trafficking in persons in the region, as well as discusses the successes and failures of some recent country and regional anti-trafficking efforts. The report concludes by raising issues that may be helpful for the 112th Congress to consider as it continues to address human trafficking as part of its authorization, appropriations, and oversight activities.

Definition

Severe forms of trafficking in persons have been defined in U.S. law as "sex trafficking in which a commercial sex act is induced by force, fraud, or coercion, or in which the person induced to perform such act has not attained 18 years of age; or ... the recruitment, harboring, transportation, provision, or obtaining of a person for labor or services through the use of force, fraud, or coercion for the purpose of subjection to involuntary servitude, peonage, debt bondage, or slavery."[2] Most members of the international community agree that the trafficking term applies to all cases of this nature involving minors whether a child was taken forcibly or voluntarily.

Trafficking vs. Human Smuggling

In 2000, the United Nations drafted two protocols, known as the Palermo Protocols, to deal with trafficking in persons and human smuggling.[3] Trafficking in persons is often confused with human smuggling. This confusion has been particularly common among Latin American officials.[4] Alien smuggling involves the provision of a service, generally procurement of transport, to people who knowingly consent to that service in order to gain illegal entry into a foreign country. It ends with the arrival of the migrant at his or her destination. The Trafficking Protocol considers people who have been trafficked, who are assumed to be primarily women and children, as "victims" who are entitled to protection and a broad range of social services from governments. In contrast, the Smuggling Protocol considers people who have been smuggled as willing participants in a criminal activity who should be given "humane treatment and full protection of their rights" while being returned to their country of origin.[5]

Many observers contend that smuggling is a "crime against the state" and that smuggled migrants should be immediately deported, while trafficking is a "crime against a person" whose victims deserve to be given government assistance and protection. The Department of Justice asserts that the existence of "force, fraud, or coercion" is what distinguishes trafficking from human smuggling.[6] Under U.S. immigration law, a trafficked migrant is a victim, while an illegal alien who consents to be smuggled is complicit in a criminal activity and may therefore be subject to prosecution and deportation.

Trafficking and Illegal Immigration

Incidences of human trafficking are often affected by migration flows, particularly when those flows are illegal and unregulated. In recent years, several factors have influenced emigration flows from Latin America and the Caribbean. Whereas a large percentage of emigrants from Latin America during the 1980s were refugees fleeing from the conflicts in Central America, a majority of the region's more recent emigrants have been economic migrants in search of better paying jobs in developed countries.[7] Primary destination countries for Latin American immigrants have included Spain, Italy, Canada, the Netherlands, Britain, and the United States. These countries, many with low birth rates and aging populations, have come to rely on migrant laborers from Latin America to fill low-paying jobs in agriculture, construction, manufacturing, and domestic service. At the same time, concerns about security and other issues related to absorbing large numbers of foreign-born populations have led many developed countries to tighten their immigration policies. These factors have led to a global rise in illegal immigration.

In the Western Hemisphere, illegal migration flows have been most evident in Mexico, particularly along its 1,951-mile northern border with the United States and its southern border with Guatemala (596 miles) and Belize (155 miles). Between 2002 and 2005, for example, the number of non-Mexican illegal migrants apprehended along the U.S.-Mexico border more than tripled.[8] Since 2007, however, both the estimated number of unauthorized immigrants entering the United States from Latin American countries other than Mexico and the size of the unauthorized population from those countries living in the United States have declined. The size of the Mexican unauthorized immigrant population living in the United

States appears to have leveled off rather than declined, even though unauthorized migration flows from Mexico to the United States have decreased significantly since mid-decade.[9]

Nevertheless, as U.S. immigration and border restrictions have tightened, illegal immigrants have increasingly turned to smugglers to lead them through Mexico and across the U.S.-Mexico border. In order to avoid detection by U.S. border patrol agents, smuggling routes have become more dangerous and therefore more costly. Some smugglers have sold undocumented migrants into situations of forced labor or prostitution in order to recover their costs. Recent studies illustrate how illegal immigrants transiting Mexico, many of whom lack legal protection because of their immigration status, have become increasingly vulnerable to human trafficking and other abuses.[10] An increasing percentage of abuses, the most violent case of which resulted in the mass murder of 72 U.S.-bound migrants in Tamaulipas in late August 2010, have been perpetrated by criminal gangs and drug traffickers, sometimes with assistance from public officials.[11]

Global Figures on Trafficking

TIP is considered to be one of today's leading criminal enterprises and is believed to affect virtually all countries around the globe. Despite limited data on the nature and severity of the problem, the U.S. government has estimated that roughly 800,000 people are trafficked across borders each year.[12] If trafficking within countries is included in the total world figures, official U.S. estimates are that 2 million to 4 million people are trafficked annually. The International Labor Organization (ILO) estimates that there are at least 2.4 million trafficked persons at any given moment, generating profits as high as $32 billion (USD).[13] The accuracy of these and other estimates, however, has been questioned.

The U.S. Government Accountability Office (GAO) released a report in 2006 casting doubt on the methodology and reliability of official U.S. government figures. It concluded that the "U.S. government has not yet established an effective mechanism for estimating the number of victims or for conducting ongoing analysis of trafficking related data."[14] Figures provided by other international organizations are unlikely to be any more accurate.

Trafficking in persons affects nearly every country and region in the world. Internal trafficking generally flows from rural to urban or tourist centers within a given country, while trafficking across international borders generally flows from developing to developed nations. Countries are generally described as source, transit, or destination countries for TIP victims. Many experts conclude that a country is more likely to become a source of human trafficking if it has recently experienced political upheaval, armed conflict, economic crisis, or natural disaster. The United Nations Children's Fund (UNICEF) and others have warned that the hundreds of thousands of Haitian children who were orphaned or abandoned after a catastrophic earthquake hit that country in January 2010 are particularly vulnerable to human trafficking.[15]

Studies have found that human trafficking disproportionately affects women and girls. A 2009 U.N. Office on Drugs and Crime (UNODC) study found that, on average, 65%-75% of human trafficking victims are women and 15%-25% are minors.[16]

The ILO estimates women and girls account for 56% of victims in forced economic exploitation, such as domestic service, agricultural work, and manufacturing—and 98% of victims in forced commercial sexual exploitation.[17] The vulnerability of women and girls is due to a number of factors in source, transit, and destination countries.[18]

HUMAN TRAFFICKING IN LATIN AMERICA AND THE CARIBBEAN

Human trafficking is a growing problem in Latin America and the Caribbean. IOM has estimated that sex trafficking in Latin America generates some $16 billion worth of business annually.[19] Internal trafficking for forced and child labor is widespread in many countries in the region. In addition, the U.S. State Department has identified several countries as major source, transit, and destination countries for victims of transnational TIP. Those countries include:

- **Source countries:** Colombia, Dominican Republic, Guatemala, Haiti, Honduras, Mexico, Nicaragua, and Paraguay
- **Transit countries:** All of Central America and the Caribbean
- **Destination countries:** Argentina, Bahamas, Barbados, Brazil, Chile, Costa Rica, Mexico, Netherland Antilles, Panama, St. Lucia, and Trinidad and Tobago.[20]

Factors that Contribute to Human Trafficking in the Region

Both individual factors and outside circumstances contribute to human trafficking within and from Latin America and the Caribbean. Individual risk factors include poverty, unemployment, illiteracy, history of physical or sexual abuse, homelessness, drug use, and gang membership. The IOM in Colombia has identified some personal characteristics common among trafficking victims. These include a tendency to take risks in order to fulfill one's goals, a focus on short-term rewards that may result from short-term risks, and a lack of familial support and/or strong social networks.[21] These risk factors that may "push" an individual towards accepting a risky job proposition in another country have been compounded by "pull" factors, including the hope of finding economic opportunity abroad, which is fueled by television and internet images of wealth in the United States and Europe.

Outside factors contributing to human trafficking include the following: (1) the high global demand for domestic servants, agricultural laborers, sex workers, and factory labor; (2) political, social, or economic crises, as well as natural disasters occurring in particular countries, such as the recent earthquake in Haiti; (3) lingering *machismo* (chauvinistic attitudes and practices) that tends to lead to discrimination against women and girls; (4) existence of established trafficking networks with sophisticated recruitment methods; (5) public corruption, especially complicity between law enforcement and border agents with traffickers and alien smugglers; (6) restrictive immigration policies in some destination countries that have limited the opportunities for legal migration flows to occur; (7) government disinterest in the issue of human trafficking; and (8) limited economic opportunities for women in Latin America. Although women have achieved the same (or higher) educational levels as men in many countries, women's employment continues to be concentrated in low-wage, informal sector jobs.

Child Trafficking

There is considerably less research on the extent and nature of trafficking in persons in Latin America and the Caribbean than there is on Asia and Europe. Most of the research that does exist has focused, at least until recently, on trafficking in children for sexual exploitation. Trafficking of children for sexual exploitation is most common in countries that are both popular tourist destinations and centers of sex tourism.[22] Street and orphaned children are particularly vulnerable to trafficking into the sex industry, although some children who have been trafficked remain living with their families and engage in commercial sex activity in order to contribute to household income. Other factors associated with children at risk of trafficking include: poverty, infrequent school attendance, physical or sexual abuse, drug or alcohol addiction, and involvement in a criminal youth gang.

Children are also trafficked both internally and across international borders for use as domestic servants. State Department officials have estimated that as many as 1 million children work as domestic servants in Latin America, many of whom are vulnerable to verbal, physical, and sexual abuse. Abuse has been particularly evident among the 225,000 or so *restaveks* (child domestic servants) in Haiti and among the thousands of Haitian *restaveks* living and working in the Dominican Republic.[23]

Latin American children have been trafficked for illegal adoptions, for use as soldiers in armed conflict, and to work for organized criminal groups.

Finally, the ILO and the U.S. Department of Labor (DOL) have documented instances from across the region of children forced to work under dangerous circumstances in agricultural or mining industries. For example, a September 2009 DOL report found continued evidence of the use of child labor in the production of a wide range of goods in many countries in Latin America. Examples of some of the goods cited in that report include bricks, gold, coffee, sugarcane, and other agro-export crops.[24] While a 2010 ILO global report estimated that the number of child laborers had declined slightly in Latin America as compared to 2006, it still estimated that some 14 million children in the region worked, 9.4 million under hazardous conditions.[25]

Trafficking for Sexual Exploitation

While trafficking for forced labor is a serious problem in Latin America and the Caribbean, trafficking for sexual exploitation has been perceived as a more widespread and pressing regional problem. Most victims are trafficked for prostitution, but others are used for pornography and stripping. Children tend to be trafficked within their own countries, while young women may be trafficked internally or internationally, sometimes with the consent of their husbands or other family members. One study estimated that some 10,000 women from southern and central Mexico are trafficked for sexual exploitation to the northern border region each year.[26] The State Department has estimated that at least 100,000 Latin Americans are trafficked internationally each year, with large numbers of victims coming from Colombia and the Dominican Republic, among others. It has identified Spain, Italy, Portugal, the United States, and Japan as major destination countries for Latin American trafficking victims.[27]

There are also intra-regional trafficking problems. A 2005 report by the International Organization for Migration (IOM) asserts that the Caribbean's relatively open borders, lax enforcement of entertainment visa and work permit rules, and legalized prostitution have contributed to the problem of trafficking there.[28] Argentina and Brazil are destination countries for women trafficked from the Andes and Caribbean countries like the Dominican Republic. Panama has been a destination for women from Colombia and Central America trafficked to work in the sex industry. Trafficking has also occurred at border crossings throughout Central America and Mexico, especially the Mexico-Guatemala border, as undocumented women who have not been able to get to the United States end up being forced into prostitution.

Trafficking for Forced Labor

The ILO reports that trafficking victims comprise 20% (or 250,000) of the 1.3 million people in Latin America engaged in forced labor. These numbers do not include the increasing numbers of Latin Americans who have ended up in situations of forced labor after migrating to Europe or the United States. Despite the relatively large number of victims trafficked for forced labor in the region, there are relatively few studies on this topic.

Since 1995, the Brazilian government has rescued more than 36,000 laborers from situations of forced labor.[29] In Brazil, forced labor is most common in isolated, rural areas. Despite government efforts, more than 25,000 Brazilian men are still being held in situations of slave labor on cattle ranches, in logging and mining camps, and on plantations where soy beans, corn, and cotton are produced. In recent years, many of the workers freed by the Brazilian government from slave-like working conditions have been employed at plantations growing sugarcane, some of which is used for ethanol production.[30]

Forced labor is also used in the mahogany, brick-making, and gold-mining industries in the Amazonian regions of Peru. In 2005, the ILO reported that more than 30,000 people work as forced laborers in Peruvian logging camps that produce mahogany, roughly 95% of which was exported illegally. Press reports have recently revealed that slave and child labor is also a major problem in several of the 2,000 or so gold mines in the Peruvian Amazon. Indigenous peoples in Peru, Bolivia, and Paraguay are particularly at risk of being trafficked for forced labor.[31] Each year, thousands of migrants flock from Haiti to the Dominican Republic to work in the construction, tourism, and agriculture industries, as well as in the informal sector. Many of those migrants lack proper documentation, rendering them vulnerable to trafficking and other abuses. In the past few years, the Department of Justice has prosecuted an increasingly large volume of cases of foreigners trafficked into forced labor in the United States. Although the majority of these cases have involved trafficking for prostitution, a significant number have involved the agricultural sector. Annually some 1.5 million seasonal farm workers, mostly from Latin America and the Caribbean, plant and harvest produce in the United States. Low wages, harsh working conditions, and a lack of legal protection, combined with an ever increasing demand for cheap labor, have resulted in growing numbers of forced labor abuses.

Relationship to Organized Crime and Terrorism

In many parts of the world, trafficking in money, weapons, and people is largely conducted by criminal gangs or mafia groups. Human trafficking can be a lucrative way for organized criminal groups to fund other illicit activities. In Latin America, Mexican drug trafficking organizations, particularly Los Zetas, have been increasingly involved in the smuggling and trafficking of people as well as drugs.[32] According to the Bilateral Safety Corridor Coalition (BSCC), criminal gangs from Mexico, Central America, Russia, Japan, Ukraine, and several other countries have been caught attempting to traffic victims across the U.S.-Mexico border. During congressional testimony, one expert on security issues in Latin America identified human trafficking as the second most serious organized criminal threat to Central America (behind drug trafficking).[33]

Some analysts maintain that criminals involved in human trafficking could eventually form ties with terrorist groups, such as Al Qaeda, thereby threatening regional security, although there has been no evidence of this to date. They argue that, just as terrorists have engaged in drug trafficking in Colombia and the Tri-Border region (Argentina, Brazil, and Paraguay), they may increasingly turn to human trafficking to fund their networks and operations. Others contend that trafficking is a type of "disorganized crime" in which traffickers are generally individuals or small groups that collaborate on an ad-hoc basis, rather than a big business controlled by organized crime.

Trafficking and HIV/AIDS

One of the serious public health effects of human trafficking is the risk of victims contracting and transmitting HIV/AIDS and other diseases. On the global level, women engaged in prostitution, whether voluntarily or not, have a high prevalence of HIV/AIDS. Some experts have noted that human trafficking may be linked to the spread and mutation of the AIDS virus. Research in Latin America and the Caribbean has shown that trafficking victims, along with other irregular migrants, are at high risk of contracting HIV/AIDS. Factors that put these groups at risk include poverty, discrimination, exploitation, lack of legal protection and education, cultural biases, and limited access to health services.

U.S. POLICY

Anti-Trafficking Legislation[34]

Anti-TIP efforts have accelerated in the United States since the enactment of the Victims of Trafficking and Violence Protection Act of 2000 (TVPA, P.L. 106-386). The TVPA established minimum standards to combat human trafficking applicable to countries that have a significant trafficking problem. The act directed the Secretary of State to provide an annual report by June 1, listing countries that do and do not comply with minimum standards for the elimination of trafficking. In the report, the act directed the Secretary to rank countries on the basis of their efforts to combat TIP, with Tier 1 as the best countries and Tier 3 as the worst. Tier 3 are the countries whose governments are deemed as not fully complying with the minimum standards and not making significant efforts to do so. The TVPA called for the United States to withhold non-humanitarian assistance and instructed the U.S. executive director of each multilateral development bank and the International Monetary Fund to vote against non-humanitarian assistance to Tier 3 countries, unless continued assistance is deemed to be in the U.S. national interest.

Congress is continuously re-evaluating the efficacy of U.S. anti-trafficking laws and programs, and since 2000, has reauthorized the TVPA several times. In 2003, for example, Congress approved the Trafficking Victims Protection Reauthorization Act (TVPRA) of 2003 (P.L. 108- 193). The TVPRA of 2003 refined and expanded the "minimum standards" for the elimination of trafficking that governments must meet and created a "Tier 2 Watch List" of countries that the Secretary of State determined were to get special scrutiny in the coming year.

Most recently, the 110th Congress passed the William Wilberforce Trafficking Victims Reauthorization Act of 2008 (P.L. 110-457). P.L. 110-457 authorized appropriations for FY2008 through FY2011 for the TVPA as amended and established a system to monitor and evaluate all assistance under the act. P.L. 110-457 requires the establishment of an integrated database to be used by U.S. agencies to collect data for analysis on TIP. In addition, it increased the technical assistance and other support to help foreign governments inspect locations where forced labor occurs, register vulnerable populations, and provide more protection to foreign migrant workers. P.L. 110-457 added a new requirement that Tier 2 Watch List countries must be dropped to the Tier 3 category after two consecutive years on the Tier 2 Watch List, unless the President issues a waiver.[35] In addition, among other measures to address the issue of child soldiers, the act prohibits military assistance to foreign governments that recruit and use child soldiers.

There have been bills introduced in the 112th Congress to reauthorize the TVPA, possibly making changes to the act and extending authorizations for some current programs. Two bills that would reauthorize the TVPA have received action. S. 1301[36] was reported by the Senate Judiciary Committee on October 13, 2001 and H.R. 2830[37] was ordered reported by the House Foreign Affairs Committee on October 5, 2011. The reported versions of both bills, due in part to the current state of the economy,[38] are less expansive than the introduced versions of the bills. In addition, there have been several other bills introduced in the 112th Congress that contain provisions related to human trafficking.

Trafficking in Persons Reports and Sanctions: Latin America

On June 27, 2011, the State Department issued its 11th annual report on human trafficking, *Trafficking in Persons Report (TIP), June 2011*, as mandated by the TVPA (P.L. 106-386 as amended). The 2011 TIP report is more comprehensive than prior reports, ranking 181 countries as compared to 177 countries in the 2010 report. As in the 2010 report, it provides a description and ranking of U.S. efforts to combat human trafficking. The report also discusses trafficking in persons in three "special case" countries—Cote D'Ivoire, Haiti, and Somalia—where sufficient information was not available to provide a ranking.

As in previous years, most Latin American countries fall somewhere in the middle of the tier rankings, with 19 countries on Tier 2, and 7 on the Tier 2 Watch List. Cuba and the Venezuela are the only two Latin American countries identified as Tier 3[39] and made subject to possible U.S. trafficking-related sanctions, while Colombia is the only country in the region to earn a Tier 1 ranking. Countries on the Tier 2 Watch List include Barbados, Costa Rica, Dominican Republic, Ecuador, Panama, St. Vincent and the Grenadines, and the

Bahamas.[40] Belize, the Dominican Republic, Guatemala, Guyana, and Nicaragua upgraded their tier rankings, whereas Bahamas, Costa Rica, Ecuador, and Venezuela were downgraded.

On September 13, 2010, President Obama issued his determination on whether to impose aid restrictions during FY2011 on the 13 listed Tier 3 countries from the 2010 TIP report, issued in June.[41] The President has the option to (1) apply a full prohibition against nonhumanitarian and nontrade-related foreign assistance, (2) withhold a portion of aid eligible for restriction by granting partial waivers, or (3) waive the restrictions entirely on the basis of national interest reasons.

For FY2011 the President determined that nonhumanitarian and nontrade-related foreign assistance would be fully withheld from two countries: Eritrea and North Korea. Four countries were granted by the President partial waivers from the aid prohibitions: Burma, Cuba, Iran, and Zimbabwe. Seven countries—the Democratic Republic of Congo, the Dominican Republic, Kuwait, Mauritania, Papua New Guinea, Saudi Arabia, and Sudan— were granted by the President full waivers from the aid prohibitions. The President determined that it remained in the U.S. national interest to continue nonhumanitarian and nontrade-related foreign assistance to these countries.

U.S. Government Anti-Trafficking Programs in Latin America

In FY2010, the U.S. government obligated approximately $85.3 million in anti-trafficking assistance to foreign governments worldwide, up from the $83.7 million obligated in FY2009. Roughly 20% ($17.1 million) of U.S. international anti-TIP funding supported projects in Latin America. Anti-trafficking programs are administered by a variety of U.S. agencies, primarily the State Department, the U.S. Agency for International Development, and the Department of Labor. The majority of the programs are either regional, or directed at countries that were placed on either Tier 3 or the Tier 2 Watch-list in recent TIP reports.

Whereas regional programs in Latin America support initiatives necessary to address the crosscutting nature of human trafficking, bilateral programs aim to help governments solve specific challenges they have had in addressing human trafficking. For example, anti-trafficking programs in the Dominican Republic are focusing on victim identification, establishing a shelter for TIP victims, and training officials from the Attorney General's office and the judiciary on how to investigate and prosecute TIP cases.

U.S. programs in Haiti are helping strengthen Haitian child protection agencies' ability to identify and rescue child trafficking victims. An anti-TIP program in Mexico supports a Resident Legal Advisor who is helping reconstruct the anti-trafficking unit within the Attorney General's Office and train Mexican officials on how to investigate and prosecute TIP cases.

In addition to foreign aid programs, various agencies within the Department of Homeland Security are stepping up joint efforts with Mexican officials to identify, arrest, and prosecute human trafficking and smuggling rings that operate along the U.S.-Mexico border and beyond.

In 2005, the Bureau of U.S. Customs and Border Protection (CBP) in DHS created a new program, the "Operation Against Smugglers (and Traffickers) Initiative on Safety and Security" (OASISS), a bilateral program that enables Mexican alien smugglers and traffickers apprehended in the United States who cannot be tried in this country to be prosecuted in

Mexico. From the time of its inception in 2005 through the end of FY2011, OASISS generated 2,617 cases, but it is unclear how many of those cases were successfully prosecuted.[42]

Various units within the Department of Justice's Civil Rights and Criminal Division have provided training and technical assistance courses to foreign officials in the United States and overseas. For example, the Office of Overseas Prosecutorial Development, Assistance, and Training (OPDAT) has helped several countries, including Brazil and Mexico, draft TIP-related legislation. OPDAT's technical assistance and training in investigating TIP cases helped Mexican officials secure their first convictions under the country's new anti-TIP law in December 2009.

REGIONAL AND COUNTRY ANTI-TRAFFICKING EFFORTS

Organization of American States

OAS efforts to combat trafficking in persons began in 1999 when the Inter-American Commission of Women (CIM) co-sponsored a research study on trafficking in persons in nine countries in Latin America that offered broad recommendations for its elimination. In 2003 and 2004, the OAS General Assembly passed two resolutions on the subject, the latter of which created an OAS Coordinator on the Issue of Trafficking in Persons, originally based in the CIM and now part of the Department of Public Security within the Secretariat for Multidimensional Security of the OAS. On a technical level, since 2005, the OAS has organized, facilitated, and implemented training programs, promoted anti-trafficking policies, and provided opportunities for the exchange of information and best practices to assist member states in their anti-TIP efforts. The OAS has developed several "tool-kits" and capacity-building programs for peacekeeping personnel, parliamentarians, law enforcement officials, migration officers, and consular and diplomatic representatives to prevent trafficking and to identify and protect victims of human trafficking. During 2008-2009, for example, the unit trained over 350 U.N. peacekeeping trainers, military, and civilian police personnel from the region on anti-TIP efforts prior to their deployment. As a self-sustaining program, the Train-the-Trainers Peacekeeping Project continues to train military and civilian police prior to deployment in peacekeeping missions throughout the world. During 2010-2011, the OAS strengthened the capacity of over 750 police, immigration officers, prosecutors, and judges from the English-speaking Caribbean and Central American countries to prevent and combat trafficking in persons. OAS programs incorporated the topic of trafficking in persons and materials developed by the OAS in the regular training curricula of the police academies of the regions covered. Some of the beneficiary countries have expressed interest in incorporating elements of the OAS tool-kits in their training curricula.

Inter-American Development Bank

In 2004, the Inter-American Development Bank (IDB) formed an internal working group to begin developing ways to support governments' anti-trafficking efforts in the region. Since

2006, the IDB has been working with the International Organization for Migration (IOM) and the Ricky Martin Foundation to raise awareness about human trafficking in the region through public service announcements, promotional materials, and the creation of hotlines to report abuses. This collaborative campaign, known as "Call and Live," has been implemented in Colombia, Costa Rica, Nicaragua, and, most recently, in the state of Mexico, Mexico. The IDB is supporting the creation of a regional framework for action to combat human trafficking, and has implemented technical cooperation projects related to TIP in Bolivia, Colombia, El Salvador, Guyana, and Paraguay. IDB efforts are coordinated with the OAS and IOM.

Country Efforts: Progress and Remaining Challenges

Over the last few years, most Latin American countries, perhaps motivated by international pressure or the threat of U.S. sanctions, have taken steps to address the growing problem of human trafficking. As evidenced in **Table 1**, a majority of countries in the region have signed and ratified several international protocols in which they have pledged to combat various aspects of the trafficking problem. Those agreements include The U.N. Protocol to Prevent, Suppress and Punish Trafficking in Persons, ILO Conventions on Abolishing Forced Labor and the Worst Forms of Child Labor; the Optional Protocol to the U.N. Convention on the Rights of the Child (CRC) on the Sale of Children, Child Prostitution, and Pornography; and The Optional Protocol to the CRC on the Involvement of Children in Armed Conflict. Six countries passed new or amended anti trafficking legislation in 2010, while several others created National TIP Coordinators or Task Forces to coordinate anti-TIP programs and initiatives.

According to some, the general problem with the new international commitments, legal reforms, and human trafficking initiatives that have emerged in Latin America is that many countries appear to lack the resources and perhaps the political will to fund and implement their anti-trafficking programs. Many governments are facing other crime problems (such as drug trafficking and gang violence) which they perceive as a bigger problem than human trafficking. Sometimes country efforts are thwarted by larger problems, such as political instability, as in the cases of Haiti, Honduras, and Guatemala. Many countries have few, if any, shelters for trafficking victims and no follow-up plans to help victims after they return from overseas to their former residences. Mexico, a large middle-income country, just recently opened its first government shelter for TIP victims. Some countries, including Guyana and Belize, have appeared to model their national TIP laws so closely to TVPA that they do not have the resources or the manpower to implement the complicated legislation. Public corruption is also a major obstacle to effective anti-trafficking programming, as there is often complicity between traffickers and corrupt border officials, customs agents, law enforcement personnel, and politicians. Finally, conviction and prosecution rates for TIP offenders are low compared to other regions, particularly for forced labor and domestic servitude crimes, but this is not surprising given the general weakness of many of the countries' police and judicial systems.

ISSUES FOR POLICY CONSIDERATION

U.S. interests in Latin America are multiple and, at times, conflicting. These interests include strengthening democracy, promoting economic growth through free trade, stemming the flow of illegal narcotics and migrants, and cooperating on border security and anti-terrorism measures. These broad interests either directly or indirectly affect all U.S. policy in the region and may at times conflict with specific human rights goals, such as fighting human trafficking. As is the case with many human rights issues, ethical concerns about human trafficking must be balanced against broader U.S. geopolitical goals and interests in each country.

There are several ways in which broader U.S. foreign policy goals may influence the TIP report and sanctions process. Some observers maintain that there are certain U.S. allies in the region that could never be sanctioned for political reasons. Others contend that the repeated inclusion of Cuba and Venezuela on the Tier 3 list has constituted "selective indignation" on the part of the U.S. government.[43] U.S. officials working in the region have noted that it is sometimes difficult to produce an unbiased account of government efforts against trafficking without being swayed by underlying foreign policy concerns. Others say that it is difficult to deal with trafficking in persons when a country is undergoing extreme political instability, and that were TIP sanctions actually enforced, that they might undermine the broader U.S. goals of preventing democratic breakdown in the hemisphere. Issues that may be considered when evaluating the implementation of U.S. anti-trafficking policies are discussed below.

Sanctions: Are They Useful?

Since 2003, no governments in Latin America except Cuba and Venezuela have been subject to partial or full sanctions for failing to meet the minimum standards of TVPA. Ecuador appeared on the Tier 3 list in both 2004 and 2005 but did not face sanctions. Some argue that sanctions will probably only be applied to countries already subject to sanctions—such as Burma, Cuba, or North Korea—and that threatening other countries with sanctions may actually encourage them to become less open to working with the United States. Others argue that this may be the case with China or Saudi Arabia, but most Latin American countries depend on good political and economic relations with the United States and fear the public humiliation that comes with a Tier 3 designation as much as actual sanctions. For example, some believe a Tier 3 designation motivated the government of Belize to take several positive steps against trafficking in the summer of 2006. Others maintain that the progress that Belize made in 2006 has not been sustained, noting that the country received a Tier 2 Watch List rating in the 2009 and 2010 TIP reports.

How to Measure Success

It is often difficult to measure success in the fight against human trafficking. Many countries in Latin America have reported increases in the number of training courses provided, conferences held, and workshops convened as evidence of their commitment to combat human trafficking. However, as stated in the 2009 TIP report, the State Department prefers countries to focus on "concrete actions" when determining the adequacy of a particular country's anti-TIP efforts. "Concrete actions" include enacting new or amended TIP legislation; expanding victim assistance and prevention programs; and, perhaps most importantly, securing prosecutions, convictions, and prison sentences for TIP offenders. While many countries in Latin America have passed or amended their existing TIP laws, until very recently, the number of TIP-related arrests, prosecutions, and convictions remained low in comparison to other regions. Some have questioned the adequacy of the State Department's indicators, asserting that more credit should be given to countries that are seeking to address the underlying factors that put people at risk for trafficking, such as gender and racial discrimination, violence against women and children, and economic inequality.[44]

Enforcement Improvement

In 2010, there were 732 prosecutions of suspected traffickers and 293 convictions in Latin America. While prosecutions and convictions have been higher in 2009 and 2010 than in previous years, they still pale in comparison to Europe, which recorded 2,803 prosecutions and 1,850 convictions in 2010. They also pale in comparison to the number of reported victims both in Latin America and globally. In order to continue improving enforcement of TIP legislation in Latin America, some observers have urged U.S. officials and other donors not to encourage countries to pass laws modeled entirely after those from other countries (such as the TVPA). Instead, countries should be given time to develop trafficking laws that respond to their particular TIP problems and law enforcement capacities. Once legislation is in place, more attention and resources may be needed to help countries implement that legislation, and that assistance may need to go beyond training for law enforcement and legal professionals. Third, attention may be needed to address the issue of police corruption that has long plagued many countries in the hemisphere. This could be addressed by stiffening penalties for police, border guards, or other officials caught assisting traffickers.

Forced Labor: Adequacy of Country Efforts

Recent research suggests that while TIP for sexual exploitation is both a highly prevalent and particularly visible form of human trafficking, TIP for forced labor exploitation may account for a large, often unreported and possibly growing share of TIP globally. Recent interest in forced labor as a form of TIP has sparked calls for greater research in analyzing the prevalence of forced labor, increased international efforts to combat this form of TIP, and more awareness to prevent and educate potential victims. The State Department's TIP reports since 2005 have placed an added emphasis on evaluating country efforts to combat trafficking for forced labor, and several other programmatic efforts to combat TIP for forced labor are underway at the State Department.

Other international groups, particularly the ILO, also play a large role in efforts to combat forced labor. Within Latin America, Brazil has been singled out by the ILO for its efforts to address forced labor.[45]

Across the region, labor trafficking prosecutions and convictions are increasing: from one prosecution and one conviction in the 2007 reporting period to 80 prosecutions and 65 convictions in 2010.[46] Despite this progress, many Latin American countries have yet to broaden their anti-TIP efforts out from focusing largely on the commercial sexual exploitation of women and children.

Debates About Prostitution and Trafficking

The current U.N. definition of TIP assumes that there are at least two different types of prostitution, one of which is the result of free choice to participate in the prostitution business while the other is the result of coercion, vulnerability, deception, or other pressures. Of these, only the latter type is considered TIP under the U.N. definition. Based on the TVPA, as amended, sex trafficking is not considered a "severe form of TIP" unless it is associated with commercial sex acts induced by force, fraud, or coercion, or in which the person induced to perform such acts is a minor.[47]

Several groups in the United States have sought to redefine TIP to include all prostitution, but many countries have thus far rejected those attempts. Proponents of this broader definition of TIP argue that prostitution is "not 'sex work;' it is violence against women [that] exists because ... men are given social, moral and legal permission to buy women on demand."[48] Several European and Latin American countries, which have legal or government-regulated prostitution, reject such a definitional change and argue that this broader definition would impede the capacity of the international community to achieve consensus and work together to combat trafficking. The U.S. State Department asserts that prostitution and TIP are inextricably linked. Most recently, in its 2008 TIP Report to Congress, the State Department states that "sex trafficking would not exist without the demand for commercial sex flourishing around the world" and that prostitution and any related activities "should not be regulated as a legitimate form of work for any human being."[49] State Department officials have identified the fact that legalized prostitution fuels sex trafficking in the region as an obstacle to anti-TIP efforts in Latin America.[50]

Is U.S. Anti-TIP Assistance for Latin America Sufficient?

Questions have been raised about the adequacy of U.S. anti-TIP assistance to Latin America. In FY2008 the percentage of U.S. international anti-trafficking program funds dedicated to Latin American and the Caribbean declined as compared to previous years, a trend that was reversed in FY2009 and FY2010. Similarly, total U.S. anti-TIP obligations for the region fell from roughly $17.5 million in FY2006 and FY2007 to some $13.7 million in FY2008, but rose again to some $17.3 million in FY2009 and $17.6 million in FY2010. Representatives from the State Department's Office to Monitor and Combat Trafficking in Persons have expressed hope that more anti-TIP programs in Mexico and Central America might be funded through the Mérida Initiative and the Central America Regional Security Initiative (CARSI).[51] To date, Congress has appropriated roughly $1.96 billion for the Mérida Initiative and CARSI. Neither initiative currently includes much funding specifically devoted to combating human trafficking.

Table 1. Latin America and the Relevant International Conventions on Human Trafficking

Country	2010 Tier Placement	2011 Tier Placement	U.N. TIP Protocol Signed	U.N. TIP Protocol Ratified	ILO Convention 105 Ratified	ILO Convention 182 Ratified	Optional Protocol of CRC Signed	Optional Protocol of CRC Ratified (a)	Optional Protocol CRC Armed Conflict Signed	Optional Protocol CRC Armed Conflict Ratified
Antigua & Barbuda	Tier 2			(a)	X	X	X	X		(a)
Argentina	Tier 2	Tier 2	X	X	X	X	X	X	X	X
Bahamas	Tier 2	Tier 2 WL	X	X	X	X				
Barbados	Tier 2 WL	Tier 2 WL	X		X	X				
Belize	Tier 2 WL	Tier 2		X (a)**	X	X	X	X	X	X
Bolivia	Tier 2	Tier 2	X	X	X	X	X	X		X(a)
Brazil	Tier 2	Tier 2	X	X	X	X	X	X	X	X
Chile	Tier 2	Tier 2	X	X	X	X	X	X	X	X
Colombia	Tier 1	Tier 1	X	X	X	X	X	X	X	X
Costa Rica	Tier 2	Tier 2 WL	X	X	X	X	X	X	X	X
Cuba	Tier 3	Tier 3			X	X	X	X	X	X
DR	Tier 3	Tier 2 WL	X	X	X	X	X	X(a)	X	
Ecuador	Tier 2	Tier 2 WL	X	X	X	X	X	X	X	X
El Salvador	Tier 2 WL	Tier 2	X	X	X	X	X	X	X	X
Guatemala	Tier 2 WL	Tier 2		X (a)	X	X	X	X	X	X
Guyana	Tier 2 WL	Tier 2		X (a)	X	X		X(a)		X(a)
Haiti	Not rated	Not rated.	X		X	X	X		X	
Honduras	Tier 2	Tier 2		X(a)	X	X		X (a)		X (a)
Jamaica	Tier 2	Tier 2	X	X	X	X	X	X	X	X
Mexico	Tier 2	Tier 2	X	X	X	X	X	X	X	X
Nicaragua	Tier 2 WL	Tier 2		X (a)	X	X		X(a)		X(a)
Panama	Tier 2 WL	Tier 2 WL	X	X	X	X	X	X		X
Paraguay	Tier 2	Tier 2	X	X	X	X	X	X	X	X
Peru	Tier 2	Tier 2	X	X	X	X	X	X	X	X
St. Vincent &Grenadines	Tier 2 WL	Tier 2 WL	X		X	X		X (a)		X(a)
Suriname	Tier 2	Tier 2		X(a)	X	X	X	X	X	X
Venezuela	Tier 2 WL	Tier 3	X	X	X	X	X	X	X	X

Source: U.S. Department of State, *Trafficking in Persons Report, 2011*, June 27, 2011.

Notes:

* (WL) indicates placement on Tier 2 Watch List as opposed to Tier 2. ** (a) indicates accession.

Treaties and Protocols:

—U.N. Protocol to Prevent, Suppress and Punish Trafficking in Persons

—ILO Convention 105 (Abolition of Forced Labor)

—ILO Convention 182 (Convention on the Worst Forms of Child Labor)

—Optional Protocol to the Convention on the Rights of the Child (CRC) on the Sale of Children, Child Prostitution, and Pornography

—Optional Protocol to the CRC on the Involvement of Children in Armed Conflict.

End Notes

[1] For more general information on human trafficking, see CRS Report RL34317, *Trafficking in Persons: U.S. Policy and Issues for Congress*.

[2] *Victims of Trafficking and Violence Protection Act of 2000 (TVPA)* (P.L. 106-386).

[3] The United Nations Convention Against Organized Crime and Its Protocols, available at http://www.unodc.org/unodc/en/crime_cicp_convention.html.

[4] The most accurate phrase in Spanish for referring to human trafficking is *la trata de personas* (the trade of people), rather than the commonly used phrase *el tráfico de personas* (the traffic of people), which means something akin to human smuggling. See: U.S. Department of State, *Trafficking in Persons (TIP) Report*, June 2009, available at http://www.state.gov/ g/tip/rls/tiprpt/2009/.

[5] http://www.unodc.org/unodc/en/crime_cicp_convention.html.

[6] U.S. Department of Justice, Human Smuggling and Trafficking Center, "Fact Sheet: Distinctions Between Human Smuggling and Human Trafficking," January 2005.

[7] There are several exceptions to this general rule, including emigrants fleeing from Cuba and Colombia.

[8] "Life on a Trouble Frontier," *Fort Worth Star-Telegram*, June 4, 2006.

[9] Jeffrey S. Passel and D'Vera Cohn, *U.S. Unauthorized Immigration Flows Are Down Sharply Since Mid-Decade*, Pew Hispanic Center, Washington, D.C., September 2010.

[10] Comisión Nacional de Derechos Humanos (CNDH), Informe Especial Sobre Secuestro de Migrantes en México, February 2011.

[11] Amnesty International, *Invisible Victims: Migrants on the Move in Mexico*, April 2010.

[12] U.S. Department of State, *Trafficking in Persons Report*, June 2008. Notably, the estimate of 600,000 to 800,000 people trafficked across borders each year is from 2003.

[13] International Labor Organization (ILO), "ILO Action against Trafficking in Human Beings," 2008.

[14] U.S. Government Accountability Office (GAO), *Human Trafficking: Better Data, Strategy, and Reporting Needed to Enhance U.S. Antitrafficking Efforts Abroad*, 06-825R, July 2006.

[15] United Nations Children's Emergency Fund (UNICEF), *Children in Haiti: One Year After – The Long Road from Relief to Recovery*, January 2011. In response, the U.S. State Department's Office to Monitor and Combat Trafficking in Persons provided $4.5 million in grants in FY2011 to organizations working to combat human trafficking in Haiti.

[16] UNODC and the United Nations Global Initiative to Fight Human Trafficking (UNGIFT), *Global Report on Trafficking in Persons*, February 2009.

[17] ILO, *A Global Alliance Against Forced Labor*, 2005.

[18] U.S. Department of State, Office to Monitor and Combat Trafficking in Persons (G-TIP), "Fact Sheet: Gender Imbalance in Human Trafficking," June 16, 2009.

[19] "Sex Trafficking Now a $16 Billion Business in Latin America," *EFE*, January 3, 2007.

[20] U.S. Department of State, G-TIP, Power Point Presentation from Briefing on TIP in the Western Hemisphere, July 2009.

[21] Sanin et al., "Condiciones de Vulnerabilidad a la Trata de Personas en Colombia," IOM, 2005.

[22] The State Department has identified Brazil, Costa Rica, the Dominican Republic, Honduras, Jamaica, Mexico, and Nicaragua as countries with significant child sex tourism industries. G-TIP, Power Point Presentation from Briefing on TIP in the Western Hemisphere, July 2009.

[23] U.S. Department of State, *TIP Report*, June 2010.

[24] U.S. Department of Labor (DOL), *The DOL's List of Goods Produced by Child Labor or Forced Labor*, September 2009.

[25] ILO, International Program on the Elimination of Child Labour (IPEC), *Accelerating Action Against Child Labour: ILO Global Report on Child Labour*, May 2010.

[26] Arun Kumar Acharya, "Tráfico de mujeres hacia la Zona Metropolitana de Monterrey: Una Perspectiva Analítica," *Revista Espacios Públicos*, Year 12, No. 24, 2009.

[27] U.S. Department of State, G-TIP, Power Point Presentation from Briefing on TIP in the Western Hemisphere, July 2009.

[28] "Exp loratory Assessment of Trafficking in Persons in the Caribbean Region," IOM, June 2005.

[29] The International Labor Organization (ILO) defines forced labor as any situation in which work is carried out involuntarily under the menace of a penalty. The terms "forced labor" and "slave labor" are often used interchangeably. For a description of the extent of forced labor in Brazil and the country's efforts to combat it,

see Patricia Trindade Maranhão Costa, "Fighting Forced Labor: The Example of Brazil," ILO Special Action Program to Combat Forced Labor, 2009; U.S. Department of State, *TIP Report*, June 2011.

[30] Repórter Brasil, "Brazil of Biofuels: Sugarcane 2008," January 2009.

[31] For information on ILO research and programs in these countries, see http://www.ilo.org/sapfl/Projects/lang--en/WCMS_082040/index.htm. See also "U.N. Permanent Forum on Indigenous Issues Calls for Urgent Action to Stop Forced Labor in Bolivia, Paraguay," *Targeted News Service*, August 31, 2009. Trip reports available at http://www.un.org/esa/socdev/unpfii/.

[32] Melissa Graham, "Mexico's New War: Sex Trafficking," *La Prensa San Diego*, October 29, 2010; Tim Johnson, Mexican Criminal Gang Turns to Migrant Smuggling," *McClatchy-Tribune News Service*, August 15, 2011.

[33] Testimony of Eric L. Olson, Senior Advisor, Security Initiative, Woodrow Wilson Center, before the House Subcommittee on National Security and Foreign Affairs, October 1, 2009.

[34] For a complete history of U.S. anti-TIP legislation and current legislation on human trafficking in the 112th Congress, see CRS Report RL34317, *Trafficking in Persons: U.S. Policy and Issues for Congress*, by Alison Siskin and Liana Sun Wyler.

[35] Such a waiver permits the President to waive the Tier 3 listing for up to two years. In exercising this waiver authority, the President must determine that such a waiver is justified because the country has a "written plan" to start making "significant efforts" to comply with the TVPA's minimum standards to combat TIP, and because the country has committed "sufficient resources" to implement the plan.

[36] S. 1301 was introduced on June 29, 2011, by Senator Patrick J. Leahy. Senator Leahy offered an amendment in the nature of a substitute during the mark-up of S. 1301. The amendment was agreed to by voice-vote.

[37] H.R. 2830 was introduced on August 30, 2011, by Representative Christopher H. Smith. Representative Smith offered an amendment in the nature of a substitute during the mark-up of H.R. 2830, and the amendment was agreed to by voice-vote. For more information on the mark-up see Joanna Anderson, "House Panel Approves U.N. Population Fund, Anti-Trafficking Measures," *CQ.Com*, October 5, 2011, http://www.cq.com/doc/committees2011100500291818?wr=Nng4dW84NzhVdzBsRlJZSTlQZUVkUQ.

[38] U.S. Congress, House Foreign Affairs, *Mark-Up of H.R. 2830*, 112th Cong., 1st sess., October 5, 2011. U.S. Congress, Senate Judiciary Committee, *Mark-Up of S. 1301*, 112th Cong., 1st sess., October 13, 2011. U.S. Congress, Senate Judiciary Committee, *TRAFFICKING VICTIMS PROTECTION REAUTHORIZATION ACT OF 2011*, report to accompany S. 1301, 112th Cong., 1st sess., November 17, 2011, S.Rept. 112-96.

[39] The other Tier 3 countries include: Algeria, Burma, Central African Republic, Democratic Republic of Congo, Equatorial Guinea, Eritrea, Guinea-Bissau, Iran, Kuwait, Lebanon, Libya, Madagascar, Mauritania, Micronesia, North Korea, Papua New Guinea, Saudi Arabia, Sudan, Turkmenistan, Yemen, and Zimbabwe.

[40] The State Department must submit an interim report by February 2012 on the Tier 2 Watch List countries in advance of the next TIP report.

[41] Barack Obama, "Presidential Determination With Respect To Foreign Governments' Efforts Regarding Trafficking In Persons," Presidential Determination 2010-15, September 13, 2010.

[42] Data provided to CRS by U.S. Border Patrol in an email, 10/17/2011.

[43] "Politics: U.S. Trafficking Report Includes Cuba and Venezuela," *Global Information Network*, June 10, 2005.

[44] David E. Guinn, "Defining the Problem of Trafficking: the Interplay of U.S. Law, Donor, and NGO Engagement and the Local Context in Latin America," *Human Rights Quarterly*, 30 (2008).

[45] Patricia Trindade Maranhão Costa, "Fighting Forced Labor: The Example of Brazil," ILO Special Action Program to Combat Forced Labor, 2009.

[46] *TIP Report*, June 2011.

[47] Sec. 103 (8-9) of P.L. 106-386, as amended.

[48] Janice G. Raymond, "Sex Trafficking is Not 'Sex Work,'" *Conscience*, Spring 2005.

[49] U.S. Department of State, 2008 TIP Report. The 2009 TIP Report does not discuss linkages between prostitution and trafficking.

[50] U.S. Department of State, G-TIP, Power Point Presentation from Briefing on TIP in the Western Hemisphere, July 2009.

[51] U.S. Department of State, G-TIP, Power Point Presentation from Briefing on TIP in the Western Hemisphere, July 2009.

In: The Persistence of Human Trafficking
Editors: Perry Simmons Foster and Kayla Brady

Chapter 4

SEX TRAFFICKING OF CHILDREN IN THE UNITED STATES: OVERVIEW AND ISSUES FOR CONGRESS[*]

Kristin M. Finklea, Adrienne L. Fernandes-Alcantara and Alison Siskin

SUMMARY

The trafficking of individuals within U.S borders is commonly referred to as domestic human trafficking, and it occurs in every state of the nation. One form of domestic human trafficking is sex trafficking. Research indicates that most victims of sex trafficking into and within the United States are women and children, and the victims include U.S. citizens and noncitizens alike. Recently, Congress has focused attention on domestic sex trafficking, including the prostitution of children—which is the focus of this report.

Federal law does not define sex trafficking per se. However, the term "severe forms of trafficking in persons," as defined in the Victims of Trafficking and Violence Protection Act of 2000 (TVPA, P.L. 106-386) encompasses sex trafficking. "Severe forms of trafficking in persons" refers, in part, to "[s]ex trafficking in which a commercial sex act is induced by force, fraud, or coercion, or in which the person induced to perform such act has not attained 18 years of age...." Experts generally agree that the trafficking term applies to minors whether the child's actions were forced or appear to be voluntary.

The exact number of child victims of sex trafficking in the United States is unknown because comprehensive research and scientific data are lacking. Sex trafficking of children appears to be fueled by a variety of environmental and situational variables ranging from poverty or the use of prostitution by runaway and "thrown-away" children to provide for their subsistence needs to the recruitment of children by organized crime units for prostitution.

---

[*] This is an edited, reformatted and augmented version of a Congressional Research Service publication, CRS Report for Congress R41878, from www.crs.gov, dated June 21, 2011.

The TVPA has been the primary vehicle authorizing services to victims of trafficking. Several agencies have programs or administer grants to other entities to provide specific services to trafficking victims. Despite language that authorizes services for citizen, lawful permanent resident, and noncitizen victims, appropriations for trafficking victims' services have primarily been used to serve noncitizen victims. U.S. citizen victims are also eligible for certain crime victim benefits and public benefit entitlement programs, though these services are not tailored to trafficking victims. Of note, specialized services and support for minor victims of sex trafficking are limited. Nationwide, organizations specializing in support for these victims collectively have fewer than 50 beds. Other facilities, such as runaway and homeless youth shelters and foster care homes, may not be able to adequately meet the needs of victims or keep them from pimps/ traffickers and other abusers.

In addition, it has been suggested that minor victims of sex trafficking—while too young to consent to sexual activity with adults—may at times be labeled as prostitutes or juvenile delinquents and treated as criminals rather than being identified and treated as trafficking victims. These children who are arrested may be placed in juvenile detention facilities instead of environments where they can receive needed social and protective services.

Finally, experts widely agree that any efforts to reduce the prevalence of child sex trafficking—as well as other forms of trafficking—should address not only the supply, but also the *demand*. Congress may consider demand reduction strategies such as increasing public awareness and prevention as well as bolstering investigations and prosecutions of those who buy illegal commercial sex ("johns"). In addition, policy makers may deliberate enhancing services for victims of trafficking. The 112th Congress may address these and other issues if policy makers choose to take up the reauthorization of the TVPA , which expires at the end of FY2011.

OVERVIEW OF SEX TRAFFICKING OF CHILDREN IN THE UNITED STATES

Human trafficking involves the exploitation of individuals for forced labor or commercial sex. The trafficking of individuals within U.S borders is commonly referred to as domestic human trafficking, and it occurs in every state in the nation.[1] Of those individuals who are victims of sex trafficking, research indicates that most victims coming into and within the United States are women and children, and the victims include U.S. citizens and noncitizens alike. This report focuses on the sex trafficking of children in the United States.

The investigation and prosecution of human trafficking has often been carried out by the states, and the majority of states outlaw human trafficking, including sex trafficking in children.[2] Congress has focused recent attention on domestic sex trafficking of children, which includes commercial sex acts involving children under the age of 18.[3] Under the Victims of Trafficking and Violence Protection Act of 2000 (TVPA), the primary law that addresses trafficking, sex trafficking of children is a federal crime—even if a child is not removed from his or her community.[4] Further, regardless of whether a child is believed to have consented to sex or whether the child represents himself/herself as an adult,[5] the child is considered a trafficking victim under federal law.

The exact number of child victims of sex trafficking in the United States is unknown because comprehensive research and scientific data are lacking.[6] According to the State Department's 2010 *Trafficking in Persons (TIP) Report*, more U.S. citizens—adults and children alike—are victims of sex trafficking than labor trafficking, and U.S. citizen child victims are often runaway and homeless youth.[7] One snapshot of the child victim population, albeit incomplete, comes from the Department of Justice (DOJ)-funded Human Trafficking Reporting System (HTRS). Data in the HTRS come from investigations opened by federally funded human trafficking task forces, and do not represent all incidences of human trafficking nationwide. In January 2008, the task forces began entering data into HTRS. Between January 1, 2008, and June 1, 2010, the task forces opened 2,515 investigations of human trafficking; 82% of these were classified as sex trafficking.[8] Of these sex trafficking cases, 83% involved U.S. citizen victims and 40% involved prostitution or sexual exploitation of a child.

Demand for prostitution (and other forms of commercial sexual exploitation) of children is steady, and profit to sex traffickers, or pimps, has increased.[9] Together, these factors have helped fuel sex trafficking of children. Pimps/traffickers prey on vulnerable youth (primarily girls) and groom their victims to enter "the life" of prostitution.[10] They manipulate and abuse—physically, mentally, and emotionally—their victims to maintain control. Additionally, technological advances such as cellular telephones and the Internet have facilitated the demand for child sex trafficking. These technologies can rapidly connect buyers of commercial sex with trafficking victims while simultaneously distancing the perpetrator from the criminal transactions.[11] The individuals who purchase sexual services from pimps/traffickers are known as clients or "johns." The johns may or may not be aware that the individuals with whom they are engaging in sex are children or trafficking victims.

Commercial sexual exploitation of children appears to be fueled by a variety of environmental and situational variables. The scholarly literature has identified those factors as including the use of prostitution by runaway and "thrown-away"[12] children to provide for their subsistence needs;

- the presence of pre-existing adult prostitution markets in the communities where large numbers of street youth are concentrated;
- prior history of child sexual abuse and child sexual assault;
- poverty;
- the presence of large numbers of unattached and transient males in communities— including military personnel, truckers, conventioneers, and sex tourists, among others;
- for some girls, membership in gangs;
- the promotion of juvenile prostitution by parents, older siblings, and boyfriends;
- the recruitment of children by organized crime units for prostitution; and
- the illegal trafficking of children for sexual purposes to the United States from developing countries.[13]

Notably, studies have found that sex trafficking (and commercial sexual exploitation) is supply-driven as well as demand-driven.[14] However, federal legislation has focused more extensively on penalizing the pimps/traffickers and has placed less emphasis on the buyers of commercial sex. Experts generally agree that any efforts to reduce the prevalence of sex trafficking—as well as other forms of trafficking—should address not only the supply, but also the demand.[15]

The TVPA, most recently amended and reauthorized in 2008, has been the primary legislative vehicle authorizing services to victims of trafficking. The TVPA historically focused on providing shelter and support services to victims within the United States—particularly noncitizens.[16] This may have been, in part, because noncitizens were not eligible for those services—including healthcare, housing, education, and legal assistance—to which U.S. citizen and lawful permanent residents (LPR) victims had access.[17] U.S. citizen victims are eligible for certain crime victim benefits and public benefit entitlement programs, though these services are not tailored to trafficking victims. Further, "there is currently little data to assess the extent to which U.S. citizen trafficking victims are accessing the benefits for which they are eligible."[18] Since its enactment in 2000, the TVPA has been reauthorized three times—in 2003 (P.L. 108- 193), 2006 (P.L. 109-164), and 2008 (P.L. 110-457). Through reauthorizations in 2006 and 2008, Congress increased focus on U.S. citizen and LPR victims and authorized services specifically to address sex trafficking of children within the United States. In addition, Congress requested a report, through P.L. 110-457, detailing any differences in services provided to noncitizens and citizens. In practice, services authorized through the TVPA for trafficking victims, which are provided primarily by the Departments of Justice (DOJ) and Health and Human Services (HHS), continue to aid primarily the noncitizen victim population.[19] This may be a result of several factors. For one, while Congress has expanded authorized funding to include victim services for trafficking victims in the United States—irrespective of immigration status—appropriations for trafficking victims services have simultaneously remained relatively stable since the TVPA passed in 2000. In other words, Congress has not appropriated additional funds for services that target a broader spectrum of victims that have been subsequently authorized.[20] Further, appropriations have not specified which services should be funded, and program funding has been an administrative decision within DOJ and HHS. Exploring the adequacy of victim services for *all* victims of sex trafficking in the United States may be of interest for Congress if policy makers choose to take up the reauthorization of the TVPA, which expires at the end of FY2011.

Another issue Congress may consider is the lack of specialized support for minor victims of sex trafficking in the United States. Organizations in the United States that specialize in serving child victims of prostitution and other forms of sex trafficking collectively have fewer than 50 beds.[21] Other facilities, such as runaway and homeless youth shelters as well as foster care homes, do not appear to be adequate for meeting the needs of victims or keeping them secure from pimps/traffickers and other abusers.[22] Further, victims of trafficking may come to the attention of child protective services (CPS), but CPS may not be able to adequately respond to the needs of sex trafficking victims if workers are not knowledgeable about human trafficking, the trafficking laws, or how to handle cases involving child victims.[23] Child victims may also be arrested and placed in juvenile detention facilities because they are perceived to be responsible for prostitution (and other types of commercial sex acts) and/or because they often need protection from sex traffickers.[24]

This report provides an overview of sex trafficking of children in the United States. It first conceptualizes the issue, discussing the victims and perpetrators involved. It then outlines the federal response to investigating and prosecuting perpetrators as well as providing services to victims. The report concludes with a discussion of select issues concerning the federal response to sex trafficking of minors in the United States.

CONCEPTUALIZING SEX TRAFFICKING OF CHILDREN

Federal law does not define sex trafficking per se. However, the term "severe forms of trafficking in persons," as defined in the TVPA, includes sex trafficking. "Severe forms of trafficking in persons" refers to

a) sex trafficking in which a commercial sex act is induced by force, fraud, or coercion, or in which the person induced to perform such act has not attained 18 years of age; or

b) the recruitment, harboring, transportation, provision, or obtaining of a person for labor or services, through the use of force, fraud, or coercion for the purpose of subjection to involuntary servitude, peonage, debt bondage, or slavery.[25]

As part of this definition, a "commercial sex act" means "any sex act, on account of which anything of value is given to or received by any person."[26] The commercial aspect of the sexual exploitation separates trafficking from other crimes such as molestation, sexual assault, and rape. There appears to be a consensus among experts that the prostitution of minors fits the definition of "severe forms of human trafficking."[27] In the case of minors, there is general agreement in the United States and much of the international community that the trafficking term applies to children, regardless of whether the child's actions are believed to be forced or voluntary.[28]

Sex Trafficking of Children: Vulnerable Populations

As mentioned, the exact number of children who are victims of sex trafficking does not exist because comprehensive research is lacking. However, several studies have attempted to measure the extent of the problem.[29] Notably, the studies are not comparable, do not measure the same populations, and do not use consistent terminology.[30] For a discussion of studies that aim to evaluate the scope of the commercial sexual exploitation and prostitution of children, see Appendix A. Runaways are particularly vulnerable to becoming victims of sex trafficking. A federally funded study found that approximately 1.7 million youth had run away from home or were forced to leave their homes at some point in 1999.[31] While away from home, an estimated 38,600 (2.2%) of these youth were sexually assaulted, were in the company of someone known to be sexually abusive, or were engaged in sexual activity in exchange for money, drugs, food, or shelter. Runaways may be perceived as easy targets for pimps/traffickers because they often cannot go home and have few resources. One study involving a nationally representative sample of shelter youth and interviews of street youth in multiple cities indicated that approximately 28% of street youth and 10% of youth in shelters reported selling sex to generate money for basic needs (often referred to as survival sex).[32] Those youth under the age of 18 would be considered victims of sex trafficking if they had sex with an adult in exchange for basic provisions. The study also pointed out that the odds of engaging in survival sex increased for youth who had been victimized (emotionally or physically),[33] had participated in criminal behavior, had a history of substance abuse, had attempted suicide, had a sexually transmitted disease (STD), or had been pregnant. The Dallas

Police Department also found a strong correlation between sex trafficking and runaway status: the more times a child runs away, the greater the likelihood that he or she will be victimized.[34] The department also found that other risk factors among child trafficking victims include their young ages, whether they had previously been sexually exploited, and whether they had previously been victims of prostitution. Other research, including studies examining the histories of prostitutes in Boston, Chicago, and San Francisco, has found that the majority of prostituted women were runaways.[35] According to a study funded by HHS, between 21% and 42% of runaway and homeless youth were victims of sexual abuse before they left their homes.[36] In the general youth population, this prevalence is 1% to 3%. The Letot Center, a juvenile justice facility in Dallas that cares for youth victims, has indicated that about nine out of 10 youth in the Center had previously been physically or sexually abused. Further, 10% of the youth had previously been involved with child protective services (CPS).[37] In addition to runaway and homeless youth, foster youth may also fall prey to traffickers. According to anecdotal reports, it appears that traffickers target group homes and other settings where foster youth congregate.[38]

Traffickers and Buyers

Victims of sex trafficking are exploited by pimps/traffickers who may operate alone or as part of a criminal network. In the United States, traffickers range from teenage boys, young men, and men and women who work for older male pimps to organized criminal syndicates operating both within and across state and national lines.[39] Pimps/traffickers profit by receiving cash or other benefits in exchange for the sexual use of an individual by another person. It is more profitable for a trafficker to prostitute a child than to commit other crimes such as dealing in drugs.[40] For one, the commodity (child) is reusable. In addition, technological innovation has allowed traffickers to reach a wider client base and connect more quickly with buyers. Of note, when referring to the trafficking of *minors*, the terms "pimp" and "trafficker" are synonymous. This does not necessarily hold true when referring to the trafficking of adults. In the context of adults, a pimp who does not use force, fraud, or coercion to induce adults to prostitute themselves would not be considered a trafficker. However, this distinction is moot when the prostituted individuals are minors, with whom a pimp need not use force, fraud, or coercion to be considered a trafficker.[41] There is no single profile of a buyer of commercial sex with a minor, making buyers particularly difficult to identify. Research has suggested that these predators are often encouraged by online solicitations, temptations, and exploitation.[42] In addition to those actively seeking out sex with minors, some buyers may engage in sex with minors unknowingly. The perpetrators may assume that a prostituted individual is an adult. Alternatively, they may or may not inquire about the age of that individual and may still decide to engage in a sex act even if she or he is a minor.[43]

Current Law

Before 2000, U.S. laws were widely believed to be inadequate for dealing with trafficking in women and children or for protecting and assisting victims. Anti-trafficking legislation and programs have since been implemented with the goal of improving the situation. The Victims of Trafficking and Violence Protection Act of 2000 (TVPA, P.L. 106-386) was enacted on October 28, 2000. The TVPA sought to punish traffickers and provide support for victims within U.S. borders. Congress reauthorized the TVPA in 2003 (P.L. 108-193), in 2006 (P.L. 109-164), and most recently in 2008 (P.L. 110-457). Of note, the Trafficking Victims Protection Reauthorization Act of 2005 (P.L. 109-164), signed into law on January 10, 2006, sought to address the special needs of child victims, as well as the plight of American victims trafficked within the United States. The act sought to remedy a perceived inequality between the services available to foreign and domestic victims by creating grant programs specifically to address the needs of U.S. citizen and LPR victims.[44] The William Wilberforce Trafficking Victims Protection Reauthorization Act of 2008 (P.L. 110-457)[45] created a new grant program for U.S. citizen and LPR victims, and it required a study identifying any gaps between services provided to U.S. citizen and noncitizen victims of trafficking. According to the Department of Justice, the TVPA is considered the seminal piece of legislation in the fight against the commercial sexual exploitation of children.[46]

FEDERAL RESPONSE TO SEX TRAFFICKING OF CHILDREN

The federal government investigates and prosecutes trafficking crimes and provides services to victims, including those who are sex trafficked. While the State Department's 2010 *Trafficking in Persons Report* indicates that the U.S. government is in full compliance with minimum standards to eliminate trafficking, it also notes that "government services for trafficked U.S. citizen children were not well coordinated; they were dispersed through existing child protection and juvenile justice structures."[47] As such, the State Department has recommended increasing government efforts to identify and assist U.S. citizen victims. As part of the response to punishing traffickers, the Departments of Justice (DOJ) and Homeland Security (DHS) have primary responsibility for investigating and prosecuting trafficking cases. Multiple federal statutes, including those enacted and amended by the TVPA, outlaw sex trafficking of minors and include penalties for individuals who are found guilty. The federal government also funds services for victims of trafficking. The TVPA, as amended, is the major federal legislation that authorizes these services, which are provided primarily by DOJ and the Department of Health and Human Services (HHS). There has been confusion regarding whether U.S. citizen, LPR, and noncitizen victims are equally eligible to receive these services. In practice, these services tend to be targeted to aiding noncitizen victims.[48] However, it appears that one program, DOJ Grants for Victim Services, has used funding specifically to serve U.S. citizen and LPR minor victims of sex trafficking. Table 1 summarizes programs authorized by the TVPA to combat and respond to trafficking of children in the United States. The majority of programs appear to be able to address the trafficking of U.S. citizen, LPR, and noncitizen victims alike.

Table 1. Programs Authorized by the Trafficking Victims Protection Act, as Amended, That Could Address Sex Trafficking of Children within the United States

Agency, Program, and Authorizing Statute	Description	Authorization of Appropriations	Appropriations for FY2011 (P.L. 112-10)[a]	Population Served (Directly or Indirectly)
		Grants for Law Enforcement		
Department of Justice (DOJ): Grants to State and Local Law Enforcement for Anti-trafficking Programs (P.L. 109-164, §204; 42 U.S.C. §14044c)	DOJ may award grants to state and local law enforcement for programs to investigate and prosecute the domestic trafficking of U.S. citizens and lawful permanent residents (LPRs). Funds may also be used to investigate and prosecute those who purchase commercial sex and to educate those individuals who have been convicted of these and related offenses. Funds may be used to train law enforcement to work specifically with trafficking victims.	$20.0 million for each of FY2008 through FY2011.	No funds appropriated.	U.S. citizen and LPR victims of trafficking.
DOJ: Grants for Law Enforcement Training Programs (P.L. 109-162 §111; 42 U.S.C. §14044f)	DOJ may award grants to state and local governments to assist law enforcement in identifying and protecting victims of trafficking. Funds may be used to train prosecutors to identify, investigate, or prosecute trafficking as well as to utilize and develop laws to prohibit trafficking.	$10.0 million for each of FY2007 through FY2011.	No funds appropriated.	Victims of trafficking generally.
DOJ: Grants for Victim Services (P.L. 106-386; 22 U.S.C. §7105(b)(2)(A))[c]	DOJ may award grants to states, Indian tribes, local governments, and nonprofit, nongovernmental victims' services organizations to develop, expand, or strengthen service programs for victims of trafficking.	$10.0 million for each of FY2008 through FY2011.	$12.3 million	Victims of trafficking generally.[b]
DOJ and Department of Health and Human Services (HHS): Victims Assistance for U.S. Citizens and Lawful Permanent Residents (P.L. 110-457, §107; 22 U.S.C. §7105(f))	DOJ and HHS (in consultation with the Department of Labor) are to establish a grant program to assist U.S. citizens and LPRs who are victims of severe forms of trafficking. The program is to facilitate communication and coordination between assistance providers, provide a means to identify such providers, and provide a means to make referrals to programs for which victims are already eligible.	$2.5 million for FY2008, $5.0 million for FY2009, $7.0 million for FY2010, and $7.0 million for FY0211 (for both DOJ and HHS).	No funds appropriated.	U.S. citizen and LPR victims of trafficking.

Authorizing Statute	Appropriations Grants for Law Enforcement	FY2011 (P.L. 112-10)[a]	(Directly or Indirectly)
	HHS and DOJ may award grants to states, Indian tribes, local governments, and nonprofit, nongovernmental victims' services organizations.		
HHS: Victims' Assistance (P.L. 106-386, §107(b)(1); 22 U.S.C. §7105(b))[b]	HHS is to expand benefits and services to certain victims of severe forms of trafficking in the United States. (The law also directs other federal agencies to expand services; however, Congress has not appropriated funds specifically for this purpose.)	$12.5 million for each of FY2008 through FY2011; and additional amounts for each of these years: $2.5 million for FY2008, $5.0 million for FY2009, $7.0 million for FY2010, and $7.0 million for FY0211 (this funding is also available for other activities under 22 U.S.C. §7105(b), including certification and victim assistance to noncitizen victims).	$9.6 million	Individuals under the age of 18 who are victims of trafficking or noncitizen adult victims who have been certified by HHS as eligible to receive services.
HHS: Grants to Assist U.S. Citizen or LPR Victims (P.L. 109-164, §202; 42 U.S.C. §14044a)	HHS may make grants to states, Indian tribes, local governments, and nonprofit, nongovernmental victims' services organizations for U.S. citizens or LPRs who are the subject of sex trafficking or severe forms of trafficking that occur, in whole, in the U.S. HHS is to give priority to applicants with experience in delivering services to victims of sexual abuse or commercial sexual exploitation and to applicants who would employ survivors of sexual abuse or commercial sexual exploitation.	$8.0 million for each of FY2008 through FY2011.	No funds appropriated.	U.S. citizen and LPR victims of trafficking.
HHS: Pilot Program for Residential Treatment Facilities for Juveniles in the U.S. (P.L. 109-164, §203; 42 U.S.C. §14044b)	HHS is to establish and carry out a pilot program to establish residential treatment facilities in the U.S. for juveniles subject to trafficking.	$5.0 million for each of FY2008 through FY2011.	No funds appropriated.	Individuals under the age of 18 who are victims of trafficking.

Table 1. (Continued)

Agency, Program, and Authorizing Statute	Description	Authorization of Appropriations	Appropriations for FY2011 (P.L. 112-10)[a]	Population Served (Directly or Indirectly)
		Grants for Law Enforcement		
	The program is to provide benefits and services to juveniles at facilities (and to assess the benefits and most efficient and cost-effective means of providing these facilities) that provide shelter, psychological counseling, and assistance in developing individual living skills; and to assess the need for and feasibility of establishing additional facilities. HHS is to provide grants to organizations that have relevant expertise in providing services to juveniles who have been subjected to sexual abuse or commercial sexual exploitation or have entered into partnerships with other organizations with this expertise.			

Source: Congressional Research Service.

[a] The Department of Defense and Full-Year Continuing Appropriations Act, 2011 (P.L. 112-10) appropriated funding at the FY2010 level, with an across-the-board rescission of 0.2%.

[b] Funding appropriated to the department for trafficking has been used to carry out this program.

[c] Funding appropriated to the department for trafficking has been used to carry out this program. This program, Services for Domestic Minor Victims of Sex Trafficking, funds a grant for U.S. citizen and LPR victims of trafficking.

The programs include grants to law enforcement for investigations and prosecutions as well as to social services and other providers of victims' services. Only selected programs, including DOJ Grants for Victim Services and HHS' Victims' Assistance program, have actually been funded. While both of these programs have served noncitizen victims, only the DOJ Grants for Victim Services—and only in FY2009—has used money to serve U.S. citizen and LPR victims.

Investigations of Child Sex Trafficking Offenses[49]

Investigations of human trafficking (including sex trafficking) are often complicated by language barriers and humanitarian issues (e.g., the victim has been traumatized and is unable to aid in the investigation), as well as logistical challenges and difficulties (e.g., transporting, housing, and processing the victims). Moreover, unlike drug trafficking cases where the contraband itself is proof of the illegal activity, the successful prosecution of trafficking in persons cases relies on the availability of witnesses who may refuse to testify for various reasons, including fear of retribution against themselves or their families.[50]

As mentioned, the investigation and prosecution of child prostitution is most often a matter of state law. Every state outlaws the prostitution of children.[51] The vast majority also outlaw human trafficking in terms sufficient to encompass sex trafficking in children.[52] Within the federal government, DHS and DOJ have primary responsibility for investigating and prosecuting sex traffickers, including those who traffic children. The majority of the cases are investigated by agents in DHS's Bureau of Immigration and Customs Enforcement (ICE) or DOJ's Federal Bureau of Investigation (FBI), who coordinate as appropriate.[53] In addition, DOJ, through the Child Exploitation and Obscenities Section (CEOS), works with the U.S. Attorneys' Offices to prosecute individuals who violate federal laws relating not only to trafficking, but also to child pornography, child prostitution, obscenity, child sex tourism, and international parental kidnapping. CEOS prosecutes sex traffickers under the TVPA and other laws relating to child sexual exploitation. With specific respect to prosecuting the domestic sex trafficking of minors, perpetrators are often prosecuted for violations of the Mann Act,[54] the Racketeer Influenced and Corrupt Organization Act (RICO),[55] or the TVPA.[56] Specific statues available to prosecute such crimes include, but are not limited to, the following:

- 18 U.S.C. §1591—Recruiting, enticing, or obtaining (including via force, fraud, or coercion) individuals to engage in commercial sex acts, or benefiting from such activities;
- 18 U.S.C. §2421—Transporting individuals across state or international lines for prostitution or other unlawful sexual activities;
- 18 U.S.C. §2422—Enticing or coercing an individual to cross a state or international line for prostitution or other unlawful sexual activities;
- 18 U.S.C. §2423—Transporting a minor across state or international lines for prostitution or other unlawful sexual activities;
- 18 U.S.C. §2424—Keeping an alien in a house or place of prostitution; and
- 18 U.S.C. §2241(c)—Engaging in interstate travel for sexual activities with a child under age 12, and sexual activities with a child under age 16.

Of these, only 18 U.S.C. §1591 is an anti-trafficking statute created in the TVPA. The provisions created in other federal laws often reference that the crime is prosecutable so long as the victim is brought across states lines; however, under the TVPA, victims do not have to be removed from their communities in order for the crime to be considered eligible for prosecution. Further, the majority of statutes used to prosecute trafficking offenses focus on prosecuting the traffickers, and not as much focus has been placed on prosecuting the clients or "johns." Another difference between the prosecution of traffickers and the prosecution of buyers appears to be that traffickers can be prosecuted whether or not a victim is brought across state lines. On the other hand, federal statutes generally used to prosecute buyers appear to require that either the buyer crosses state lines or that she/he entices the victim to cross state lines. In short, there may be more flexibility and options for federal prosecutors to prosecute traffickers than to prosecute johns.

The following sections discuss efforts by DOJ and DHS to combat trafficking, including prostitution and other forms of child sex trafficking.

Department of Justice (DOJ)

Federal Bureau of Investigation (FBI), Civil Rights Unit

The Civil Rights Unit (CRU) of the FBI is responsible for investigating cases of domestic minor sex trafficking as well as other trafficking offenses. The CRU coordinates with other FBI units, such as the Organized Crime and Crimes Against Children units to investigate these sex trafficking cases. In 2005, the FBI launched the Human Trafficking Initiative. This initiative employs the FBI field offices to use a threat assessment to determine the existence and scope of trafficking in their region, participate in an anti-trafficking task force (discussed below), and conduct investigations and report significant case developments to the CRU. According to the most recent data, in FY2009 the FBI opened 167 human trafficking cases, resulting in 93 convictions.[57] The data do not, however, identify the proportion of arrests that were made for violations related to minors or adults, the proportion of arrests for sex trafficking or labor trafficking, or the proportion of cases involving domestic or international victims. In FY2009, the FBI also reported rescuing 13 minor victims of trafficking and dismantling seven human trafficking organizations.[58]

The FBI, along with the Child Exploitation and Obscenities Section of DOJ and the National Center for Missing and Exploited Children (NCMEC) (both discussed below), participates in the Innocence Lost Initiative, an initiative dedicated specifically to combating sex trafficking of minors within the United States. The FBI has established 39 Innocence Lost Task Forces around the country.[59] This has led to the conviction of 625 perpetrators as well as the rescue of 1,200 children.[60]

Anti-Trafficking Task Forces

Through the Anti-Human Trafficking Task Force Initiative, DOJ (via the Bureau of Justice Assistance) funds 42 anti-trafficking task forces nationwide.[61] These task forces are composed of federal, state, and local law enforcement investigators and prosecutors and NGO victims service providers. The task forces coordinate cases and conduct law enforcement training on the identification, investigation, and prosecution of human trafficking cases.

Research has reportedly shown that locales with task forces are more likely to identify and prosecute trafficking cases.[62]

Internet Crimes Against Children (ICAC) Task Force Program[63]

The Internet Crimes Against Children (ICAC) Task Force program was first funded in 1998 to provide federal support for state and local law enforcement agencies to combat online enticement of children and the proliferation of pornography.[64] To date, 61 regional task forces have been created, each of which are comprised of multiple affiliated organizations (most of which are city and county law enforcement agencies).[65]

In 2008, ICAC task forces processed 345 complaints related to child prostitution.[66] From 2004 through 2008, the number of child prostitution complaints that were processed increased by 914%. According to DOJ, this could be due to the increase in the number of ICAC task forces over this period. This increase could also be due to heightened awareness about child prostitution and the use of the Internet to facilitate child prostitution.

In FY2010, ICAC funding was awarded to four task forces to develop strategies to protect children from child prostitution and other forms of commercial sexual exploitation.[67] The funding was intended to (1) improve training and coordination activities; (2) develop policies and procedures to identify victims of commercial sexual exploitation; (3) investigate and prosecute cases against adults who sexually exploit children for commercial purposes; and (4) adopt best practices to intervene appropriately with and compassionately serve victims, including providing essential services in cases where technology is used to facilitate the child's exploitation. Grants will also be awarded in FY2011 for these same purposes.[68]

Department of Homeland Security (DHS)

U.S. Immigration and Customs Enforcement (ICE)

The Human Smuggling and Trafficking Unit (HSTU) in ICE is primarily responsible for sex trafficking investigations within DHS. HSTU coordinates with other units within ICE—such as the Cyber Crimes Center; the Law Enforcement Support Center; and the Financial, Narcotics, and Public Safety Division—and units in other agencies to combat this form of trafficking. In FY2009, ICE arrested 388 individuals for human trafficking offenses, more than double the 189 arrests in FY2008.[69] The data, however, do not distinguish the proportion of arrests for sex trafficking or labor trafficking, nor do they distinguish the proportion of cases involving domestic or international victims. They also do not distinguish the proportion of arrests that were made for violations related to minors or adults.

Human Smuggling and Trafficking Center

In July 2004, the Attorney General and the Secretaries of the Departments of State (DOS) and Homeland Security signed a charter to establish the Human Smuggling and Trafficking Center (HSTC). The Intelligence Reform and Terrorism Protection Act of 2004 (P.L. 108-458, §7202), signed into law on December 17, 2004, formalized the HSTC. The HSTC serves as the federal government's information clearinghouse and intelligence center for all federal agencies addressing human smuggling, human trafficking, and the potential use of smuggling routes by terrorists. It is unclear how much of the HSTC's resources are focused on minor victims of sex trafficking. While the HSTC is the information repository for matters including trafficking, there is no centralized database housing information on trafficking perpetrators, victims, outreach, and other matters—although Congress mandated the creation of such a database in the TVPA reauthorization of 2008.[70] In DOJ's 2010 report on the *National Strategy for Child Exploitation Prevention and Interdiction*, DOJ indicates that the creation of a database is currently underway.[71]

Services for Child Victims of Sex Trafficking

As referenced in Table 1, the TVPA, as amended, authorizes services (primarily through DOJ and HHS) to assist victims of trafficking within the United States. Some of these programs are aimed at child victims of trafficking, particularly sex trafficking.[72] In practice, funds appropriated to HHS and DOJ for trafficking have been used to carry out those programs authorized under 22 U.S.C. §7105(b) and 22 U.S.C. §7105(b)(2). Under 22 U.S.C. §7105(b), it appears that HHS may provide assistance to two distinct categories of victims: (1) any victim under the age of 18 and (2) any adult who HHS has certified[73] as a victim—a noncitizen adult victim.[74] The statute does not specify the citizenship of children. In practice, HHS provides services to noncitizen children. Although noncitizen trafficking victims under the age of 18 do not have to be certified to receive benefits and services, it is HHS policy to issue eligibility letters to such victims.

Because adult domestic victims do not go through the process of certification, there is some confusion over whether U.S. citizens are eligible for services provided by HHS and other federal agencies (including, as referenced under 22 U.S.C. §7105(b), the Department of Labor, the Legal Services Corporation, and other federal agencies). Adult U.S. citizen and LPR trafficking victims are not required to be certified by HHS, and indeed would not meet the criteria to be certified because certification applies only to foreign nationals who need an immigration status (e.g., T status or continued presence) [75] to remain in the United States. Nonetheless, a 2007 report by the Senior Policy Operating Group on Trafficking in Persons (SPOG) states, "there are not many differences in trafficking victims' eligibility for the services we reviewed when one looks at the relevant statutes." However, the report does note that U.S. citizen victims may have less intensive case management services compared to noncitizens.[76] In addition, only *noncitizen* trafficking victims are eligible for refugee-specific programs.[77]

For services authorized under 22 U.S.C. §7105(b)(2), DOJ can use funds to provide services to "victims of trafficking," which appears to include both citizens and noncitizens as well as both adults and minors. Of the money it has received to combat trafficking in persons, DOJ has targeted funds toward the Grants for Victim Services. These grants are used to provide emergency services to victims as soon as they have been identified, prior to certification by HHS (for more information, see Appendix B). Under the umbrella of this program, DOJ has used some funding to serve domestic minor victims of sex trafficking through a program called Services for Domestic Minor Victims of Human Trafficking.[78] In FY2009, DOJ's Office for Victims of Crime awarded cooperative agreements, each for $800,000, for a period of three years to three organizations that work with domestic minor victims of sex trafficking.[79] Three additional organizations have received DOJ support through other programs for these same purposes.[80] The purposes of the grant are to (1) provide a comprehensive array of timely and high-quality services, including intensive case management and shelter, to victims of sex and labor trafficking who are U.S. citizens or LPRs under the age of 18; (2) develop, enhance, or expand the community response to domestic minor victims of all forms of human trafficking; and (3) produce a final report about the implementation of the project so that OVC may disseminate lessons to the trafficking victims' services field.

While other HHS and DOJ programs authorized under TVPA (and referenced in Table 1) could provide services to minor victims of sex trafficking, it does not appear that these programs have received funding. For instance, the act directs the Secretary of HHS to carry out a grant program for states, tribal governments, local governments, and nonprofit nongovernmental victims' service organizations to establish, develop, expand, and strengthen assistance programs for U.S. citizens or LPRs who are the subject of sex trafficking or severe forms of trafficking in persons that occur, in whole or in part, within the United States.[81] The act further directs the Secretary of HHS to establish a pilot program to establish residential treatment facilities in the United States for juveniles subjected to trafficking within the United States.[82] The William Wilberforce Trafficking Victims Protection Reauthorization Act of 2008 (P.L. 110-457) reauthorized the two programs through FY2011.[83] In addition, the act also created a new grant program to be administered jointly by the Secretary of HHS and the Attorney General to provide services to U.S. citizen victims of severe forms of trafficking.[84] These programs, however, have not received appropriations. Other programs, outside of the TVPA, that may provide assistance to minor victims of sex trafficking (but are not directed to do so in authorizing statute or elsewhere) in the United States are discussed in Appendix C.

SELECTED ISSUES

Funding and Authority to Assist U.S. Citizen and LPR Victims of Trafficking

One overriding issue concerning minor victims of sex trafficking is the extent to which federal agencies can and do provide services to U.S. citizen and lawful permanent resident (LPR) trafficking victims. Originally, the Victims of Trafficking and Violence Protection Act of 2000 (TVPA, P.L. 106-386) primarily targeted services toward noncitizen victims because they were not eligible for existing federal human service programs for which U.S. citizen and LPR victims may have been eligible. As mentioned, U.S. citizen victims are eligible for certain crime victim benefits and public benefit entitlement programs, though these services are not tailored to trafficking victims. Further, the extent to which U.S. citizen victims rely upon these services is unknown.

There has been disagreement over whether the services and programs authorized by the TVPA are available to all victims, regardless of citizenship status. A recent U.S. Department of Justice (DOJ) report noted that U.S. citizen and foreign national victims of trafficking are treated differently when they are identified, characterized, and offered services.[85] In addition, service providers and advocates report that federal legislation on commercial sexual exploitation often focuses on foreign victims; as a result, providers often have difficultly securing social services for U.S. citizen victims.[86] Contributing to this concern may be the limited response provided by agencies such as child protective services (CPS) that many may assume would be able to serve these U.S. victims—discussed in detail below.

In response to perceived inequities between services provided to U.S. citizen and noncitizen trafficking victims,[87] the Trafficking Victims Protection Reauthorization Act of 2005 (P.L. 109- 164) enacted policies to assist U.S. citizen and LPR victims.[88] In the conference report to accompany the law, Congress highlighted concerns with the commercial sexual exploitation of U.S. and LPR children in particular:

> The United States not only faces an influx of international victims of sex and labor trafficking, but also has a problem of internal trafficking (also referred to as domestic trafficking), particularly of minors, for the purpose of commercial sexual exploitation. In consultation with the committees of jurisdiction over domestic programs, the Committee amended Title II of the bill, which addresses trafficking in persons that occurs within the borders of the United States and victimizes United States citizens or permanent residents.... Among youth living on the streets in the United States, involvement in commercial sex activity is a problem of epidemic proportion.... The Committee is concerned about U.S. persons who become subjects of trafficking for commercial sexual exploitation and encourages the law enforcement community at the State and local levels to focus efforts on prosecuting individuals who exploit others through prostitution and trafficking. New strategies and attention are needed to prevent the victimization of U.S. persons through domestic trafficking.[89]

As mentioned, P.L. 109-164 authorized two programs specifically to provide services to minor victims, one of which targets U.S. citizen and LPR trafficking victims. Despite explicit language in the TVPA, as amended, regarding assistance to U.S. citizen and LPR victims, appropriations language has been unclear as to whether funds are available for this purpose. Each year since FY2008, Congress has appropriated between $9.4 million and $12.5 million to DOJ for programs for victims of trafficking and between $9.8 million and $10.0 million to the Department of Health and Human Services (HHS) to "carry out the Trafficking Victims Protection Act of 2000." DOJ funds have been used by the Office for Victims of Crime (OVC) to provide services to noncitizens before they are certified and, beginning in FY2009, to carry out the Services for Domestic Minor Victims of Human Trafficking program.[90] Funds have also been used to support the Anti-Human Trafficking Task Forces. HHS funds have been used by the Office of Refugee Resettlement (ORR) to provide certification and victim services and to carry out a public awareness campaign about trafficking.[91] ORR has said that services are not provided for U.S. citizens and LPRs because it believes that Congress has not provided funding specifically for this purpose. In fact, HHS funding to combat trafficking has remained stable at approximately $10 million since FY2002: appropriated funding did not increase after Congress authorized additional programs for minor victims of sex trafficking, including U.S. citizens and LPRs.

Further, the *FY2009 Attorney General's Annual Report to Congress on U.S. Government Activities to Combat Trafficking in Persons* states, "the funds provided under the TVPA by the federal government for direct services to victims are dedicated to assist non-U.S. citizen victims and may not currently be used to assist U.S. citizen victims."[92] However, it appears likely that the funding may be available for benefits and programs for U.S. citizens and LPRs, given that the TVPA authorizes services for these victims. In fact, DOJ began funding a three-year grant in FY2009, Services for Domestic Minor Victims of Human Trafficking,[93] for U.S. citizen and LPR victims.[94] According to DOJ, this grant is authorized under 22 U.S.C. §7105(b)(2)(A), which was included in the TVPA as enacted in 2000. The authorizing language of this grant program does not appear to differentiate between U.S. citizen and noncitizen victims:

> IN GENERAL.—Subject to the availability of appropriations, the Attorney General may make grants to States, Indian tribes, units of local government, and nonprofit, nongovernmental victims' service organizations to develop, expand, or strengthen victim service programs for victims of trafficking.[95]

Authorized funding for this grant appears to be inconsistent with the statement in the FY2008 Attorney General's report that the funds appropriated under the TVPA can only be used for noncitizen victims. Due to the apparent confusion over the authority and funding available to provide services to U.S. citizen trafficking victims, Congress may choose to clarify the authorities to provide services to these victims under the TVPA.

Resources for Trafficking Victims' Services

A corollary issue is the overall breadth of funding for victims' services. It has been estimated that there are approximately 14,000 noncitizens trafficked into the United States each year.[96] And this estimate does not include U.S. citizen and LPR victims. In addition, it is estimated that the number of child victims of sex trafficking in the United States could be in the hundreds of thousands. As the focus on sex trafficking has broadened to include victims of child prostitution, funding has increasingly become an issue. In FY2011, Congress appropriated to HHS and DOJ approximately $22.3 million for services to trafficking victims. For information on current authorizations and appropriations for trafficking victims' services through HHS and DOJ, see Table 1.

This raises several questions. For one, are the resources for trafficking victims, both citizen and noncitizens, adequate? The State Department's 2010 Trafficking in Persons Report recommends that the U.S. government "increase funding for victims services," among other things, to more effectively combat trafficking in persons.[97] If funds were allocated based on estimated citizen populations and noncitizen populations, would certain victims have more difficulty obtaining services? To what extent are the needs of U.S. citizen and noncitizen victims similar, and to what extent do they differ? As mentioned U.S. citizen and LPRs are more likely to be victims of sex trafficking and noncitizens are more likely to be victims of labor trafficking. As such, should funding for victims of trafficking generally be targeted to serve specific populations based on immigration status, or should it be targeted to providing specialized services for victims of a particular form of trafficking (sex or labor trafficking) without regard to immigration status?

Lack of Adequate Shelter and Services

At a 2010 hearing before the Senate Committee on the Judiciary, Subcommittee on Human Rights and the Law, a social service provider for sex-trafficked youth stated that 12 organizations throughout the country specialize in providing services for minor victims of sex trafficking, and collectively they have fewer than 50 beds for victims.[98] In its 2009 report on domestic child sex trafficking, Shared Hope International identified five residential facilities nationwide that provide protective shelter, defined as a facility with the ability to separate a victim from a pimp/trafficker and provide the victim with a restorative home.[99] According to the report, the facilities are able to provide youth protection because they often are isolated from major transportation centers and common trafficking/pimping areas. They also have a high ratio of staff to minors that can help keep youth from being re-trafficked and/or from running away. Such facilities also have security systems, including outdoor and indoor cameras that can hinder outsiders from entering and can discourage youth from running away.

As part of HHS's work on sex trafficking of minors within the United States, contracted researchers have identified—based on discussions with shelter providers, law enforcement officials, case workers, and directors and staff of four residential facilities that serve minor victims of domestic sex trafficking—promising elements for residential facilities for victims:

- Residential facilities should be designed to serve homogenous populations of trafficking victims. Victims may benefit from smaller, more intimate settings so they can develop relationships more easily with staff and other victims.
- Facilities must be secure in order to establish physical and emotional safety, and should include an undisclosed location, security cameras and alarm systems, 24- hour staffing and presence of security guards, unannounced room searchers and drug screens, and limited phone use.
- Services must be available to trafficking victims, including basic needs such as clothing, food, and shelter; intensive case management; mental health counseling and treatment; medical screenings and routine care; life skills and job training programs; youth development programming; educational programming; and services to assist youth in reunifying with their families or other appropriate support persons, as appropriate.[100]

Other facilities, such as runaway and homeless youth shelters, child welfare group homes, and other foster care settings, do not appear to be able to adequately meet the needs of youth or keep them from pimps/traffickers and other abusers.[101] In addition, these settings are often not equipped to provide intensive services for victims or recognize the trauma they have experienced. Runaway shelters often have time restrictions on the length of stay imposed by funding sources, which, given their unique needs, makes serving victims of sex trafficking difficult. Runaway shelter providers and other providers may not recognize the signs of sex trafficking or that trafficking is a crime. Even if they do, youth may choose to leave, given that shelter providers are required to report suspected abuse and neglect, including sexual exploitation.[102] In one HHS study, contractors with the department found that HHS-funded Runaway and Homeless Youth (RHY) providers tended to report that they served no sex trafficking victims, citizen or noncitizen, and often equated trafficking victims with being foreign born.[103]

Congress may wish to consider explicitly designating trafficking or alternate funds for victims' services, or amending current law to further specify that funds under the existing (and unfunded) pilot program for residential facilities are available for these victims.[104] Historical examples appear to exist in which individuals were specifically classified as victims in order to receive shelter and other services. For example, before the Violence Against Women Act (VAWA) was enacted, law enforcement officials generally did not know how to adequately respond to victims of domestic violence and often did not protect victims from their abusers. With VAWA, law enforcement officials received training on domestic violence, and the law authorized federal funding for domestic violence shelters. Similarly, prior to the enactment of the Juvenile Justice and Delinquency Prevention Act (JJDPA), runaways were generally processed through the juvenile justice system instead of being referred for social services to address the reasons they ran away and to provide needed services.

Efforts are underway at the state level to provide unique responses to victims of sex trafficking, particularly prostitution. These responses seek to extend greater social service support to youth victims, in combination with assistance from other stakeholders, including law enforcement. At least one state, New York, has passed a law that would provide certain protections for child victims of prostitution. New York's Safe Harbor for Exploited Children Act requires that children under age 18 who engage in prostitution be considered *victims* of sexual exploitation.[105] This presumption permits the child to avoid criminal charges of prostitution and instead be considered a person in need of supervision by the state. The statute also provides support and services to sexually exploited youth. These services include safe houses, crisis intervention programs, community-based programs, and law enforcement training to help officers identify sexually exploited youth.[106]

Limited Response by Child Protective Services (CPS)

Child victims of trafficking may come to the attention of child protective services (CPS). However, as discussed above, CPS may not be able to adequately respond to the needs of sex trafficking victims. Research of CPS workers in a small number of cities found that these workers are not familiar with human trafficking terms and laws or how to handle cases involving trafficking of children.[107]

Reports of abuse and neglect can be screened in and referred for investigation by CPS only if they concern actions that meet the state statutory definition of abuse and neglect. States that receive state grant funds under the Child Abuse Prevention and Treatment Act (CAPTA) must define "child abuse and neglect" to be consistent with this federal definition of abuse and neglect under CAPTA: "at a minimum, any recent act or failure to act on the part of a parent or caretaker, which results in death, serious physical or emotional harm, sexual abuse or exploitation, or an act or failure to act which presents an imminent risk of serious harm."[108] The law also expands on the term "sexual abuse," which refers to "the employment, use, persuasion, inducement, enticement, or coercion of any child to engage in, or assist any other person to engage in, any sexually explicit conduct or simulation of such conduct for the purpose of producing a visual depiction of such conduct; or the rape, and in cases of caretaker or inter-familial relationships, statutory rape, molestation, prostitution, or other forms of sexual exploitation of children, or incest with children."[109] The law does not, however, define "parent" or "caretaker."

While some states refer to sexual abuse in general terms, others refer to more specific types of abuse, including sexual exploitation.[110] Forms of sexual exploitation include the production of child pornography or allowing a child to engage in prostitution. Several states also define persons who can be reported to CPS as perpetrators. These are individuals who have a relationship with or regular responsibility for the child and generally include parents, guardians, foster parents, relatives, or other caregivers responsible for the child's welfare. It appears that in some cases, this could mean an adult over the age of 18 who is living with the child, but it is unclear whether a pimp/trafficker could be included in this definition.

Despite challenges with involving CPS in these types of cases, some states have recently taken steps to track commercial sexual exploitation and/or prostitution cases under the broader category of sexual abuse.[111] Further, some states and localities have begun to provide specialized foster care services for victims of sex trafficking. For example, in August 2010 the Illinois Safe Children Act was enacted, which makes all children (under the age of 18) in Illinois immune from prosecution for prostitution, under any circumstances, and requires these children to be considered "abused" for purposes of being screened in by the state child welfare agency. In Georgia, the Governor's Office for Children and Families provides case management, referrals, and funding for all children identified as victims of commercial sexual exploitation.[112] Leveraging funds from private organizations, the office also helps to place children in residential facilities that are equipped to address sex trafficking. In addition, the office provides training to law enforcement officials and others (e.g., mental health providers) about sex trafficking of children.

One policy response could be to encourage or require state child welfare agencies to screen in reports of commercial sex trafficking, including child prostitution, as a form of sexual abuse, regardless of whether this abuse is perpetrated or facilitated by a parent or guardian. This would enable states to track cases involving commercial sex trafficking. States could additionally be required to have in place policies to respond to children who are victims of child prostitution, including while they are in care. The federal government could compel states to make these changes through amendments to federal child welfare programs (under Titles IV-B and IV-E of the Social Security Act or CAPTA), which provide funding for state child welfare programs.

Requiring state child welfare agencies to respond to child victims of commercial sexual exploitation would raise questions about how to fund this response and how best to prepare child welfare workers to meet the needs of these children. Federal law does not appear to prohibit the use of federal foster care dollars for specialized services for victims of commercial sexual exploitation who have contact with CPS, including foster care placements. However, Congress may consider clarifying that foster care funding could be used specifically for this purpose. Alternatively, Congress could provide funding through other sources that may not restrict services to a specific population, such as select programs under Title IV-B of the Social Security Act (notably, the Title IV-E federal foster care program is available only for children who meet certain family income and other criteria). Regardless of whether the federal government provides additional funding, states may face challenges in collecting data on victims of commercial sexual exploitation who are under the control of a pimp/trafficker. States could also have difficulties in placing children in specialized foster or group homes, given that few facilities exist for victims generally.

Further, given the lack of awareness in the child welfare field about trafficking, the federal government could compel or require states to provide training to CPS workers on this topic. Loyola University Chicago's Center for the Human Rights for Children and the International Organization for Adolescents issued a publication in 2011 that provides guidance to the Illinois Department of Children and Family Services, the state child welfare agency, on trafficking. Specifically, the publication seeks to increase identification of trafficking cases overall; ensure that victims receive full access to protections and services, including foster care, public benefits, assistance in the criminal justice system, and restitution; and prevent further child trafficking.[113]

The publication provides guidance on procedures for identifying and investigating cases of trafficking, providing case management, addressing criminal justice procedures and issues, and referring children to other resources.

Trafficking Victims Treated as Criminals or Delinquents

Through the Trafficking Victims Protection Act of 2000, Congress legislated, essentially, that juveniles who are involved in commercial sexual crimes are to be considered the *victims* of these crimes.[114] However, researchers have cited disparities in the ways that exploited children are labeled at the state and local levels. It has been suggested that victims of child sexual exploitation—even though these children are too young to consent to sexual activity with adults—may at times be labeled as child prostitutes or juvenile delinquents and treated as criminals rather than being labeled and treated as victims. These children who are arrested may then be placed in juvenile detention facilities with juveniles who have committed serious crimes instead of in environments where they can receive needed social and protective services.[115] As Shared Hope International observes, "while this sometimes is viewed as the only option available to arresting officers, it is a practice that pulls the victim deeper into the juvenile justice system, re-victimizes [the young person], and hinders access to service."[116] Like runaway and homeless youth shelters, juvenile detention facilities provide treatment and services (in this instance, services aligned with a youth's pending charges) that are often unrelated to sex trafficking. Consequently, these services may be ineffective at addressing the deeper issues facing victims.[117]

Further, victims may enter into the juvenile justice system in situations where law enforcement does not know that the juvenile is a trafficking victim as well as in situations where law enforcement *is* aware that the juvenile is a victim. For instance, a law enforcement officer who has not been trained in identifying children as victims of commercial sexual exploitation may mistakenly charge these children with a crime. Children may hide their identities by using fake identification cards to protect the pimp, further reducing the likelihood that the children will be identified as victims or that that the pimp will be prosecuted. On the other hand, an officer who recognizes that an individual is a victim may charge the individual with a crime so as to place the victim into one of the only available safe and secure environments—a detention facility within the juvenile justice system. As mentioned previously, there are few safe facilities for child victims of sex trafficking.

Results from the 2009 study conducted by Shared Hope International suggest that, in nine out of 10 U.S. cities evaluated with respect to prostitution and other forms of commercial sexual exploitation, victims had been placed in juvenile detention centers.[118] There are no comprehensive data, however, that address the number of prostituted or otherwise sexually trafficked juveniles who are treated as offenders. Two studies do provide some insight into this number and how law enforcement agencies process children who are prostituted. One of the only studies that has attempted to gather this data relies on National Incident-Based Reporting System (NIBRS)[119] data from 76 law enforcement agencies in 13 states. Findings from this study, conducted by the Department of Justice, reveal that 229 juveniles were implicated as offenders in prostitution incidents, and arrests were made in about 74% of those cases between 1997 and 2000.[120] Although the percentage of juveniles involved in prostitution who were arrested is lower than the percentage of adult prostitutes arrested (90%),[121] this nonetheless suggests that in the sample examined, juveniles were more likely to be treated as offenders than as victims.

In addition, as part of the National Juvenile Prostitution Study,[122] juveniles were categorized as victims, as delinquents, or as both victims and delinquents based on how they were treated by police. Juveniles were categorized as being treated as victims if (1) only the exploiter was arrested or (2) the juvenile and exploiter were arrested but the charge against the juvenile was not a prostitution-related charge (e.g., disturbing the peace or a drug charge). Juveniles were categorized as being treated as delinquents if they were the only ones arrested or detained. They were categorized as being treated as both victims and delinquents if the exploiter was arrested on a charge specific to a sexual assault against a minor and the juvenile was also arrested on a prostitution-related charge. Based on this classification, 53% of juveniles were classified as victims, 31% as delinquents, and 16% as both victims and delinquents. For the cases where a child was classified as both a victim and delinquent, researchers examined the case summaries more carefully to see whether they could be classified more accurately as victims or as delinquents. In all cases, researchers were prompted to change the status to victim only because either (1) the initial charges were dropped or (2) there was a specific comment from the investigator that the only reason the juvenile was charged was so they could get needed services. Overall, 69% of juveniles were ultimately classified as victims and 31% as delinquents.

The study found a strong and significant association between how the case came to the police's attention and how the juvenile was treated by law enforcement. Cases that began through a police report (i.e., a report by the juvenile, a family member, a social service provider, or others) were almost eight times more likely to result in the juvenile being treated as a victim than those cases that began through action taken by the police (i.e., surveillance or undercover operations). Juveniles were also more likely to be treated as victims if they were younger, female, frightened, or were dirty or had body odor at the time of the initial encounter with police.

Congress provides grants to states for juvenile justice through several avenues such as grants within the Juvenile Justice and Delinquency Prevention Act (JJDPA) and the Juvenile Accountability Block Grant (JABG) program.[123] These grant programs provide funding for an array of purposes including counseling, mentoring, and training programs; community-based programs and services; after school programs; education programs; substance and drug abuse prevention programs; mental health services; gang-involvement prevention programs; and coordinating local service delivery among the different agencies involved, among other purposes. However, none of the purposes directly specify services for victims of trafficking or commercial sexual exploitation. As such, if victims of trafficking continue to be placed into the juvenile justice systems, policy makers may consider whether to expand or specify the list of purpose areas for which states may utilize juvenile justice grant funding.

Several policy options exist to address the issues in labeling victims of trafficking as perpetrators of crimes. For example, Congress may consider whether to provide grant money for the purposes of researching or establishing alternatives to detention for victims of child sex trafficking. A related question that may arise is whether these alternatives should be available for domestic victims and/or international victims, or whether this distinction should be made at all. Another option Congress may consider is whether to provide funding for programs to train law enforcement and social service providers to recognize possible indicators of trafficking and subsequently identify the victims. If Congress decided to appropriate funds for these types of programs, research would be needed to assess the reliability and validity of any trainings utilized.[124]

Reducing Demand for Minor Sex Trafficking in the United States

It is widely agreed upon that any efforts to reduce the prevalence of child sex trafficking—as well as other forms of trafficking—must include efforts to reduce not only the supply, but also the *demand*.[125] Research has identified various factors that contribute to the demand for commercial sex. One such factor contributing to the demand for younger girls is that buyers believe they are less likely to contract a sexually transmitted disease from a younger girl.[126] Another factor influencing the demand for commercial sex is the technology boom; commercial sex is advertised extensively on the Internet, and buyers are connected with victims through cell phones—allowing traffickers to conduct business quickly and anonymously over the phone rather than face-to-face.

Experts have provided recommendations for demand reduction strategies that involve increasing public awareness and prevention as well as bolstering investigations and prosecutions of those buying illegal commercial sex. The federal government has already taken steps to address demand reduction. For example, in FY2009 DOJ's Office of Justice Programs funded a national assessment of sex trafficking reduction efforts. This program plans to assess over 435 national sites that have engaged in some form of demand reduction programs in order to assess their effectiveness and inform future programs.[127]

Policy makers may consider other policy options to reduce the demand for commercial sex with minors. For instance, Congress may consider whether to provide further grant money designated specifically for campaigns to increase public awareness of the issue. Also, some researchers have suggested that increasing the age of consent in all commercial sex activities would be an effective means of reducing the risk of misidentifying a minor as an adult.[128] Congress may debate whether this would also decrease the rate at which johns seek out minors for commercial sex or whether it would only decrease the genuine misidentification of a minor as an adult. Yet another option that Congress may consider is whether strengthening the federal anti-trafficking laws, particularly with respect to the investigation and prosecution of buyers of commercial sex with minors.

As mentioned, one distinction between the prosecution of traffickers and the prosecution of buyers appears to be that traffickers can be prosecuted whether or not a victim is brought across state lines.

On the other hand, federal statutes generally used to prosecute the buyers of commercial sex appear to require that either the buyer crosses state lines or that he entices the victim to cross state lines. Congress may also consider whether encouraging states to strengthen their laws to provide harsher penalties for engaging in commercial sex activities with minors would deter individuals from doing so. Policy makers may also debate whether providing funding to assist states with investigations and prosecutions of these crimes would in turn reduce the prevalence of buyers who are willing to engage in commercial sex with minors.

Data on Victims and Perpetrators

Studies of sex trafficking, including those involving sex trafficking of children in the United States, are scarce. Those studies that do provide insight into the number of victims of child sexual exploitation, such as those conducted by Estes and Weiner and Shared Hope International (see Appendix A), provide estimates based on the number of youth who are at risk of trafficking or were identified as victims in a small number of cities. Given the nature of sex trafficking, estimating the number and characteristics of victims, pimps/traffickers, and johns is difficult. Nonetheless, the TVPA requires that the Department of Justice provide demographic and other information related to sex trafficking in reports to Congress.[129] Specifically, the act requires "review and analysis of sex trafficking and unlawful commercial sex acts in the United States" in two reports. One of the two reports is to address severe forms of trafficking in persons, including the estimated number and demographic characteristics of persons engaged in severe forms of trafficking. The other report is to address sex trafficking, including the number and demographic characteristics of persons engaged in sex trafficking and those who purchase sex acts; the estimated value in dollars of the "commercial sex economy," and the number of investigations, arrests, and incarcerations of persons engaged in sex trafficking, including purchasers of sex trafficking. The TVPA authorizes up to $1.5 million annually for the studies.

APPENDIX A. SELECTED STUDIES MEASURING SEX TRAFFICKING OF CHILDREN

Estes-Weiner Study

Richard J. Estes and Neil Alan Weiner estimated in their 2001 study that more than 244,000 youth in the United States were at risk of becoming victims of prostitution and other forms of trafficking.[130] Importantly, the authors noted that this number did not reflect the *actual* number of child exploitation cases. The study noted that the majority of victims tended to be runaway or thrown-away youth who lived on the streets and became victims of prostitution. Generally, these children came from homes where they had been abused or abandoned and often became involved in prostitution as a way to support themselves.[131]

Estes and Weiner found that approximately 55% of girls living on the streets in the United States engaged in formal prostitution, and of these girls, approximately 75% worked for a pimp/trafficker.[132] The average age at which girls first entered into prostitution was between 12 and 14 years, and the average age of entry into prostitution for boys was between 11 and 13 years. The researchers also estimated that in the United States, approximately 156,200 homeless youth were at risk of commercial sexual exploitation.[133]

National Juvenile Prostitution Study

The National Juvenile Prostitution Study surveyed nearly 2,600 law enforcement agencies regarding individuals involved in juvenile prostitution in 2005. Data were collected on whether agencies arrested or detained—in conjunction with a juvenile prostitution case—(1) youth under age 18 or (2) adults ages 18 and older.[134] In total, the study calculated 1,450 arrests and detentions for crimes related to juvenile prostitution that year, including crimes committed by adults. The study further found that 95% of the law enforcement agencies sampled made no arrests in cases involving juvenile prostitution; in large jurisdictions where researchers assumed such cases would be most likely, 56% of agencies reported no arrests or detentions. Based on these findings, the researchers suggested that, at least in larger communities, police were not doing enough to address the problem of child prostitution in particular.[135]

To gather more information and data on victim characteristics, researchers followed up with law enforcement officials from agencies that had reported arrests or detentions in juvenile prostitution cases. They randomly sampled these agencies and spoke with case investigators for 138 cases. Cases were classified under three categories: third-party exploiters, solo juveniles, and child sexual abuse (CSA) cases with payment. Most of the cases (57%) were classified as third-party exploiters. This category involved pimps or others who profit financially from selling juveniles for sex, and included small-time or less formal operations and well-organized criminal and commercial enterprises, such as massage parlors. The solo juvenile category, which involved 31% of the cases, encompassed juveniles who offered themselves for sexual services (including pornography production), typically to people they did not know, for money or other items of monetary value.[136] This group included juveniles who lacked a stable residence and juveniles living in a home or institution, such as a foster home. Finally, the remaining 12% of youth were engaged in CSA with payment cases, whereby children were sexually abused by family members, acquaintances, and caretakers and who were paid money as inducements to engage in or continue these sexual acts. Researchers found that of the entire sample, nine out of 10 youth were female and more than half (55%) were ages 16 or 17. Most (60%) had a history of running away; in 12% of the cases, officials did not know about the runaway history.

Shared Hope International Study

In 2006, Shared Hope International, a nonprofit organization that seeks to prevent and eradicate sex trafficking, began working with 10 Department of Justice-funded human trafficking task forces[137] to assess the scope of sex trafficking of children. The study defined domestic minor sex trafficking (DMST) as the commercial sexual exploitation of American children within U.S. borders, which includes prostitution, pornography, and/or stripping.[138] While the study used a broad definition of DMST, it focused primarily on the prostitution of children.[139] Researchers requested that the 10 task forces identify the number of minors who qualified as DMST victims.

No further information was provided about how victims were identified, except to say that an accurate count of the number of victims was not available due to many factors, including a lack of protocols to track victims and misidentification of victims. Table A-1 presents the findings from the 10 study sites. Notably, the data collected are not uniform and represent different time periods.

Ohio Trafficking in Persons Study Commission

In 2009, Ohio Attorney General Richard Cordray tasked the Ohio Trafficking in Persons Study Commission to explore the scope of human trafficking within Ohio. Using methodologies developed in other studies—including the Estes and Weiner study discussed above—the Commission estimated that of the American-born youth in Ohio, nearly 3,000 (2,879) were at risk for sex trafficking, or prostitution. Further, 1,078 Ohio youth were estimated to have been victims of sex trafficking over the course of one year.[140] The researchers also estimated that 3,437 foreign-born persons (adults and juveniles) in Ohio were at risk for sex or labor trafficking, of which 783 were estimated to be trafficking victims.[141] Additionally, they estimated that 945 homeless youth in Ohio may be at risk for trafficking.[142] Importantly, the report states, "due to the very nature of human trafficking, it is virtually impossible to determine the exact number of victims in Ohio at any given time and with any degree of certainty."[143]

Table A-1. Number of Suspected Child Sex Trafficking Victims in Selected Locations Shared Hope International Study

Research Site	State/Territory	Number of Suspected DMST[a] Victims	Time Period
Dallas	Texas	150	2007
San Antonio/Bexar County	Texas	3-4	2005-2008
Fort Worth/Tarrant County	Texas	29	2000-2008
Las Vegas	Nevada	5,122	1994-2007
Independence/Kansas City area	Missouri	227	2000-2008
Baton Rouge/New Orleans area	Louisiana	105	2000-2007
Saipan/Rota/Tinian	Northern Mariana	1	2008
Salt Lake City	Utah	83	1996-2008
Buffalo/Erie County	New York	74-84	2000-2008
Clearwater/Tampa Bay area	Florida	36	2000-2008

Source: Linda A. Smith, Samantha Healy Vardaman, and Melissa A. Snow, "The National Report on Domestic Minor Sex Trafficking: America's Prostituted Children," Shared Hope International, May 2009, p. 11.

Notes: Due to a lack of formal tracking protocols, some DMST victims may be duplicated within a city and some may not have been included in the counts. These numbers were obtained through an interview process in addition to official government records.

[a] Domestic Minor Sex Trafficking (DMST)

Prostitution of Juveniles: Patterns from the
National Incident-Based Reporting System (NIBRS)

In 2004, DOJ's Office of Juvenile Justice and Delinquency Prevention published a report examining characteristics of juvenile prostitution incidents that had come to the attention of law enforcement.[144] Data referenced in the report are from the National Incident-Based Reporting System (NIBRS), years 1997–2000. With the caveat that the data included in this study were limited,[145] findings suggest that juvenile prostitution and adult prostitution are distinctive. Compared to adult prostitution, the prostitution of juveniles was more likely to occur indoors, to occur in large cities, and to involve multiple offenders. Within the category of juvenile prostitution, the study also noted differences between boys and girls. Male juvenile prostitutes were often older than female juvenile prostitutes, and they were more likely to operate outdoors. When arresting juveniles for prostitution, law enforcement more often arrested males than females. Researchers also found that police were more likely to characterize juveniles engaged in prostitution as offenders rather than as victims of crime. However, those characterized as victims were more likely to be younger and female.

APPENDIX B. TRAFFICKING VICTIM
SERVICES FOR NONCITIZENS

The TVPA, as amended, is the major federal legislation that authorizes these services, which are provided primarily by the Departments of Justice (DOJ) and Health and Human Services (HHS).

In practice, these services tend to be targeted to *noncitizen victims*.

Department of Justice (DOJ)

Office for Victims of Crime (OVC)

The TVPA of 2000 created a grant program administered by the Attorney General to provide grants to states, Indian tribes, local governments, and nonprofit victims' services organizations to develop, expand, or strengthen victims' service programs for trafficking victims.[146] This grant program, known as the Services for Victims of Human Trafficking Program, is administered through DOJ's Office for Victims of Crime (OVC) and provides emergency services—including temporary housing, medical care, crisis counseling, and legal assistance—to victims as soon as they have been identified, prior to certification by HHS. According to DOJ, OVC awards grants to non-governmental organizations to provide trafficking victims with comprehensive or specialized services and provide training and technical assistance to grantees for program support and enhancement.[147] According to the *Attorney General's Annual Report to Congress on U.S. Government Activities to Combat Trafficking in Persons: Fiscal Year 2009,* one of the goals of this program is to "provide timely, high-quality direct services to pre-certified foreign national victims of severe forms of human trafficking...."[148] This goal would imply that only *noncitizens* are eligible for this grant program. However, since certification is not a requirement to receive services through DOJ,

U.S. citizens, LPRs, and noncitizens may all be eligible for services. In fact, using the same authority provided for the Trafficking Victims Discretionary Grant Program (22 U.S.C §7105(b)(2)(A)), DOJ has funded a grant for child victims of sex trafficking—Services for Domestic Minor Victims of Human Trafficking.[149] Additionally, U.S. citizen and LPR trafficking victims may be eligible for victims' assistance and compensation from OVC through the Crime Victims Fund.[150] This fund provides a direct reimbursement on behalf of a crime for crime-related expenses, including medical costs, mental health counseling, lost wages or loss of support, and funeral or burial costs.

In addition, as of the end of December 2009 OVC had 37 active grants to victims' services organizations working in collaboration with human trafficking task forces to coordinate services on behalf of the victims. These task forces are funded through DOJ's Bureau of Justice Assistance.

Department of Health and Human Services (HHS)

In practice, HHS administers grant programs to nonprofit and other organizations that directly serve *noncitizen* trafficking victims and provides information to the public about trafficking. The grants for victims' services, as well as certain benefits solely for noncitizen victims, are provided by the Office of Refugee Resettlement (ORR) in the Administration of Children and Families. According to ORR, the office does not provide any services to U.S. citizen victims of trafficking even though such services are authorized under TVPA. ORR notes that this is because Congress has not appropriated any money specifically for these services.[151]

Certification

To receive benefits and services through HHS under the TVPA (22 U.S.C. §7105(b)), victims of severe forms of trafficking who are at least 18 years of age must be certified by the Secretary of HHS, after consultation with the Secretary of Homeland Security.[152] Certified victims must be willing to assist in every reasonable way in the investigation and prosecution of severe forms of trafficking. They must have made a bona fide application for a T-visa (that has not been denied). Further, they must have been granted continued presence in the United States in order to effectuate the prosecution of traffickers in persons.[153] ORR provides certification and eligibility letters for victims.

Under the law, noncitizen trafficking victims under the age of 18 do not have to be certified to receive benefits and services, but it is HHS policy to issue eligibility letters to such victims. As discussed in this report, the concept of certification does not apply to U.S. citizen and LPR victims.

Victims' Services through the Office of Refugee Resettlement (ORR)

Once trafficking victims are certified, they may be eligible for certain victims' services through ORR.[154] ORR funds and facilitates a variety of programs to help refugees achieve "economic and social self-sufficiency in their new homes in the United States." These programs are intended to help needy refugees who are ineligible to receive benefits under two federal programs available to U.S. citizens: Temporary Aid for Needy Families (TANF) and Medicaid.[155]

For trafficking victims, ORR also provides grants to organizations that render assistance specific to the needs of these victims, such as temporary housing, independent living skills, cultural orientation, transportation needs, access to appropriate educational programs, and legal assistance and referrals. ORR may also supply trafficking victims with intensive case management programs to help the victim find housing and employment, and provide mental health counseling and specialized foster care programs for children. These services are not currently available to U.S. citizen trafficking victims.

In addition, ORR provides grants to organizations to provide street outreach services to help identify victims of trafficking among populations they already service. In FY2008, these grantees made contact with approximately 1,660 victims or suspected victims: 1,209 U.S. citizens, 373 foreign citizens, and 78 persons whose citizenship could not be determined.[156] ORR piloted a program in which community outreach workers who located a citizen/LPR child or adult victim of sex trafficking were given a letter from ORR stating that the individual may be a victim of human trafficking and might qualify for services as such. Nonetheless, ORR does not provide any services to U.S. citizen or LPR child victims of trafficking.[157]

Rescue and Restore Victims of Human Trafficking Campaign

HHS, through ORR, also conducts outreach to inform victims of available services and to educate the public about trafficking.[158] HHS established the Rescue and Restore Victims of Human Trafficking public awareness campaign, which promotes public awareness about trafficking and the protections available for trafficking victims. The goal of the campaign is to help communities identify and serve victims of trafficking and support them in coming forward to receive services and aid law enforcement. HHS funds three contracts to "intermediary" organizations to foster connections between the Rescue and Restore campaign and local service providers. These intermediaries serve as the focal points for regional public awareness campaign activities and aid in victim identification.

In addition to promoting public awareness about trafficking, HHS, through the Rescue and Restore campaign, has established anti-trafficking coalitions in 25 areas.[159] These coalitions are intended to increase the number of trafficking victims who are identified and assisted. Coalition members include social service providers, local government officials, health care professionals, leaders of faith-based and ethnic organizations, and law enforcement personnel. Along with identifying and assisting victims, coalition members use the Rescue and Restore campaign messages to educate the general public about human trafficking.

Another component of the campaign is the creation of a toll-free National Human Trafficking Resource Center (NHTRC) available for advice and victim-care referrals 24-hours a day.[160] In FY2009, the NHTRC received 7,257 phone calls. These calls included 1,019 tips, of which approximately 300 were referred to law enforcement, and 697 requests for victim-care referrals. It is unknown how many of the calls to NHTRC were related to situations involving child prostitution or other forms of sex trafficking.[161]

APPENDIX C. OTHER POSSIBLE FEDERAL RESPONSES TO SEX TRAFFICKING OF MINORS

Policy makers and researchers have begun viewing commercial child sexual exploitation as a form of human trafficking. Nonetheless, while anti-trafficking statutes are fairly new, having first been enacted in 2000, the issue of commercial child sexual exploitation is not. Thus, there are other laws and programs that attempt to address the issues surrounding the commercial sexual exploitation of children, some of which have been in existence for several decades. While these laws and programs target exploited children, they do not focus exclusively on trafficking victims. This Appendix contains a discussion of selected programs.

Department of Health and Human Services (HHS)

Runaway and Homeless Youth Program[162]

As discussed, runaway youth are particularly at risk of becoming victims of sex trafficking. The Runaway and Homeless Youth (RHY) program, administered by the Family and Youth Services Bureau (FYSB) of HHS, includes three programs to assist runaway and homeless youth. For FY2011, Congress appropriated $115.7 million for the program. Two of the programs—the Basic Center program (BCP) and Transitional Living program (TLP)— provide shelter, counseling, and related services to youth.[163] While the BCP and TLP generally do not specialize in services for runaway and homeless victims of prostitution and other forms of sexual exploitation, a small number of BCP and TLP grantees provide services for these victims. For example, YouthCare, a TLP grantee in Seattle, provides beds and services specifically for runaway and homeless youth who are victims of commercial sexual exploitation.[164]

The third RHY program, the Street Outreach program (SOP), provides street-based outreach and education, including treatment, counseling, provision of information, and referrals for runaway, homeless, and street youth who have been subjected to or are at risk of being subjected to sexual abuse and exploitation. Trained workers, some of whom are employed by BCPs and TLPs (and other runaway and homeless youth shelters that are not federally funded), visit youth on the street to provide these services and referrals.[165]

The RHY program also funds the National Runaway Switchboard (NRS), which serves as the national communication system for runaway and homeless youth. The NRS mission is to keep runaway and at-risk youth safe and off the streets. NRS operates a 24-hour hotline to provide crisis intervention, referrals to community resources, and family reunification. NRS staff are trained on issues involving child sexual exploitation and provide training to RHY and other grantees about the forms of sexual exploitation among runaway and homeless youth.[166]

Office of Refugee Resettlement (ORR) and Family and Youth Services Bureau (FYSB) Coordination

In 2008, staff from the Family and Youth Services Bureau and Office of Refugee Resettlement provided training to five RHY grantee sites.[167] The grantees were funded under the BCP, TLP, and/or SOP. According to HHS, the training familiarized ORR staff with the work of FYSB grantees. Further, the training developed and tested a training module for new ORR and FYSB grantees on ORR procedures in processing or certifying trafficked youth. The training highlighted the differences between domestic and foreign trafficking victims, the different services they can receive, and emerging issues related to providing services to these youth—including the labeling of youth as victims or offenders as well as defining trafficking.

Department of Justice (DOJ)

Missing and Exploited Children's Program[168]

The Missing Children's Assistance Act (P.L. 98-473), as amended, authorizes funding for the Missing and Exploited Children's (MEC) program. The act is the centerpiece of federal efforts to prevent the abduction and sexual exploitation of children, and to recover those children who go missing.[169] Since 1984, the National Center for Missing and Exploited Children (NCMEC) has served as a national resource center and has carried out many of the objectives of the act in collaboration with OJJDP. NCMEC operates the CyberTipline, which allows the public and electronic communication service providers (e.g., search engines and email providers) to report child victims of prostitution, enticement of children for sexual acts, child sexual molestation occurring outside the family, child pornography, and sex tourism involving children. NCMEC analysts from the Exploited Children's Unit send verified reports to the appropriate Internet Crimes Against Children Task Forces (see discussion elsewhere in this report) or, when appropriate, the local police agencies. The CyberTipline also accepts reports of misleading domain names and unsolicited materials sent to children, which are then referred to the Child Exploitation and Obscenities Section (CEOS) of DOJ. Federal law enforcement agents and analysts co-located at NCMEC prepare and serve subpoenas based on leads from the CyberTipline, and reported leads are referred to field offices.[170] The FBI uses CyberTipline reports to gain leads for their Innocence Lost Project on domestic child trafficking. Between March 1998 (when the CyberTipline began) and December 2010, nearly one million (995,493) reports were received, of which 9,343 (0.9%) were for child prostitution.[171] The majority of reports were for child pornography.

The MEC program also supports the Internet Crimes Against Children (ICAC) Task Force program to assist state and local law enforcement cyber units in investigating possible incidents of online child sexual exploitation (discussed above). The MEC also provides technical assistance for the AMBER Alert system, which coordinates state efforts to broadcast bulletins in the most serious child abduction cases. In some years, the MEC program supports, or has supported, additional activities. For example, in FY2009 the program funded grants for researching and combating child sexual exploitation and promoting child safety in general.

In addition to funding its major components (the National Center for Missing and Exploited Children, the ICAC Task Force Program, etc.), the Missing and Exploited Children's program provides funding for smaller grant programs, some of which have targeted victims of commercial sexual exploitation. According to the funding announcement for the grants, commercial sexual exploitation describes a range of crimes of a sexual nature committed against victims younger than age 18, primarily or entirely for financial or other economic reasons, including trafficking for sexual purposes, prostitution, sex tourism, mail-order bride trades and early marriage, pornography, stripping, and performances in sexual venues such as peep shows or clubs.[172]

In FY2009, DOJ allocated funding for two competitive grant programs that address commercial sexual exploitation. One of the grants provided funding to three communities to assist in developing policies and procedures for identifying victims of commercial sexual exploitation.[173] Another grant, Research on the Commercial Sexual Exploitation of Children, is used to support research on the scope and consequence of the commercial sexual exploitation of children and youth.[174] For FY2011, the MEC program is providing funding through a grant, the Technical Assistance Program to Address Commercial Sexual Exploitation/Domestic Minor Sex Trafficking. The program will fund a grantee to provide training and technical assistance to OJJDP grantee organizations and other entities to implement or enhance efforts to identify youth at risk of commercial sexual exploitation (defined above) and domestic minor sex trafficking (not defined); develop or enhance mentoring service models for youth at risk; provide an array of services for youth victims; and develop and deliver prevention programming in a variety of community settings.

End Notes

[1] For more information about trafficking generally, see U.S. Department of State, *Trafficking in Persons Report*, June 2010. See also CRS Report RL34317, *Trafficking in Persons: U.S. Policy and Issues for Congress*, by Alison Siskin and Liana Sun Wyler.

[2] See, for example, Ala. Code §13A-6-152; Ala. Code §13A-6-151(7); Alaska Stat. §§11-41-360 to 11-41-370; Ariz. Rev. Stat. Ann. §13-1307; Ark. Code Ann. §5-11-108; and Cal. Penal Code §§236.1 to 237.

[3] In the 112th Congress, legislation on sex trafficking of minors in the United States (e.g., S. 596) has been introduced. Also, the Senate held a March 16, 2011, briefing on "Domestic Minor Sex Trafficking." In the 111th Congress, policy makers convened briefings and hearings on the topic, including a December 14, 2009, Senate briefing and panel, "Understanding Domestic Minor Sex Trafficking Issues"; a February 16, 2010, House Human Trafficking Caucus briefing, "Child Sex Trafficking in America"; a February 24, 2010, hearing, "Child Prostitution and Sex Trafficking," for the Senate Judiciary Committee, Subcommittee on Human Rights and the Law; and a September 15, 2010, hearing, "Domestic Minor Sex Trafficking," for the House Judiciary Committee, Subcommittee on Crime, Terrorism, and Homeland Security. In addition, two bills (H.R. 5575 and S. 2925) were introduced to address the topic.

[4] P.L. 106-386. This act is also called the Trafficking Victims Protection Act. The TVPA is codified under 22 U.S.C. §7101 et seq., 42 U.S.C. §14044 et seq., and 18 U.S.C. §1591 et seq. (the criminal statute pertaining to sex trafficking of children). Of note, sex trafficking may encompass a range of activities including prostitution, pornography, and stripping. However, for purposes of this report, sex trafficking is discussed primarily in terms of prostitution. Further, federal agencies have recently discussed sex trafficking in the context of the prostitution of children. For instance, see U.S. Department of Justice, *The National Strategy for Child Exploitation Prevention and Interdiction: A Report to Congress*, August 2010, pp. 34-35, http://www.justice.gov/ag/annualreports/tr2009/agreporthumantrafficking2009.pdf. (Hereinafter, U.S. Department of Justice, *The National Strategy for Child Exploitation Prevention and Interdiction*.)

[5] The law provides that in prosecutions involving a child victim, the government is not required to prove that the defendant knew that the person was under the age of 18. See 18 U.S.C. §1591(c).

[6] U.S. Department of Justice, Child Exploitation and Obscenity Section, *Child Prostitution: Domestic Sex Trafficking of Minors*, http://www.justice.gov/criminal/ceos/prostitution.html.

[7] U.S. Department of State, *Trafficking Persons Report*, 10th Edition, June 2010, http://www.state.gov/documents/organization/142979.pdf.Conversely, noncitizens are more likely to be victims of labor trafficking.

[8] Duren Banks and Tracey Kyckelhahn, *Characteristics of Suspected Human Trafficking Incidents, 2008-2010*, Department of Justice, Office of Justice Programs, Bureau of Justice Statistics Special Report, Washington, DC, April 2011, http://bjs.ojp.usdoj.gov/content/pub/pdf/cshti0810.pdf. Subject to appropriations, the Trafficking Victims Protection Reauthorization Act of 2005 (P.L. 109-164 §201) required the Attorney

General to use available data to perform a comprehensive analysis of the incidence of sex trafficking and unlawful commercial sex acts within the United States. In response to this requirement, DOJ funded the creation of the HTRS.

[9] U.S. Department of Justice, *The National Strategy for Child Exploitation Prevention and Interdiction*, pp. 32-33, http://www.justice.gov/ag/annualreports/tr2009/agreporthumantrafficking2009.pdf. For the purposes of this report, the terms "pimp" and "trafficker" are used interchangeably when referring to the sex trafficking of minors.

[10] Richard J. Estes and Neil Alan Weiner, *Commercial Sexual Exploitation of Children in the U.S., Canada and Mexico*, University of Pennsylvania, Philadelphia, PA, September 19, 2001 (revised February 20, 2002), p. 16. (Hereinafter, Estes and Weiner, *Commercial Sexual Exploitation of Children in the U.S., Canada and Mexico*.) Still, boys appear to be just as likely to be victims of sex trafficking, even if they are not under the control of a pimp. See Taya Moxley-Goldsmith, "Boys in the Basement: Male Victims of Commercial Sexual Exploitation," *Update*, vol. 2, no. 1, U.S. District Attorneys Association, American Prosecutors Research Institute, 2005. Traffickers may be part of a criminal network or ring or they may operate independently. They can be strangers, acquaintances, or family members.

[11] U.S. Department of Justice, *The National Strategy for Child Exploitation Prevention and Interdiction*. See also Shared Hope International, *DEMAND. A Comparative Examination of Sex Tourism and Trafficking in Jamaica, Japan, the Netherlands, and the United States*, Arlington, VA, July 2007. (Hereinafter, Shared Hope International, *DEMAND. A Comparative Examination of Sex Tourism and Trafficking in Jamaica, Japan, the Netherlands, and the United States*.) Note: The Shared Hope report was supported by a grant from the Department of State, Office to Monitor and Combat Trafficking in Persons. Shared Hope is a nonprofit advocacy and policy organization founded by former Congresswoman Linda Smith.

[12] A "thrown-away" child is a child who is asked or told to leave home by a parent or other adult in a household, no adequate alternative care is arranged for the child, and the child is out of the household overnight; or a child who has run away and is prevented from returning home. Heather Hammer, David Finkelhor, and Andrea J. Sedlak, "Runaway/Thrownaway Children: National Estimates and Characteristics," U.S. Department of Justice, Office of Juvenile Justice and Delinquency Prevention, OJJDP NISMART Bulletin, October 2002, http://www.missingkids.com/ en_US/documents/nismart2_runaway.pdf.

[13] Estes and Weiner, *Commercial Sexual Exploitation of Children in the U.S., Canada and Mexico*, p. 1.

[14] Polaris Project, *Why Trafficking Exists*, http://www.polarisproject.org/human-trafficking/ overview/why-trafficking-exists. The Polaris Project is a nonprofit organization that works on human trafficking issues. See also Shared Hope International, *DEMAND. A Comparative Examination of Sex Tourism and Trafficking in Jamaica, Japan, the Netherlands, and the United States*.

[15] Ibid. See also Iris Yen, "Of Vice and Men: A New Approach to Eradicating Sex Trafficking by Reducing Male Demand Through Educational Programs and Abolitionist Legislation," *Journal of Criminal Law and Criminology*, vol. 98, no. 2 (Winter 2008).

[16] For more information on the history of the TVPA, see CRS Report RL34317, *Trafficking in Persons: U.S. Policy and Issues for Congress*, by Alison Siskin and Liana Sun Wyler. Services authorized by the TVPA are available to victims of both labor and sex trafficking.

[17] H.Rept. 106-487 to accompany H.R. 3244 outlined these services as necessary for the "safe reintegration of domestic trafficking victims into the larger society."

[18] U.S. Department of Justice, *Attorney General's Annual Report to Congress on U.S. Government Activities to Combat Trafficking in Persons: Fiscal Year 2009*, p. 17, http://www.justice.gov/ag/annualreports/ tr2009/agreporthumantrafficking2009.pdf.

[19] It appears that one program, DOJ Grants for Victim Services, has used funding specifically to serve U.S. citizen and LPR victims. See Appendix B for further information about services for noncitizen victims. See also CRS Report RL34317, *Trafficking in Persons: U.S. Policy and Issues for Congress*, by Alison Siskin and Liana Sun Wyler. Other federal programs provide services to certain vulnerable populations such as children who have run away and/or are sexually exploited. These programs, described in Appendix C, do not target minor victims of sex trafficking per se but serve a broad population.

[20] For funding information, see CRS Report RL34317, *Trafficking in Persons: U.S. Policy and Issues for Congress*, by Alison Siskin and Liana Sun Wyler.

[21] U.S. Congress, Senate Committee on the Judiciary, Subcommittee on Human Rights and the Law, *Child Prostitution and Sex Trafficking*, testimony of Rachel Lloyd, Executive Director and Founder of Girls Educational & Mentoring Services (GEMS), 111th Cong., 2nd sess., February 24, 2010.

[22] Heather J. Clawson and Lisa Goldblatt Grace, *Finding a Path to Recovery: Residential Facilities for Minor Victims of Domestic Sex Trafficking*, U.S. Department of Health and Human Services, Office of the Assistant Secretary for Planning and Evaluation, September 2007, http://aspe.hhs.gov/hsp/07/humantrafficking/ResFac/ib.htm. (Hereinafter, Clawson and Grace, *Finding a Path to Recovery: Residential Facilities for Minor Victims of Domestic Sex Trafficking*.)

[23] Loyola University Chicago, Center for the Human Rights of Children and the International Organization for Adolescents (IOFA), *Building Child Welfare Response to Child Trafficking*, 2011, http://www.luc.edu/chrc/pdfs/BCWR_Handbook_Final1_forjosting_1.pdf (hereinafter, Loyola University Chicago, Center for the Human Rights of Children and the International Organization for Adolescents (IOFA), *Building Child Welfare Response to Child Trafficking*).

[24] Clawson and Grace, *Finding a Path to Recovery: Residential Facilities for Minor Victims of Domestic Sex Trafficking*.

[25] Sec. 103(8) of Div. A of P.L. 106-386, Victims of Trafficking and Violence Protection Act of 2000; approved October 28, 2000; 22 U.S.C. §7102. The remainder of the definition section relates to labor trafficking.

[26] Examples include money, drugs, shelter, and food. P.L. 106-386, §103(3); 22 U.S.C. §7102. The money or item of value given for the sex act does not need to be received by the child (i.e., can be received by a pimp/trafficker).

[27] Child pornography for profit and stripping also fall under the definition of severe forms of trafficking.

[28] Smith, Vardaman, and Snow, "The National Report on Domestic Minor Sex Trafficking: America's Prostituted Children," p. iv.

[29] The U.S. Department of State *Trafficking in Persons Report* (June 2010) states that "[d]espite the mandates of the 2005 and 2008 amendments to the TVPA, uniform data collection for trafficking crimes or number of victims among federal, state and local law enforcement agencies did not occur...." P.L. 109-164 (§201) requires biennial reporting on human trafficking, using available data from state and local authorities. As previously mentioned, in response to this requirement, DOJ funded the creation of the Human Trafficking Reporting System (HTRS).

[30] Some have argued that the lack of reliable estimates is the result of (1) the hidden nature of the problem, (2) the questionable methodologies of the studies, and (3) the lack of sufficient attention to the issue. Michelle Stransky and David Finkelhor, *How Many Juveniles are Involved in Prostitution in the U.S.?*, Crimes Against Children Research Center, University of New Hampshire, Durham, NH, 2008, http://www.unh.edu/ccrc/prostitution/Juvenile_Prostitution_factsheet.pdf. (Hereinafter, Stansky and Finkelhor, *How Many Juveniles are Involved in Prostitution in the U.S.?*)

[31] Heather Hammer, David Finkelhor, and Andrea J. Sedlak, "Runaway/Thrownaway Children: National Estimates and Characteristics," U.S. Department of Justice, Office of Juvenile Justice and Delinquency Prevention, OJJDP NISMART Bulletin, October 2002, http://www.missingkids.com/en_US/documents/ nismart2_runaway.pdf. These are the most recent survey data available. For purposes of this study, a runaway episode is one that meets any one of the following criteria: a child leaves home without permission and stays away overnight; a child 14 years old or younger (or older and mentally incompetent), who is away from home, chooses not to come home when expected to and stays away overnight; and a child 15 years old or older who is away from home, chooses not to come home, and stays away two nights. Nearly all (99%) of the children returned home, and most (58%) did so within one week.

[32] Jody M. Greene, Susan T. Ennett, and Christopher Ringwalt, "Prevalence and Correlates of Survival Sex Among Runaway and Homeless Youth," *American Journal of Public Health*, vol. 89, no. 9 (September 1999), p. 1406. These youth were ages 12 to 21 and spent at least one night in the previous year in a youth or adult shelter, an improvised shelter, or with a stranger. Youth under age 18 who had spent one night in the past year away from home without the permission of their parents or legal guardians were also sampled.

[33] This includes having been victims of assault or robbery.

[34] Smith, Vardaman, and Snow, *The National Report on Domestic Minor Sex Trafficking: America's Prostituted Children*, p. 34.

[35] Heather J. Clawson and Lisa Goldblatt Grace, *Human Trafficking Into and Within the United States: Review of the Literature*, U.S. Department of Health and Human Services, Office of the Assistant Secretary for Planning and Evaluation, August 2009, http://aspe.hhs.gov/hsp/07/HumanTrafficking/LitRev/index.shtml.

[36] U.S. Department of Health and Human Services, Administration for Children and Families, Administration on Children, Youth, and Families, Commissioner's Office of Research & Evaluation and the Family and Youth Services Bureau, "Sexual Abuse Among Homeless Adolescents: Prevalence, Correlates, and Sequelae," November 2002, http://www.acf.hhs.gov/programs/opre/fys/sex_abuse/ reports/sexabuse_hmless/sex_abuse_

hmless.pdf. (Hereinafter, HHS, "Sexual Abuse Among Homeless Adolescents: Prevalence, Correlates, and Sequelae.")

[37] Smith, Vardaman, and Snow, *The National Report on Domestic Minor Sex Trafficking: America's Prostituted Children*, p. 35.

[38] Ibid.

[39] See Federal Bureau of Investigation press releases regarding domestic minor sex trafficking cases involving individual perpetrators (e.g., http://atlanta.fbi.gov/dojpressrel/pressrel10/ at042110.htm) and perpetrators acting within criminal organizations (e.g., http://newyork.fbi.gov/dojpressrel/pressrel10/nyfo042010.htm). For more information on organized crime in the United States, see CRS Report R41547, *Organized Crime: An Evolving Challenge for U.S. Law Enforcement*, by Jerome P. Bjelopera and Kristin M. Finklea. See also Shared Hope International, *DEMAND: A Comparative Examination of Sex Tourism and Trafficking in Jamaica, Japan, the Netherlands, and the United States*, p. 4.

[40] U.S. Department of Justice, *The National Strategy for Child Exploitation Prevention and Interdiction*, p. 33.

[41] Human Smuggling and Trafficking Center, *Domestic Human Trafficking—An Internal Issue*, December 2008, p. 5, http://www.state.gov/documents/organization/113612.pdf.

[42] Smith, Vardaman, and Snow, *The National Report on Domestic Minor Sex Trafficking: America's Prostituted Children*, p. 17.

[43] Ibid.

[44] See U.S. Congress, *Report to Accompany H.R. 972*, 109th Cong., 1st sess., November 18, 2005, H.Rept. 109-317, p. 11.

[45] P.L. 110-457 was signed into law on December 23, 2008.

[46] William Adams, Colleen Owens, and Kevonne Small, *Effects of Federal Legislation on the Commercial Sexual Exploitation of Children*, U.S. Department of Justice, Office of Justice Programs, Office of Juvenile Justice and Delinquency Prevention, Washington, DC, July 2010, p. 1.

[47] U.S. Department of State, *Trafficking Persons Report*, 10th Edition, June 2010, p. 338, http://www.state.gov/documents/organization/142979.pdf.

[48] See Appendix B for further information about services for noncitizen victims. See also CRS Report RL34317, *Trafficking in Persons: U.S. Policy and Issues for Congress*, by Alison Siskin and Liana Sun Wyler. Other federal programs provide services to certain vulnerable populations such as children who have run away and/or are sexually exploited. These programs, described in Appendix C, do not target youth victims of sex trafficking per se.

[49] This section is based on information in the U.S. Department of State, *Trafficking in Persons Report*, June 2010; U.S. Department of Justice, U.S. Department of Health and Human Services, U.S. Department of State, U.S. Department of Labor, U.S. Department of Homeland Security, and U.S. Agency of International Development, *Assessment of U.S. Government Efforts to Combat Trafficking in Persons*, September 2007; and U.S. Department of Justice, *Attorney General's Annual Report to Congress on U.S. Government Activities to Combat Trafficking in Persons: Fiscal Year 2009*.

[50] U.S. Government Accountability Office (GAO), *Combating Alien Smuggling, Opportunities Exist to Improve the Federal Response*, GAO-05-305, May 2005, p. 10. (Hereinafter cited as GAO, *Combating Alien Smuggling, Opportunities Exist to Improve the Federal Response*.)

[51] U.S. Department of State, *Trafficking in Persons Report*, June 2010.

[52] For example, Ala. Code §13A-6-152 ("(a) A person commits the crime of human trafficking in the first degree if: (1) He or she knowingly subjects another person to ... sexual servitude through use of coercion or deception. (2) He or she knowingly obtains, recruits, entices, solicits, induces, threatens, isolates, harbors, holds, restrains, transports, provides, or maintains any minor for the purpose of causing a minor to engage in sexual servitude.... "); Ala. Code §13A-6-151(7)("Sexual servitude [is] ... any sexual conduct ... for which anything of value is directly or indirectly given, promised to, or received by any person, which conduct is induced or obtained by coercion or deception form a person.... "); see also, Alaska Stat. §§11-41-360 to 11-41-370; Ariz. Rev. Stat. Ann. §13-1307; Ark. Code Ann. §5-11- 108; Cal. Penal Code §§236.1 to 237.

[53] The division of responsibilities between these two agencies is not clearly delineated, which may lead to a lack of coordination between the agencies and possibly to some duplicative efforts. In addition, according to an ICE Office of Investigations (OI) official, the Border Patrol only has a minor role in alien smuggling and trafficking investigations and is required to coordinate with OI before initiating anti-smuggling investigations. U.S. Government Accountability Office, *Immigration Enforcement: DHS, GAO-05-66 Has Incorporated Immigration Enforcement Objectives and Is Addressing Future Planning Requirements (2004)*, p. 9.

[54] The Mann Act is codified at 18 U.S.C. § 2421 et seq. The Mann Act was enacted in 1910 to fight against forced prostitution. As currently written, the Mann Act makes it a felony to knowingly transport "an individual who has not attained the age of 18 years in interstate or foreign commerce, or in any Territory or Possession of the United States, with intent that such individual engage in prostitution, or in any sexual activity for which any person can be charged with a criminal offence." The FBI investigates possible Mann Act violations and refers them to the U.S. Attorneys. CEOS supervises the prosecution of these cases. William Adams, Colleen Owens, and Kevonne Small, *Effects of Federal Legislation on the Commercial Sexual Exploitation of Children*, U.S. Department of Justice, Office of Justice Programs, Office of Juvenile Justice and Delinquency Prevention, Washington, DC, July 2010, p. 3.

[55] RICO is codified at 18 U.S.C. §1961-1968 and is Title IX of the Organized Crime Control Act of 1970 (P.L. 91-452). RICO allows for the prosecution of anyone who participates or conspires to participate in a criminal enterprise/organization through two acts of "racketeering activity" within a 10-year period of time. The predicate offenses for racketeering include various state and federal crimes listed in the U.S. Code. For more information on RICO, see CRS Report 96-950, *RICO: A Brief Sketch*, by Charles Doyle.

[56] U.S. Department of Justice, *The National Strategy for Child Exploitation Prevention and Interdiction*, pp. 33-34.

[57] U.S. Department of Justice, *Attorney General's Annual Report to Congress on U.S. Government Activities to Combat Trafficking in Persons: Fiscal Year 2009*, pp. 41-43. The arrest, indictment, and conviction statistics are in trafficking cases. Not every arrest, indictment, or conviction is for a trafficking charge; rather, they occurred in a case opened based on an allegation of trafficking.

[58] Ibid., p. 42.

[59] Ibid.

[60] These data are current as of November 2010. For more information, see http://www.fbi.gov/about-us/investigate/vc_majorthefts/cac/innocencelost.

[61] U.S. Department of Justice, Civil Rights Division, *Report on the Tenth Anniversary of the Trafficking Victims Protection Act*, October 29, 2010, pp. 9-10, http://www.justice.gov/crt/about/crm/trafficking_news letter/tvpaanniversaryreport.pdf. For more information on the Initiative, see http://www.ojp.usdoj.gov/BJA/grant/httf.html.

[62] The number of investigations and prosecutions among the task forces varies widely. More investigations are for sex trafficking than labor trafficking, which may be a result of law enforcement's ability to rely upon pre-existing vice units devoted to prosecution enforcement. U.S. Department of State, *Trafficking in Persons Report*, June 2010, p. 340.

[63] For more information on the task force program, see CRS Report RL34050, *Missing and Exploited Children: Background, Policies, and Issues*, by Adrienne L. Fernandes-Alcantara.

[64] The program was formally authorized by the PROTECT Our Children Act of 2008 (P.L. 110-401). As outlined in the law, program purpose areas include (1) increasing investigative capabilities of state and local law enforcement officers in the detection, investigation, and apprehension of internet crimes against children offenses or offenders—including technology-facilitated child exploitation offenses; (2) conducting proactive and reactive internet crimes against children investigations; (3) providing training and technical assistance to ICAC task forces and other law enforcement agencies for investigations, forensics, prosecutions, community outreach, and capacity building, using recognized experts to assist in the development and delivery of training programs; (4) increasing investigations and prosecutions of internet crimes against children offenses; and (5) developing and delivering public awareness and prevention programs regarding internet crimes against children, among other purposes.

[65] U.S. Department of State, *Trafficking in Persons Report*, June 2010, p. 58.

[66] Ibid., p. D-7.

[67] U.S. Department of Justice, Office of Justice Programs, Office of Juvenile Justice and Delinquency Prevention, *OJJDP FY2010 ICAC Program – Law Enforcement Strategies for Protecting Children from Commercial Sexual Exploitation*, http://www.ojjdp.gov/grants/solicitations/FY2010/ICACCSEC.pdf; and U.S. Department of Justice, Office of Justice Programs, *Office of Justice Programs Funding Resources*, http://www.ojp.usdoj.gov/fundingfunding.htm.

[68] U.S. Department of Justice, Office of Justice Programs, Office of Juvenile Justice and Delinquency Prevention, *OJJDP FY2011 ICAC Program – Law Enforcement Strategies for Protecting Children from Commercial Sexual Exploitation*, http://www.ojjdp.gov/grants/solicitations/FY2011/LawEnforcement.pdf.

[69] U.S. Department of Justice, *Attorney General's Annual Report to Congress on U.S. Government Activities to Combat Trafficking in Persons: Fiscal Year 2009*, pp. 43-44.

[70] Ibid., p. 46.

[71] U.S. Department of Justice, *The National Strategy for Child Exploitation Prevention and Interdiction: A Report to Congress*, August 2010, pp. 45-46, http://www.justice.gov/ag/annualreports/tr2009/agreporthumantrafficking2009.pdf. See also U.S. Department of Justice, *Attorney General's Annual Report to Congress on U.S. Government Activities to Combat Trafficking in Persons: Fiscal Year 2009.*

[72] These statutes include 22 U.S.C. §7105(b), 22 U.S.C. §7105(f), 42 U.S.C. §14044a, 42 U.S.C. §14044b, 42 U.S.C. §14044c, and 42 U.S.C. §14044f.

[73] For more information on victim certification, see Appendix B. Certification of *adult* victims by HHS appears to be a necessary condition of receiving trafficking victims' services from HHS under 22 U.S.C. §7105(b).

[74] 22 U.S.C. §7105(b)(1)(C). The statute specifies that HHS, Department of Labor (DOL), the Legal Services Corporation (LSC), and other federal agencies are to "expand benefits and services to victims of severe forms of trafficking in persons," defined as individuals who are under the age of 18 and adults who are the subject of certification. For further information on services provided by DOL and LSC, see CRS Report RL34317, *Trafficking in Persons: U.S. Policy and Issues for Congress*, by Alison Siskin and Liana Sun Wyler.

[75] TVPA of 2000 created a new nonimmigrant category, known as T status or T-visa, for aliens who are victims of severe forms of human trafficking. Federal law enforcement officials who encounter victims of severe forms of trafficking and are potential witnesses to that trafficking may request that DHS grant the continued presence of the alien in the United States. Historically, the Attorney General has had the discretionary authority to use a variety of statutory and administrative mechanisms to ensure the alien's continued presence. For more on immigration relief for trafficking victims, see CRS Report RL34317, *Trafficking in Persons: U.S. Policy and Issues for Congress*, by Alison Siskin and Liana Sun Wyler.

[76] Senior Policy Operating Group on Trafficking in Persons: Subcommittee on Domestic Trafficking, *Final Report and Recommendations*, Washington, DC, August 2007, http://www.acf.hhs.gov/trafficking/SPOGReport-Final9-5-07.pdf.

[77] CRS correspondence with the U.S. Department of Health and Human Services, Administration for Children and Families, Congressional Affairs, April 2, 2007.

[78] The grant is authorized under 22 U.S.C. §7105(b)(2)(A), pertaining to grants made by the Attorney General to develop, expand, or strengthen victim service programs for victims of trafficking in the United States.

[79] The three organizations include Safe Horizon, a youth-service provider for runaway and homeless youth and other vulnerable youth in New York; Salvation Army in Chicago, which seeks to combat sex trafficking of children; and Standing Against Global Exploitation (SAGE), a provider of services to minor and adult victims of commercial sexual exploitation in San Francisco. As part of their grant applications, the grantees demonstrated how comprehensive services will be provided to both male and female victims of sex and labor trafficking, and documented how the grantees will work collaboratively with juvenile justice system professionals, child welfare service providers, and other youth-serving organizations to ensure that a comprehensive array of services are provided to victims. U.S. Department of Justice, Office of Justice Programs, Office for Victims of Crime, "Announcing the Awardees from OVC's Services for Domestic Minor Victims," press release, 2009; and U.S. Department of Justice, Office of Justice Programs, Office for Victims of Crime, *OVC FY09 Services for Domestic Minor Victims of Human Trafficking Funding Announcement*, 2009.

[80] See U.S. Department of Justice, Office for Victims of Crime, *Grants & Funding: OVC-Funded Grantee Programs To Help Victims of Trafficking*, http://www.ojp.usdoj.gov/ovc/grants/traffickingmatrix.html.

[81] §202, 42 U.S.C. §14044a. In authorizing this program, Congress emphasized the importance of serving U.S. citizen and LPR victims: "The Committee notes that, as a result of the TVPA, foreign victims of severe forms of trafficking in the United States are legally required to be treated as victims, rather than as criminals. The same should be true for American citizens. Nonetheless, a nongovernmental organization which advocates for exploited children, ECPAT-USA, issued a 2005 report (*Who Is There to Help Us? How the System Fails Sexually Exploited Girls in the United States*), which concluded, in relevant part, that 'the implementation of the TVPA to date, both in terms of services and prosecutions, has assisted girls from abroad while ignoring girls in similar situations from the U.S.'" Ibid., p. 24.

[82] §203, 42 U.S.C. §14044b. In authorizing this program, Congress emphasized the importance of serving U.S. citizen and LPR victims: "The Committee has learned from both governmental and nongovernmental sources who work with trafficked children in the United States that a lack of housing options for such children is a debilitating impediment to providing effective rehabilitative and restorative help to escape commercial sexual exploitation. This section [of the law] responds to that need."

[83] The current authorization levels for each year, FY2008 through FY2011, are $8 million for HHS grants for victims' services for U.S. citizens and LPRs, $5 million for the residential treatment pilot program, and $20 million to DOJ grants for law enforcement.

[84] P.L. 110-457, §213, 22 U.S.C. §7105(f).

[85] William Adams, Colleen Owens, and Kevonne Small, *Effects of Federal Legislation on the Commercial Sexual Exploitation of Children*, Department of Justice, Office of Justice Programs, Office of Juvenile Justice and Delinquency Prevention, Washington, DC, July 2010, p. 4. This information comes from DOJ meetings with commercial child sexual exploitation service providers.

[86] Ibid., p. 7.

[87] See, for example, Sarah Ann Friedman, *Who Is There to Help Us? How the System Fails Sexually Exploited Girls in the United States*, ECPAT-USA, 2005, http://ecpatusa.org/wp-content/uploads/2010/11/Who-Is-There-to-Help-Us.pdf.

[88] The law also sought to encourage prosecutions of trafficking of U.S. citizens and LPRs. P.L. 109-164 directs the Attorney General (as described in Table 2) to make grants to state and local law enforcement agencies to establish, develop, expand, or strengthen programs to investigate and prosecute acts of severe forms of trafficking in persons that involve United States citizens, or LPRs, and that occur in the United States, including investigating and prosecuting persons who engage in the purchase of commercial sex acts. §204, 22 U.S.C. §7105(f).

[89] U.S. Congress, House Committee on International Relations, *Trafficking Victims Protection Act Reauthorization of 2005*, committee print, 105th Cong., November 18, 2005, H.Rept. 109-317, p. 23.

[90] P.L. 112-10, P.L. 111-117, P.L. 111-8, P.L. 110-161. See Appendix B for further information about the pre-certification services.

[91] See Appendix B for further information. ORR also provides services for victims of torture, certain U.S. citizens seeking to repatriate to the U, unaccompanied alien children, and unaccompanied refugee minors. For further information on the programs pertaining to children, see these archived CRS reports: CRS Report RL33896, *Unaccompanied Alien Children: Policies and Issues*; and CRS Report RL34414, *Unaccompanied Refugee Minors*.

[92] U.S. Department of Justice, *Attorney General's Annual Report to Congress on U.S. Government Activities to Combat Trafficking in Persons: Fiscal Year 2009,* p. 17.

[93] DOJ also funded two projects for case management assistance to children found in prostitution, and one training and technical assistance project targeted at 10 youth service organizations assisting children found in prostitution. It is unclear if funding for these grant programs came from appropriations for the TVPA. U.S. Department of State, *Trafficking in Persons Report*, June 2010, p. 342.

[94] The grant is authorized under §22 U.S.C. 7105(b)(2)(A), which pertains to grants made by the Attorney General to develop, expand, or strengthen victim service programs for victims of trafficking in the United States. It is a program that was in the TVPA as enacted in 2000. U.S. Department of Justice, Office of Justice Programs, Office for Victims of Crime, "Announcing the Awardees from OVC's Services for Domestic Minor Victims," press release, 2009.

[95] 22 U.S.C §7105(b)(2)(A).

[96] U.S. Department of Justice, U.S. Department of Health and Human Services, U.S. Department of State, U.S. Department of Labor, U.S. Department of Homeland Security, and U.S. Agency of International Development, *Assessment of U.S. Government Efforts to Combat Trafficking in Persons,* June 2004, p. 4. This is the most recent estimate of noncitizens trafficked into the United States.

[97] U.S. Department of State, *Trafficking Persons Report*, 10th Edition, June 2010, pp. 338-339, http://www.state.gov/documents/organization/142979.pdf.

[98] U.S. Congress, Senate Committee on the Judiciary, Subcommittee on Human Rights and the Law, *Child Prostitution and Sex Trafficking*, testimony of Rachel Lloyd, Executive Director and Founder of Girls Educational & Mentoring Services (GEMS), 111th Cong., 2nd sess., February 24, 2010.

[99] Smith, Vardaman, and Snow, "The National Report on Domestic Minor Sex Trafficking: America's Prostituted Children," p. 67.

[100] Clawson and Grace, *Finding a Path to Recovery: Residential Facilities for Minor Victims of Domestic Sex Trafficking*. At the time of the study in 2007, the researchers identified only four facilities specific to the population across the country: Girls Educational and Mentoring Services (GEMS) Transition to Independent Living (TIL) program in New York; Standing Against Global Exploitation (SAGE) Safe House in San Francisco; Children of the Night in Los Angeles County; and Angela's House in a rural community outside Atlanta.

[101] Clawson and Grace, *Finding a Path to Recovery: Residential Facilities for Minor Victims of Domestic Sex Trafficking*, pp. 2-4, 9.

[102] Heather J. Clawson et al., *Study of HHS Programs Serving Human Trafficking Victims*, U.S. Department of Health and Human Services, Office of the Assistant Secretary for Planning and Evaluation, December 2009, p. iv,

http://aspe.hhs.gov/hsp/07/HumanTrafficking/Final/index.pdf.

[103] Ibid.

[104] This program is authorized at 42 U.S.C. §14044b.

[105] Sections 447-a and 447-b of the New York State Social Services Law.

[106] Legislation has been introduced in the 112th Congress to assist states in providing services to minor victims of sex trafficking in the United States. For instance, S. 596 would authorize the Assistant Attorney General for DOJ's Office of Justice Programs, in consultation with the Assistant Secretary for Children and Families in HHS, to award one-year grants to six eligible entities in different regions of the United States to combat the sex trafficking of children in the United States. Under the bill, some of the grants would be allocated to non-governmental organizations (NGOs) to provide counseling, legal services, shelter, clothing and other social services to minor victims of sex trafficking. Funds could also be used for training for law enforcement; investigative and prosecution expenses; case management; salaries for law enforcement officers and state and local prosecutors; and outreach, education, and treatment programs, all related to cases involving the sex trafficking of children in the United States.

[107] Smith, Vardaman, and Snow, "The National Report on Domestic Minor Sex Trafficking: America's Prostituted Children; " Loyola University Chicago, Center for the Human Rights of Children and the International Organization for Adolescents (IOFA), *Building Child Welfare Response to Child Trafficking*, 2011, http://www.luc.edu/chrc/pdfs/BCWR_Handbook_Final1_forjosting_1.pdf (hereinafter, Loyola University Chicago, Center for the Human Rights of Children and the International Organization for Adolescents (IOFA), *Building Child Welfare Response to Child Trafficking*).

[108] Section 111(2) of CAPTA, 42 U.S.C. §65101 et seq.

[109] Section 111(4) of CAPTA, 42 U.S.C. §5106g. All states receive CAPTA state grants. For further information about CAPTA, see CRS Report R40899, *The Child Abuse Prevention and Treatment Act (CAPTA): Background, Programs, and Funding*, by Emilie Stoltzfus.

[110] For further information about state definitions of abuse and neglect and procedures for screening abuse and neglect, see Child Welfare Information Gateway, *Definitions of Child Abuse and Neglect: Summary of State Laws* (current through July 2009), http://www.childwelfare.gov/systemwide/laws_policies/statutes/define.pdf; and Child Welfare Information Gateway, *Making and Screening Reports of Child Abuse and Neglect: Summary of State Laws* (current through January 2009,

http://www.childwelfare.gov/systemwide/laws_policies/statutes/repproc.pdf.

[111] Smith, Vardaman, and Snow, *The National Report on Domestic Minor Sex Trafficking: America's Prostituted Children*, pp. 72-73.

[112] For further information, see Georgia Governor's Office for Children and Families, Georgia Care Connection Office, http://www.georgiacareconnection.com/Index.html.

[113] Loyola University Chicago, Center for the Human Rights of Children and the International Organization for Adolescents (IOFA), *Building Child Welfare Response to Child Trafficking*, http://www.luc.edu/chrc/pdfs/BCWR_Handbook_Final1_ forjosting_1.pdf.

[114] See remarks by Senator Richard Durbin, Hearing before the U.S. Congress, Senate Committee on the Judiciary, Subcommittee on Human Rights and the Law, *In Our Own Backyard: Child Prostitution and Sex Trafficking in the United States*, 111th Cong., 1st sess., February 24, 2010.

[115] Smith, Vardaman, and Snow, "The National Report on Domestic Minor Sex Trafficking: America's Prostituted Children."

[116] Clawson and Grace, *Finding a Path to Recovery: Residential Facilities for Minor Victims of Domestic Sex Trafficking*.

[117] Ibid., p. 2.

[118] Ibid., p. 54.

[119] NIBRS is part of the FBI's Uniform Crime Reporting (UCR) program. Although both NIBRS and UCR are incident-based reporting systems, NIBRS presents more detailed information about crime incidents than does the UCR. NIBRS does not have as widespread of participation from state and local police, and the FBI has indicated that the data are not sufficiently robust to make broad generalizations about crime in the United States. See the FBI's website at http://www.fbi.gov/ucr/ucr.htm#nibrs. For more information about UCR and

NIBRS, see archived CRS Report RL34309, *How Crime in the United States Is Measured*, by Nathan James and Logan Rishard Council.

[120] David Finkelhor and Richard Ormrod, *Prostitution of Juveniles: Patterns From NIBRS*, U.S. Department of Justice, Office of Justice Programs, Office of Juvenile Justice and Delinquency Prevention, June 2004, p. 5.

[121] Ibid.

[122] Mitchell, Finklehor, and Wolak, "Conceptualizing Juvenile Prostitution as Child Maltreatment: Findings from the National Juvenile Prostitution Study."

[123] The JJDPA was enacted by P.L. 90-415 and was most recently reauthorized by P.L. 107-273. JABG was codified within the Omnibus Crime Control and Safe Streets Act of 1968 (42 U.S.C. 3796ee); as such it resides outside the immediate purview of the JJDPA despite the fact that it is administered by the Office of Juvenile Justice and Delinquency Prevention. For more information on these programs, see CRS Report RL33947, *Juvenile Justice: Legislative History and Current Legislative Issues*, by Kristin M. Finklea.

[124] For instance, according to Shared Hope International, after receiving training on identifiers of domestic minor sex trafficking, one runaway youth shelter in Louisiana identified 57% of the youth in the shelter as trafficking victims. Smith, Vardaman, and Snow, "The National Report on Domestic Minor Sex Trafficking: America's Prostituted Children," p. 50. It is unknown, however, how these results may generalize to other social service and law enforcement agencies that may receive such training.

[125] One grant program under the TVPA (P.L. 109-164, 42 U.S.C. 14044c) includes strengthening demand reduction as one of the allowable activities. This program would assist state and law enforcement to enhance their anti-trafficking efforts, but the program has not been funded.

[126] Shared Hope International, *Demand: A Comparative Examination of Sex Tourism and Trafficking in Jamaica, Japan, the Netherlands, and the United States*, p. 5.

[127] U.S. Department of Justice, *Attorney General's Annual Report to Congress on U.S. Government Activities to Combat Trafficking in Persons: Fiscal Year 2009*, p. 97.

[128] Shared Hope International, *Demand: A Comparative Examination of Sex Tourism and Trafficking in Jamaica, Japan, the Netherlands, and the United States*, p. 148.

[129] 42 U.S.C §14044(a)(1).

[130] The study was revised in 2002. The researchers use the term commercial sexual exploitation. Their definition of commercial sexual exploitation of children includes child pornography, juvenile prostitution, and trafficking in children. Estes and Weiner estimated that 244,000 children in the United States are at risk of becoming victims of sex trafficking, but then reduced the estimate by 25% to minimize duplications in the counts of runaway and thrown-away youth. Estes and Weiner, *Commercial Sexual Exploitation of Children in the U.S., Canada and Mexico*, pp. 10, 144-151. This study has been criticized because, among other issues, the authors lack any evidence on how many of the "at risk" youth actually become involved in prostitution. In addition, some have noted that there is duplication among the counts of "at risk" youth. Michelle Stansky and David Finkelhor, *How Many Juveniles are Involved in Prostitution in the U.S.?*, Crimes Against Children Research Center, University of New Hampshire, 2008, http://www.unh.edu/ccrc/ prostitution/ Juvenile_ Prostitution_factsheet.pdf. (Hereinafter, Stransky and Finkelhor, *How Many Juveniles are Involved in Prostitution in the U.S.?*)

[131] Ibid., pp. 2-4.

[132] Ibid., p. 60.

[133] To calculate this estimate, the researchers used findings from their field research that 30% of shelter youth and 70% of homeless youth are victims of commercial sexual exploitation. This study has been criticized because, among other issues, the authors lack any evidence on how many of the "at risk" youth actually become involved in prostitution. In addition, some have noted that there is duplication among the counts of "at risk" youth. Stransky and Finkelhor, *How Many Juveniles are Involved in Prostitution in the U.S.?*

[134] Kimberly J. Mitchell, David Finklehor, and Janis Wolak, "Conceptualizing Juvenile Prostitution as Child Maltreatment: Findings from the National Juvenile Prostitution Study," *Child Maltreatment*, vol. 15, no. 1 (February 2010), http://www.unh.edu/ccrc/pdf/Mitchell%202010%20conceptualizing.pdf. (Hereinafter, Mitchell, Finklehor, and Wolak, "Conceptualizing Juvenile Prostitution as Child Maltreatment: Findings from the National Juvenile Prostitution Study.")

[135] The fact that many police agencies are not actively arresting juveniles for prostitution means data related to prostitution arrests cannot fully characterize the problem of juvenile prostitution. For a detailed discussion of this argument, see Stansky and Finkelhor, *How Many Juveniles are Involved in Prostitution in the U.S.?*

[136] Although police did not find evidence for a third-party exploiter, some of these youth may have been exploited by a commercial operator.

[137] There are 42 task forces in total. The Department of Justice makes awards to law enforcement agencies to form these victim-centered human trafficking task forces. Department of Justice, *Attorney General's Annual Report to Congress on U.S. Government Activities to Combat Trafficking in Persons: Fiscal Year 2009*, June 2010.

[138] In other words, foreign children are not included in their definition of DMST victims. Smith, Vardaman, and Snow, *The National Report on Domestic Minor Sex Trafficking: America's Prostituted Children*, p. iv.

[139] Ibid., p. 11. Focusing on other aspects of DMST, such as pornography, may increase the number of suspected victims in a given area.

[140] Celia Williamson, Sharvari Karandikar-Chheda, and Jeff Barrows, et al., *Report on the Prevalence of Human Trafficking in Ohio To Attorney General Richard Cordray*, Ohio Trafficking in Persons Study Commission, Research and Analysis Sub-Committee, Toledo, OH, February 10, 2010, http://www.ohioattorneygeneral.gov/ TraffickingReport.

[141] Ibid., p. 5. The researchers identified four factors that may increase a child's risk of becoming a victim of sex trafficking in the United States: (1) Ohio's weak response to trafficking victims; (2) evidence that first responders to sex trafficking incidents in Ohio are unaware and unprepared; (3) customers who purchase services from youth receive minimal charges and are rarely prosecuted, and traffickers suffer minimal consequences; and (4) the high rates of vulnerable youth in Ohio.

[142] Ibid., p. 42.

[143] Ibid., p. 7.

[144] David Finkelhor and Richard Ormrod, *Prostitution of Juveniles: Patterns from NIBRS*, U.S. Department of Justice, Office of Justice Programs, Office of Juvenile Justice and Delinquency Prevention, Juvenile Justice Bulletin, Washington, DC, June 2004, http://www.ncjrs.gov/pdffiles1/ojjdp/203946.pdf.

[145] The data in this study are from a limited number of cases (13,814 prostitution incidents involving identified offenders—both adults and juveniles) and from only 76 agencies in 13 states. The NIBRS collects data, including data on offense(s), offender(s), victim(s), arrestee(s), and any property involved in an offense, for 46 different Group A offenses (those that include data on victims, offenders, circumstances, etc.) and 11 different Group B offenses (those that include data only on the arrestee). Despite the detailed crime data that the NIBRS can provide, nationwide implementation of the program has been slow, for a variety of reasons, including cost considerations. For more information, see archived CRS Report RL34309, *How Crime in the United States Is Measured*, by Nathan James and Logan Rishard Council. See also http://www.fbi.gov/about-us/cjis/ucr/frequently-asked-questions/nibrs_faqs.

[146] P.L. 106-386, §107(b)(2); 22 U.S.C §7105(b)(2)(A).

[147] U.S. Department of Justice, *Attorney General's Annual Report to Congress on U.S. Government Activities to Combat Trafficking in Persons: Fiscal Year 2009*, p. 26.

[148] U.S. Department of Justice, *Attorney General's Annual Report to Congress on U.S. Government Activities to Combat Trafficking in Persons: Fiscal Year 2009*, p. 6.

[149] The grant is authorized under 22 U.S.C. §7105(b)(2)(A), pertaining to grants made by the Attorney General to develop, expand, or strengthen victim service programs for victims of trafficking in the United States.

[150] For a description of services offered by OVC, see archived CRS Report RL32579, *Victims of Crime Compensation and Assistance: Background and Funding*, by Celinda Franco.

[151] CRS correspondence with the U.S. Department of Health and Human Services, Administration for Children and Families, Office of Refugee Resettlement, June 17, 2011.

[152] The Homeland Security Act of 2002 (HSA; P.L. 107-296) abolished the Immigration and Naturalization Service (INS) and transferred most of its functions to various bureaus in the newly created Department of Homeland Security (DHS) effective March 1, 2003. In addition, due to HSA much of the Attorney General's authority in immigration law is currently vested in or shared with the Secretary of Homeland Security. For more information on the role of the Attorney General and Secretary of Homeland Security in immigration law, see archived CRS Report RL31997, *Authority to Enforce the Immigration and Nationality Act (INA) in the Wake of the Homeland Security Act: Legal Issues*, by Stephen R. Vina.

[153] TVPA §107(b)(1)(E); 22 U.S.C. §7105(b)(1)(E).

[154] For more information, see CRS Report R41570, *U.S. Refugee Resettlement Assistance*, by Andorra Bruno.

[155] For a discussion of the eligibility of trafficking victims for state and federal means-tested benefits, see CRS Report RL33809, *Noncitizen Eligibility for Federal Public Assistance: Policy Overview and Trends*, by Ruth Ellen Wasem.

[156] U.S. Department of Justice, *Attorney General's Annual Report to Congress on U.S. Government Activities to Combat Trafficking in Persons: Fiscal Year 2008*, p. 19.

[157] CRS correspondence with the U.S. Department of Health and Human Services, Administration for Children and Families, Office of Refugee Resettlement, June 17, 2011.

[158] U.S. Department of Justice, *Attorney General's Annual Report to Congress on U.S. Government Activities to Combat Trafficking in Persons: Fiscal Year 2008,* June 2009, p. 10.

[159] These areas are Houston, TX; Las Vegas, NV; New York, NY; Milwaukee, WI; Newark, NJ; Philadelphia, PA; Phoenix, AZ; Portland, OR; St. Louis, MO; San Francisco, CA; Sacramento, CA; Louisville, KY; Nashville, TN; Columbus, OH; Cincinnati, OH; San Diego, Los Angeles, and Orange Counties in California; and statewide in Colorado, Idaho, Florida, Georgia, Illinois, Minnesota, and North Carolina. DOJ, *Attorney General's Annual Report to Congress on U.S. Government Activities to Combat Trafficking in Persons: Fiscal Year 2008*, p. 14.

[160] The NHTRC is carried out by the Polaris Project, a nonprofit organization that works on human trafficking issues.

[161] U.S. Department of State, *Trafficking in Persons Report*, June 2010, p. 343.

[162] For further information, see CRS Report RL33785, *Runaway and Homeless Youth: Demographics and Programs*, by Adrienne L. Fernandes-Alcantara.

[163] Congress appropriated $97.7 million for the two programs in FY2010, which funded 364 BCP shelters and 216 TLPs in all 50 states, the District of Columbia, American Samoa, Guam, and Puerto Rico. That same year, nearly 45,000 youth received BCP services and approximately 4,000 received TLP services. U.S. Department of Health and Human Services, Administration for Children and Families, *Children and Families Services Program Justification of Estimates for Appropriations Committees*, pp. 106, 112.

[164] CRS correspondence with the U.S. Department of Health and Human Services, Administration for Children and Families, Administration on Children, Youth, and Families, Family and Youth Services Bureau, March 2010.

[165] Approximately $18.0 million was appropriated to fund 160 grantees in FY2010, many of which operate in coordination with the two shelter programs. In FY2010, street workers with the grantee organizations made 838,414 contacts with street youth. Most of these received written materials about referral services, health and hygiene products, and food and drink items. No other information is collected about the youth who receive assistance through SOP. U.S. Department of Health and Human Services, Administration for Children and Families, *Children and Families Services Program Justification of Estimates for Appropriations Committees*, p. 111.

[166] CRS correspondence with the National Runaway Switchboard, April 2010.

[167] The sites were in San Diego, CA; and Austin, Galveston, and San Antonio in Texas. CRS correspondence with the U.S. Department of Health and Human Services, Administration for Children and Families, Administration on Children, Youth, and Families, Family and Youth Services Bureau, March 2010.

[168] For further information, see CRS Report RL34050, *Missing and Exploited Children: Background, Policies, and Issues*, by Adrienne L. Fernandes-Alcantara.

[169] The act directed DOJ's Office of Juvenile Justice and Delinquency Prevention (OJJDP) to establish both a toll-free number to report missing and exploited children and a national resource center for missing and exploited children; coordinate public and private missing and exploited children's programs; provide training and technical assistance to recover missing children; and assist law enforcement entities in combating child exploitation. For FY2011, Congress appropriated $70 million for the MEC program.

[170] Federal law enforcement officials from five agencies (FBI, U.S. Postal Inspection Service, U.S. Marshals Service, Immigration and Customs Enforcement Agency, and the State Department) work full- or part-time at NCMEC investigating missing and exploited children cases, as they pertain to their federal jurisdiction.

[171] National Center for Missing and Exploited Children, *NCMEC Quarterly Progress Report Covering Activity Through December 2010*, January 26, 2011, p. 34.

[172] See, for example, U.S. Department of Justice, Office of Justice Programs, Office of Juvenile Justice and Delinquency Prevention, *FY 09 Improving Community Response to the Commercial Sexual Exploitation of Children and Research on the Commercial Sexual Exploitation of Children, Funding Announcements*, 2009.

[173] The grantees are Multnomah County, OR; Alameda County, CA; and Kristi House, a child advocacy center for sexually abused children, in Miami, FL. An FY2009 technical assistance grant through the ICAC program awarded funds to the Girls Education and Mentoring Services (GEMS) to provide technical assistance to the grantees.

[174] The grantee is the Fund for the City of New York, a nonprofit organization that funds projects to advance the "functioning of government and nonprofit organizations in New York and beyond."

INDEX

G

H

I

J

K

O

P

Q

R

S

T

U

V

W